7.95
01

D0072120

Societies in Change

SOCIETIES IN CHANGE

An Introduction
to Comparative Sociology

BY

BRIGITTE BERGER

WITHDRAWN

Basic Books, Inc., Publishers

NEW YORK   LONDON

Hm
101
.B472

71-4726

© 1971 by Basic Books, Inc.
Library of Congress Catalog Card Number: 77-126946
SBN 465-07941-5
Manufactured in the United States of America

NOV 11 1980

Preface

THIS BOOK is intended to serve as a textbook in comparative sociology. In recent years there has been a great increase of both undergraduate and graduate courses in comparative sociology, but so far no textbook on the subject is available. Thus the present book is intended to fill a gap. Whether one regards this intention as improperly audacious or as meritorious, it is clear that a book of this kind has no precedent to fall back upon. Quite different approaches could have been used to realize the basic intention. After a good deal of experimentation, the approach chosen has been in terms of social change; that is, societies are compared in terms of overall processes of change in the modern world. This has the advantage of avoiding the static implications of much social-scientific comparison and of placing the comparative analyses in the historical context which, for most people today, makes comparison interesting in the first place.

Thus, in addition to its primary purpose of serving as a textbook for comparative sociology courses, the book might also be of interest in courses devoted to social change. Since the latter frequently attract students with little or no previous acquaintance with sociology, the book nowhere presupposes such acquaintance. Sociological concepts are explained as they come up. Conceivably, then, the book might also be of interest in introductory sociology courses emphasizing the study of comparison or change.

The book makes no pretense of providing an exhaustive survey of the, by now, enormous literature in comparative sociology. Rather, it introduces the student to the field by means of a conceptual frame of reference (mainly derived from Max Weber). If the student grasps the latter (even if he disagrees with some or all of it), he will have learned to ask what the phenomena in question mean, that is, he will have learned how to go about interpreting social processes. Needless to say, different empirical materials could be substituted almost everywhere in the book, and indeed it is hoped that instructors will often do just this. In other words, both student and instructor can use the conceptual framework presented here to organize different comparative materials than the ones selected for illustration in the book.

Some people would argue that any conceptual framework implies a political position. Be this as it may, the attempt has been made here to stay clear as much as possible of political standpoints or evaluations of the material. It is hoped that people with politically or ideologically discrepant views of contemporary processes of change in the world will find the book useful.

This book has been discussed with a number of colleagues, but, although this is not customary, a special acknowledgment should be made here of the help given to the book by its editor, William Gum. His advice, patience and encouragement have been invaluable all along.

BRIGITTE BERGER

Fall 1970
New York

Contents

Societies in Change

[1] Introduction: The Uses of Comparative Sociology

Comparative Sociology and the Social Sciences

THE social sciences have undergone an amazing expansion in recent years. This expansion has been triggered largely by the dramatic political, economic, and social changes that have been taking place all over the world. There is an urgent need to understand and to cope with these new realities, and the social sciences are expected to play a part in dealing with them.

In the political sphere more than fifty former colonial territories have become independent states and others are expecting to be granted sovereignty. Many of the new nations face the task of establishing a workable political system and of integrating diverse social groups into a political community. In addition, well-established nations that are undergoing political changes need research about the nature of political processes to predict their possible future development. Furthermore, terms such as "democracy," "nationalism," and "totalitarianism" have become ambiguous and need clarification, so that the radical transformations going on today can be adequately understood. In all these matters the political scientist plays a central role.

In the economic sphere the term "industrialization" defines the fundamental transformation that many societies in the world are experiencing today. Industrialization has become a reality of its own, seemingly releasing forces that affect men everywhere in more or less the same way, regardless of political or cultural di-

TABLE 1-1

Nations Newly Established since 1950[a]

Algeria	Malawi
Barbados	Malaysia
Botswana	Maldive Islands
Burundi	Mali
Cambodia	Malta
Cameroons	Mauritania
Central African Republic	Morocco
Chad	Niger
Congo (Brazzaville)	Nigeria
Congo (Democratic Republic of the)	Ruwanda-Urundi
Cyprus	Senegal
Dahomey	Sierra Leone
Gabon	Singapore
Gambia	Somalia
Ghana	Sudan
Guinea	Togo
Guyana	Trinidad and Tobago
Ivory Coast	Tunisia
Jamaica	Uganda
Kenya	United Republic of Tanzania (including
Kuwait	Tanganyika and Zanzibar)
Laos	Upper Volta
Lesotho	Vietnam (North)
Libya	Vietnam (South)
Madagascar	Zambia

[a]As of 30 December 1966.
Source: United Nations Yearbooks.

viding lines. Economists, for their part, have been engrossed in studying the different forms of industrialization and in arguing about the best ways of rapidly achieving industrialization, which is the overriding desire of most new nations. Some vital issues in this area are the choices between heavy industry and village-based economic programs and between centralized and decentralized development, as well as the dynamics of capital formation and the problem of balancing trade. These are economic questions, but they also give rise to political and social questions of great scope. So the economist might argue, on purely economic grounds, whether concentration on heavy industry or development of industrial activities that can be carried on in villages is more likely to achieve rapid industrialization. But it would be difficult in this debate to ignore noneconomic issues, such as the political and cultural effects of rapid urbanization that inevitably result from the heavy-industry option.

Change in the social sphere has everywhere paralleled political and economic change. The transitory and tenuous character of all patterns of social life has become especially evident. This is observed in the societies that are being rapidly transformed from traditional to modern ones. But even in those societies that achieved this transformation to "modernity" a long time ago, there have been far-reaching changes in patterns previously taken for granted, changes in life styles, social roles, ideas, attitudes, and moral values. Consequently, sociologists have become much concerned with the dynamics of social change. They have tried to develop theories to describe and account for such phenomena as bureaucratization, urbanization, and social mobility.

Comparative sociology has been a natural outgrowth of these concerns. It seems clear that sociologists, if they wish to develop theories of social change that will be useful in understanding what goes on in the world today, cannot limit themselves to monographic studies of isolated societies. Of course, some sociologists will continue to do this, but eventually their findings will have to be integrated horizontally, so that it may be seen how one basic phenomenon appears differently in different societies. Only in this way will there be some advance toward comprehensive theories of social change. And it might even be argued that the sociologist interested in only one particular society will not actually grasp the significance of his own investigations until he places them in a broader comparative framework. For the American student, comparative sociology is important not only to grasp what is going on in the societies of the so-called Third World, but also to develop a broad perspective on what is going on in American society.[1]

The Development of Comparative Sociology

Comparative sociology, then, is a "timely" discipline; however, it is not a new development in sociology. During the "classical" period of sociology (roughly between 1890–1930, when many of the root insights of the discipline were developed), there was a keen recognition of the importance of comparative studies. Emile Durkheim, the leading figure in French sociology of this period, insisted that the comparative method was essential.[2] Max Weber, the foremost "classical" German sociologist, maintained the method of comparison was for the sociologist what the controlled experiment was for the physical scientist. (He included societies of the past as well as those of his time in his comparative studies.) [3] Other sociologists of this period, such as Vilfredo Pareto, George Simmel, and Thorstein Veblen, practiced a form of comparative sociology, although they did not pay as much methodological attention to comparison as Durkheim and Weber. All of the classical sociologists were interested in making broad statements about man's social life, rather than merely describing or explaining a particular social development. Comparison was a methodological necessity for them.

This necessity actually existed even before sociology was recognized as a distinct scientific endeavor. As far back as Herodotus and Thucydides, men who wanted to explain human social behavior in broad terms were compelled to compare societies. Aristotle, in his *Politics,* may have been the first to make a method of this, and it has been used by such diverse figures as Polybius (the historian of Rome), Ibn-Khaldun (the Arab philosopher), and Machiavelli (the Florentine statesman).

Sociology, beginning with its founder, Auguste Comte (1798–1857), has only systematized technique and made it primary. Perhaps more than any other discipline, sociology thinks in terms of comparisons, and because of this, it is closer to the way people think in everyday life. (This is why many laymen, erroneously, think that they *already* know what the sociologist tells them.)

Most people, if they reflect about social life at all, engage in some sort of comparative sociology—without the logical sharpness and scientific accuracy of the professional. Max Weber (1864–1920), interested in isolating the variables that brought about modern capitalism, felt compelled to look at a great number of nonmodern, noncapitalist societies. Ibn-Khaldun (1332–1406) was interested in various peculiarities of the Arab, which led him to careful comparison between nomadic and nonnomadic societies.

In our time, the ordinary man or woman thinks in a similar fashion; for example, an American tourist or television viewer, with limited education, will be struck by the difference in the woman's role in the Middle East and in America. If he reflects on what he knows about the American woman's behavior, he may hit on one variable to explain some of the differences: for instance, the availability of household machinery that frees the American from domestic drudgery, allowing her to work outside the home at a job, to participate in politics, and to have plentiful leisure. Thinking further, as to how household machinery became so accessible in America, he may come upon variables of broader scope, like technological development or the capitalist economic system. If he is inclined toward generalization, he may then evolve a theory: the role of women changes as a result of technological development or as a result of capitalism. In effect, whether or not his theory is valid or scientifically precise, the man in the street will have used comparative sociology, accounting for the differences he observed in his travels or on his television screen. This is exactly what comparative sociology seeks to do—with refinement and accuracy.

Let us examine what happened in American sociology. Early American sociology, much like classical sociology in Europe, was eager to develop broad all-embracing theories of human social life. However, it became apparent that many of the theories it developed rested on dubious evidence, making them useless in coping with actual social problems. The empirical, pragmatic genius of American culture reacted strongly against this type of sociology, especially in the period between the two world wars. The grand explanatory schemes of the classical sociologists, both European and American, were discarded. It was then that American sociologists concentrated on the development of rigorous empirical methods (increasingly quantitative and statistical) and on the study of the small-scale social phenomena that were most amenable to these methods. In addition, the Americans concentrated almost exclusively on their own society, leaving the past to the historians and anthropologists. Consequently, American sociology became narrowly empiricist and narrowly ethnocentric at the same time. The cosmopolitan sweep of classical sociology seemed for a while irretrievably lost—lamented by only a few.

It gradually became clear to a growing number of scholars that this was not, on the whole, a fortunate turn, even if one welcomed a sharpening of methods and a restraint of generalization. After World War II there has been a strong reversal in the trend of the preceding three decades. There has been an increasing interest in theory and, concomitantly, in comparative studies. The latter was undoubtedly accelerated by the new international role of the United States and the creation of high-paying research possibilities for American sociologists. But there has also been a growing realization that there can be no adequate science of sociology without theory, and that there can be no adequate sociological theory without a broadly comparative perspective.

In the last few years there has been a particularly sharp rise of interest in comparative sociology, which has been reflected in publications and research projects and in college and graduate courses as well. Comparative sociologists have, of course, individual styles and use diverse theoretical frameworks and methods, but the overall picture reveals a rediscovery of past approaches that had been discarded, rejected, and even forgotten. Old theories have been found highly relevant to the study of rapidly changing societies.

Let us examine some of these "old" theories. The notion of social evolution, once discarded as an intellectual aberration of the Darwinian age, has become respectable again, as seen in the recent writing of Talcott Parsons, who is probably the foremost American sociological theorist today.[4] The forgotten problem of the stages of socioeconomic development has been looked at again, especially in the work of Walt Rostow, the economist and a major policy advisor of President Johnson.[5] The old Marxian attempt to discern a "dialectical" process in societal change has been revived by W. F. Wertheim, the Dutch sociologist.[6] And the old Weberian quest for explanations of the differential developments of entire national societies is under way again by sociologists in various countries: Reinhard Bendix and Robert Bellah in the United States, S. Andreski in England, and S. N. Eisenstadt in Israel.[7]

Thus, the revival of sociological theory and comparative sociology have been closely linked. It seems that this is necessarily so: theorizing necessitates a comparative approach, while comparative analyses lead to theory construction. It follows that the comparative approach is important for the sociologist in at least two ways. First, it seems to provide, from an international perspective, descriptions and explanations of social processes that are of foremost importance in the world today. Here its importance is pragmatic, even political. Second, comparative sociology offers a contribution to the construction of sociological theory, and this ought to interest even the sociologists who are not directly concerned with problems of rapid social change. For the nonsociologist, the student, and the lay reader with a nonprofessional interest in these questions, the theoretical and political nature of comparative sociology shows a side of sociology that is both intriguing to the inquisitive mind and fascinating with its "realness."

Comparative Sociology Defined

Comparative sociology is, as the term directly suggests, the study of social phenomena not just in one society but in several. Its belief is that a clearer understanding of the social phenomena may come about by seeing them in different societal, cultural, and historical variations. There are different ways in which the endeavors of comparative sociology can be carried on.

First, the comparative sociologist can analyze one particular phenomenon that he considers important in a given society, comparing it with corresponding phenomena in other societies. It is his hope that with this approach the causes or conditions for the phenomenon in the society he is studying will become more "visible." This was Max Weber's method in his studies of world religions, all having one basic purpose: to clarify the peculiar development of capitalism in Western civilization. Weber thought that the key variable in the emergence of capitalism in the West was Protestantism, and more specifically, the peculiar ethical orientation of Calvinist Protestantism that he called "inner-worldly asceticism." If that were the key variable, simple logic would lead to the supposition that this variable would be *missing* in all non-Western societies. This was what Weber contended that he had found in his comparative studies, which ranged over modern Western societies, as well as China, India, the ancient Near East, and classical antiquity. In a sense, one may say that all these societies served as "control groups" for Weber's analysis of the modern West, and all his comparative studies constituted a laboratory-type experiment performed in the mind of the analyst.

Second, the comparative sociologist may concentrate on a type or class of social process, tracing its form in different societies and in different periods of history. Here the goal is not to establish the causes or conditions for a particular phenomenon, as in the first approach, but rather to arrive at general statements about it that will be valid cross-societally or cross-culturally. Here the goal is typological and systematic rather than explanatory and historical. There is a good deal of this in Weber too, often as a by-product of his mental experiment. For example, when Weber developed such typical constructs as charismatic authority or bureaucracy, he always developed the type by reference to phenomena in several societies. This method is evident in Weber's examples: in discussing charismatic authority, he will jump from the Israelite prophets to a contemporary demagogue; in discussing bureaucracy, he will range from ancient China to contemporary Germany. This kind of approach allows the comparative sociologist to compare societies in terms of common concepts. The danger of the approach is that sole attention to the concepts can obfuscate the unique historical circumstances of each society, making them all disappear into a conceptual "night" which makes all cats look grey. However, if sensitively used, as in Weber, the opposite occurs, the uniqueness of each historical context becomes more visible to explain why in each society the phenomenon varies as it does from the typical.

Third, the comparative sociologist may have the goal of discovering and isolating some universal and necessary categories of social life. The comparativist endeavor is in this case motivated by a search for sociological constants that are present in every society, regardless of historical variations. In classical sociology this was characteristic of both Durkheim and Pareto, the former being concerned primarily with the discovery of the factors determining societal integration, the latter with the determination of recurring motives and behavior patterns ultimately rooted in human nature. In contemporary sociology it is above all the functionalists (or, as they are called in the United States, structural-functionalists) who are engaged in this kind of comparative sociology; their goal is to arrive at a determination and understanding of cross-culturally valid "functional imperatives," that is, necessary social factors that every society must take into account.

Fourth, the comparative sociologist may compare societies within the framework of some comprehensive theory of historical development, viewing each society in terms of a different stage or modification. Such a theory could be a theory of historical cities, assuming that societies will inevitably pass through a number of phases that basically resemble each other. Or, alternatively, it could be a theory of progress, in which societies represent different stages on the universal journey toward some sort of predictable outcome. The former kind of theory, of course, will tend toward pessimism and conservatism, the latter toward optimism and social or political activism. On the whole, historians and philosophers have been much more inclined to form this type of theory than have sociologists. However, Pitirim Sorokin, the Russian sociologist who came to Harvard in the 1920s, nicely represents the first kind of approach, and Marxist sociologists of every hue represent the second. What both approaches have in common, despite their opposite "moods," is that empirical findings about the various societies are all subsumed under grand schemes of interpretation that remain intrinsically inaccessible to empirical verification. Empirically, it is just as impossible to demonstrate, say, that the social convulsions of our time are nothing but the inevitable reiterations of a perennial historical script as it is to demonstrate that, on the contrary, they are the birth pangs of something entirely new in history. Of course, it is just because of the meta-empirical character of these approaches that sociologists, with few exceptions, have shied away from them.

In this book, a combination of the *first* and *second* approaches to comparative sociology will be used. The *third* approach is too ambitious and inappropriate for a textbook; consequently it will not be used. Since we believe that sociology should be an empirical science and should limit its theoretical framework to propositions that are empirically verifiable, the *fourth* approach will be avoided. Logic demands that the work of Max Weber is relied upon, as his theoretical approach is similar to ours.

We propose to take as our subject that historical reality which sparked the whole current interest in comparative sociology, not in order to be fashionable, but because it seems to us that this interest is legitimate and offers the broadest access to the field: we shall study the processes of change. It is futile in the present moment of history to compare societies without attending to the processes of continuous, radical, and rapid change that nearly all of them are undergoing. Thus our entire analysis is founded on change, and particularly on that aspect of change that is most dominant today: the process of modernization. Obviously, a textbook is not the place to develop a theory of social change. Rather, we will limit ourselves to what should be the purpose of any textbook, to present and order the available information in a given field. But such a presentation must be within some sort of theoretical framework, if it is not to be an incoherent aggregation of unrelated facts. And, since it is impossible to present *all* the facts, the *choice* of facts will necessarily be grounded theoretically, either implicitly or explicitly. It seems much better to state our theoretical basis explicitly, rather than have the reader struggle with hidden implications.

Theoretical Framework: The Concept of Rationalization

Our basic theoretical framework is derived from Weber's concept of *rationalization,* as his notion of rationality has an important place in his typology of social actions. He distinguishes among four: the affectual, the traditional, the utility-rational, and the value-rational. This differentiation is made in terms of the meanings actors attach to their own actions. *Affectual action* derives its meaning from some overriding emotion, as, for example, action taken under the influence of love or hatred. *Traditional action* obtains its meaning from the past; that is, the actor, if asked about his behavior, can only point to the fact that things have always been done in this way in his society or group. Rational action is characterized by the presence in the mind of the actor of a logical bond between means and end; that is, the actor explains the meaning of his action in terms of a specific purpose to be achieved as a result of the action. In *utility-rational action* this purpose is strictly practical; for instance, a technological change is introduced to increase economic productivity. In *value-rational action* the purpose is defined in terms of the actor's values; for instance, a political program is undertaken to maximize some good that the actor believes in.

Rationalization, then, is the historical process in which rational actions become increasingly important in a society. Weber viewed this process as the foremost factor in recent history. Even more specifically, modern rationalization refers primarily to the increase in *utility-rational actions.* To be sure, value-rational behavior has also increased, but value is less significant than utility in explaining the forces at work in the modern world. The most important reason for this has been the development of modern economic and technological systems, as shown historically in the growth of capitalism and industrialism. Furthermore, since affectual action never accounts for any large proportion of social behavior, it is above all traditional action that is decreased as a result of rationalization. The process of rationalization, then, is one in which traditional patterns of social action are increasingly replaced by utility-rational patterns.

We follow Weber also in believing that rationalization constitutes the distinguishing element in what is commonly called modernization. Various social, economic, and political forces have been singled out by various scholars as the defining characteristics of modernity: for instance, an increasingly complex and differentiated institutional structure; sophisticated technology and financial organization; the substitution of secondary occupations (industrial and commercial) and tertiary occupations ("service" occupations) for the primary occupations that extract subsistence from the natural environment (farming, fishing); the growth of bureaucratic forms of organization; the growth of cities; mass education and mass communications. Undoubtedly, all of these are important elements in any society that can be called modern, and we will study them all. We submit, however, that they all not only involve but actually depend upon rationalization for their emergence. In the ensuing analysis we will show more clearly why we take this position.

There have been two major recent controversies about the processes of social change. The first, which concerns whether modernization is inevitable and must always proceed in fixed stages, is important in regard to the societies of the Third World. The second, questioning whether all modern societies are converging in some of their central sociological characteristics, concerns the comparability of the American and Soviet societies, as well as the comparability of all industrial societies. Both debates have obvious political implications. We do not take a doctrinaire position on either issue, but we do have a general approach to these questions. Modernization does not *necessarily* occur in fixed, universal stages, for the effect of the historical peculiarities of different societies and cultures cannot be minimized; therefore, we have little faith in any alleged "laws of history."

However, we do take the position that all modern societies tend to converge sociologically. Such convergence is one of the more visible consequences of modernization. Our position does *not* mean, though, that we expect world-wide standardization or leveling to result from modernization. Nor do we assume that modernization operates as a uniform or irresistible force. Every society experiences modernization in terms of its unique history and culture;

also, the political system and the conscious social plans of each society will modify, deflect, and, in rare cases, stop the modernization process. Nevertheless, even *partially successful* modernization will result in sociological patterns that resemble those of other modern or modernizing societies throughout the world. It may be argued that even various *resistances* to modernization resemble each other. For example, critics of the "convergence theory" have pointed to cases in which contact with modernity has led to a resurgence of traditional patterns, as in "nativistic" movements in which old customs and beliefs are belligerently reasserted in the face of modernizing trends. The point is well taken. However, it must be recognized that the resurgent traditions are imbued with new meanings by the very fact that they are consciously maintained where once they were taken for granted as the unconscious background of social life. Rather, the traditions are now marched out precisely because they are no longer taken for granted. They are intensively reflected upon. What is more, their worth and superiority are supposed to have articulated purposes—for a better life, for political independence, or even for economic development. In such cases, the traditions themselves are *rationalized,* in Weber's sense; subtly, they become part of the general movement into modernity.

Thus, when we speak of modernization, we are concerned with an almost universal process. There are few islands of undisturbed traditionalism left today and none that are unthreatened. Most of the economically underdeveloped countries are frantically struggling to modernize themselves. And the economically developed countries are undergoing social transformations rooted in the modernity they have already achieved; modernization seems to be a permanent and cumulative revolution. Since most of the world is either modernized or modernizing, there are very great pressures on the remaining traditional societies or subsocieties to follow suit. The pressure is partly economic and political, as these "backward" regions become entangled in the worldwide economic and political process. But the pressure develops so quickly because modern mass communications are capable of reaching almost anywhere on the surface of the earth—where they arouse by invidious comparisons a need to join the modern world. This, of course, is the dynamics of what has been called the "revolution of rising expectations." Indeed, it can be said only *half*-facetiously that one

TABLE 1-2

Developing Countries[a]

Afghanistan	Mauritius
Albania	Mexico
Bolivia	Mongolia
Brazil	Nepal
British Caribbean Territories	Nicaragua
Bulgaria	Pacific Island Countries and Territories
Burma	Pakistan
Chile	Panama
China	Papua and New Guinea
Colombia	Paraguay
Costa Rica	Peru
Cuba	Philippines
Ecuador	Poland
El Salvador	Rumania
Ethiopia	Saudi Arabia
Guatemala	Surinam
Haiti	Swaziland
Honduras	Syria
India	Thailand
Iran	Turkey
Iraq	United Arab Republic
Jordan	Venezuela
Korea (North)	Vietnam (North)
Korea (South)	Vietnam (South)
Lebanon	Yemen
Liberia	Yugoslavia

[a]This list varies according to the criteria used. For instance, Czechoslovakia, Hungary, Greece, and Spain could be included in this list; or an argument could be made to exclude such countries as Poland and Yugoslavia.

aspect of modernization and its revolution of the imagination is that *everybody* becomes a comparative sociologist.

Finally, in this textbook we will follow Weber's approach by making extensive use of historical materials. It is certainly possible to make sociological analyses without reference to the past, but, in our opinion, it is not desirable, particularly for comparative sociology. We contend that one cannot adequately compare societies without an adequate grasp of the major historical forces that shaped them. Otherwise, one constantly runs the danger of misperceiving, distorting, even overlooking crucial features.

The design of the book is simple. It involves two levels of sociological analysis: first, the institutional structures in the process of social change; second, ideas and personality in the same process. Our concept of "institutional structure" follows general sociological usage. By an "institution" we mean a patterned, regulative arrangement of social relationships. By an "institutional structure" we mean such an arrangement when it extends over so long a period of time and embraces such a large number of people that it is considered coextensive with a particular historical society. We will examine various key institutions: to wit, political, economic, and class institutions, and particular institutionalization of social life that accompanies urbanization, and the institutional structures of family and youth.

In the second part of the book, we will explore certain changes in ideational and psychological patterns that develop from modernization. Since this second level of analysis is not customary in sociology, we will present at length the theoretical considerations that have led us to our belief that the modern world can only be fully understood if we grasp that a new, a modern man lives in it.

Clearly, in such an undertaking it is impossible to consider everything. What is included and what is omitted will be determined by our theoretical framework and by the overall process we are concerned with. Said differently, the material we will present will have the character of illustrations, designed to make clearer overall processes that are relevant to different societies. The reader will add his own knowledge to the illustrations presented here, and the book will have served its purpose if this knowledge can now be placed in the context of interpretation. For example, when discussing the American class system, we omit the dramatic racial issue. This is not because it is deemed trivial. It is simply that the author believes the American racial situation to be unique in the world; as such, it does not lend itself to a discussion of intersocietal patterns and trends.[8] We make prominent note of this and other such omissions, lest our concentration on comparable features exaggerate the convergence of all societies. Nevertheless, the task of comparative sociology is to compare, and we must concentrate on those features that lend themselves to comparison.

The comparative sociologist is in a position vis-à-vis the sociologist who has specialized in one society that is rather similar to that of any sociologist vis-à-vis the historian. He is subject to being reproached, as the sociologist with his penchant for generalization, has long been by the historian—as a "terrible simplifier." It must be admitted that there is usually a certain justification to this reproach. Generalization simplifies, comparison simplifies. The scholar who spends his life concentrating with utmost precision on unique phenomena will always be annoyed by such simpli-fication. On the other hand, this kind of scholar rarely is capable of, or concerned enough with, making statements of a more general scope. Comparative sociology must, therefore, almost by defini-tion, annoy some "experts." Their criticism will not be intolerable, though, if comparative sociology does what we believe it can: pro-vide a better grasp of a world undergoing radical transformation and provide the materials of theory-building in sociology.

NOTES

1. The term "Third World" is commonly used to refer to the existence of the so-called underdeveloped or developing countries that are neither of the East or West.

2. Emile Durkheim, *The Rules of the Sociological Method* (Glencoe: Free Press, 1950).

3. See Max Weber, *Gesammelte Aufsaetze zur Wissenschaftslehre* (Tue-bingen: Mohr und Siebeck, 1951).

4. Talcott Parsons, *Societies: Evolutionary and Comparative Perspec-tives* (Englewood Cliffs, N. J.: Prentice-Hall, 1966).

5. Walt W. Rostow, *The Stages of Economic Growth* (Cambridge: Cam-bridge University Press, 1960).

6. W. F. Wertheim, *East-West Parallels* (Chicago: Quadrangle Books, 1965).

7. R. Bendix, *Work and Authority in Industry* (New York: John Wiley, 1965), and *Nation-Building and Citizenship* (New York: John Wiley, 1964); R. Bellah, *Tokugawa Religion* (Glencoe: Free Press, 1957); S. An-dreski, *The Uses of Comparative Sociology* (Berkeley: University of Cali-fornia Press, 1964); S. N. Eisenstadt *Essays on Comparative Institutions* (New York: John Wiley, 1965) and *The Political Systems of Empires* (New York: Free Press, 1962).

8. A number of studies have been published in recent years that attempt to come to some cross-cultural understanding of the phenomenon of race segregation and integration. Although we have refrained from attempting to incorporate the findings of these studies in this book, for the reasons given, the interested student may wish to consult Guy Hunter, ed., *Indus-trialization and Race Relations* (New York: Oxford University Press, 1965). Here is a good bibliography on race relations in general for Brazil, the Ca-ribbean area, the United States, South Africa, India, Asia, and Malaya.

PART I

*Social Change
and Institutional
Structures*

[2] The Political Structure

Even among social scientists and social historians there is no general agreement as to which social institution—the political state,[1] the military,[2] the economy,[3] the social mores[4]—is most significant in the process of social change. For example, Marxists claim that economic development is fundamental, that the structure of the state reflects the economic-technological structure. But some historians feel that economic changes are merely expressions of changes in international relations. And yet other social historians believe that the changing values and mores of a people produce the changes in all other sectors of social life. In this book we are not concerned with discussing the validity of any one theory. Our position is that all the structures which make up a given society are interrelated; in accordance with the specific historical configuration, one aspect or another of this social structure may take on different degrees of importance in the process of change. However, let us note that, regardless of which institutional area a scientific observer may believe the crucial one, in the consciousness of ordinary people the political state is the one most closely associated with the notion of "modernity."

The notion of "modernity" is most significant and demands elaboration.[5] When a state becomes independent today, the foremost concern of her inhabitants and leaders is the creation of symbols characteristic of the modern state. Much energy—which to outside observers often seems misspent, unrelated to the "actual needs" of the country—goes into such costly and spectacular projects as the establishment of a modern army that may not be needed or of a modern national airline that will probably never make a profit. Or, they will construct chrome and glass administrative buildings, despite the fact that ample space for government offices already exists, or they will issue colorful, striking postage stamps. All of these symbols of the modern state have one common, crucial element, regardless of which ideology is used to further legitimate them (nationalism, democracy, communism). They symbolize that the state is capable of administering the country in an efficient and forward-looking manner. The particular ideology under which the state has been proclaimed has, in this matter, little bearing on a "modern" structure.

Let us illustrate this point briefly. What, for instance, do postage stamps stand for? If a country has her own postage stamps, the implication is given that I, a citizen of Nigeria and a resident of the city of Kaduna, can send a letter to a possible future employer in Lagos and can—hopefully—depend upon my letter getting there within a reasonable period of time. Or, the streamlined administrative buildings supply the imagery of government officials sitting behind orderly desks with five telephones, constantly calling up everybody in the country, getting things done in order to ensure a golden future for the country which will eventually bear comparison with other modern states. The fast-moving luxury limousines, which some of the functionaries of the new state have imported at great expense and in which they race up and down the ten miles of the only existing paved and cemented road the country can boast of, do not symbolize waste and prodigious luxury. Rather, they symbolize that we in this country also have roads, and limousines, and officials who know how to drive them. At this point in our analysis we are not concerned with the degree to which this imagery corresponds to reality. It may very well be that the limousine-riding government official squanders much-needed funds for his own private purposes and vanities. This is a problem of no concern to us here. What we wish to bring out is simply that one of the key characteristics of a modern state is the need to create an imagery which reflects the rational and modern manner in which the affairs of the state are handled. The rational-modern way of communication implies the frequent use of the telephone, the rational-modern way of transportation is by means of a high-powered car on a modern highway or by means of a modern airline, and the rational-modern way of sending mail is through a postal service which issues its own postage stamps.

We can state that the image of the modern state is, to a large degree, based upon the presupposition of rationality. This is a recent phenomenon in the history of mankind as we have shown before. It is a concept largely unknown to the political structures of the past. In the work of Max Weber, we find a differentiation of types of political structures in terms of the underlying type of political power exercised within them. In general, Weber distinguishes charismatic, traditional, and legal-rational power.[6] These are abstract concepts that social scientists use as methodological tools to compare political situations in different societies at different times in history. Abstractions, it should be understood, do not exist in any "pure" form in reality; that is to say, no state has entirely traditional, charismatic, or legal-rational power. In reality, these forms of political authority always are mixed and often in modified combinations. Although a society may correspond, in part, to an underlying sociological pattern, each is always unique in the expression of this pattern.

To make Weber's highly theoretical and complex approach to the nature of power more accessible to the beginning student of political sociology, we may see it in terms of the question: Why does any political authority (tribal chief, king, elected president, or dictator) have the right to do what he is doing? The *traditional* answer is: because it has always been done so. The *charismatic* answer is: because the gods say so, or because this person has extraordinary powers. The *legal-rational* answer is: because he has been elected to his job, or because he has gotten it in accordance with legal, regulated procedures, further explaining that he is qualified to carry out the job.

An interesting historical example of traditional power is the rulers of the Portuguese kingdom toward the end of the Middle Ages. Even though the blood of the Portuguese dynasty was clearly tainted with insanity, the right to rule of such disturbed men as Dom Sebastian was never challenged. He was a rightful holder of authority because his dynasty had ruled the country, for better and for worse, for hundreds of years, that is, traditionally.

Napoleon Bonaparte ruled charismatically. Extraordinary powers—genius—attributed to him by his followers, supported and justified his singular and dramatic career. By virtue of his charismatic qualities Napoleon rose from the lowly rank of corporal in the revolutionary army to that of general, consul, and finally emperor. And when his unusual powers seemed to fail him after the unfortunate war against Russia and the final defeat at Water-

Aspects of Political Modernization

In the political sphere, "modernity" implies the institutionalization of three essential elements:

1. Rationalized authority. The replacement of multiple authorities such as family, tribe, race, religion—"traditional" authorities—by a single national authority.
2. Differentiated national structure. The rise of a separate, complex political structure—the government bureaucracy—to perform the increasing number of political functions. These are now specialized and differentiated from other areas of competence.
3. Increased participation. Citizens now become directly involved in and affected by government. New organizations and interest groups develop. The type of mass participation may vary and will find differential legitimation in accordance with the ideological superstructure.

Source: Based on the illuminating discussion of forms of political modernization by Samuel P. Huntington, "Political Modernization: America vs. Europe," *World Politics* 18 (April 1966): 378–414.

loo, the belief in the "genius" of Napoleon waned, and he was forced to abdicate and ultimately was exiled from his country.

Legal-rational authority is well exemplified by the process of the election of a president in the United States. The administrative and political background of a candidate as well as his overall personal capacity are supposed to assure competent and forward-looking leadership. But, regardless of the actual existence of the qualities claimed for the candidate, his authority after his election does *not* rest upon these, but rather on the fact that he has been legally elected according to the procedures laid down by the Constitution.

In our era, the image of the modern state is that of a *rationalizing force.* By virtue of this rational force the modern state is able to transform and validate the varied political structures out of which it has emerged. This process of transformation may at times be accompanied by the great violence of a revolution, but frequently it occurs peacefully and gradually. In fine, the process generally described as the rise of the "modern state" may, from the sociological perspective, be seen as the transformation of various forms of nonrational power to more rational ones.[7]

The Legitimation of
the "Modern State"

THE IDEOLOGICAL PERSPECTIVE

The arguments advanced to justify or legitimate the modernization of the state are different in different countries. Moreover, the legitimating arguments for the process of political rationalization, though they are usually advanced in the form of an overall ideology (communism, socialism, democracy, nationalism), need *not* be rational themselves. Even in the case of the democratic ideology, which social philosophers generally agree is predominantly rational, the rational elements may have disappeared by the time the masses have adopted it. For instance, the French revolution of 1789 was engendered by largely democratic ideas which culminated in the haunting battle cry "Liberty, Equality, Fraternity." But when the fervent citizens of Paris manned the barricades, the rational elements were completely absent. Furthermore, some ideologies (nationalism, for instance) are irrational from the start. However, even an irrational ideology can be used for rational purposes, that is, for the transformation of traditional structures into the form of rationality.

We are not suggesting that ideological differences are completely unimportant. Within a democratic ideology rationalization assumes different forms than it does, for instance, within a communist one.[8] But the crucial point is that ideological differences only modify the process of rationalization, which has an underlying uniformity wherever it takes place. Regardless of the extent to which a particular ideology may be considered rational or irrational, all ideologies have the same purpose, namely, to help unify a population, to help develop a "we-consciousness." For example, the task of the Nigerian government is to "govern" the roughly thirty-four million people of diverse tribal and cultural backgrounds who happen to live within the arbitrarily imposed boundaries of the former colonial territory; to do this, the government must "invent" a Nigerian people. In the absence of a common culture, language, or religion, one way to unify a great number of diverse people is to develop nationalism—that is, to "invent" a nation. In other situations a common language or a common religion facilitates unification, as is true of Arab nationalism.[9] The ideology may be grossly irrational, a welter of illusions; nevertheless, its purpose may be the highly rational one of preventing such different tribes as the Hausa, the Ibo, and the Yoruba, to mention only a few of the multitude of tribes in Nigeria, from cutting each other's throats. Indeed, as recent events have shown, even the idea of Nigerian nationalism is not quite strong enough to prevent precisely such occurrences.

THE HISTORICAL PERSPECTIVE

Although not always successful, an ideological factor is essential to the unification of any large, heterogeneous number of people and groups, if they are to be administered by a single government. The "nation state" is a concept that fulfills this requirement.[10]

We today think of the nation-state as a self-evident political unit; at least in the Western world people think of themselves as Frenchmen, Americans, Danes, Russians. This was not always so. Only a few hundred years ago, until the end of feudalism, Western people did not think of themselves mainly in terms of large national groups. The largest common unifying element was religion. For instance, under the banners of Christianity or Islam, wars were fought with those who were not true believers. However, most people found their group identities in much smaller and more immediate units, such as the family, village, or province. Above all was the family: people slaved, fought, married, lived, and even died for the greater glory of their family.

This has changed fundamentally in the course of the last four hundred years, which has witnessed the rise of the national state and its ideology, first in Europe and then in almost all other parts of the world. Soviet Russia—in a cross-national manner similar to that of feudal Christianity—originally proclaimed itself a state founded on a communist ideology inimical to nationalistic principles. However, twenty years later Stalin had redefined communism in nationalistic Russian terms. Hans Kohn, in numerous studies, has explored the rise of nationalism and its meaning,[11] as have many other scholars.[12] The phenomenon of "national consciousness" has changed the map and mind of Europe completely in the past two hundred years, and it is about to influence dramatically the fate of many African and Asian people today. Nationalism is best understood from an historical perspective. This perspective provides us with a better understanding of the essential differences between the forces that produced European nationalism, in what may now be called the classical pattern, and the forces producing and shaping nationalism in the new states of Asia and Africa.

The original movement to bring all people of a "nation" together appeared in Europe. One interesting feature of European nationalism is the close, almost simultaneous growth of political, administrative territories called nations, and of national languages and of national cultures. In this process, the traditional village communities and the narrow provincial boundaries that had limited the lives of most people dissolved. They were integrated into increasingly larger political, economic, and cultural areas, whose many languages were incorporated into or replaced by the single national language. This language then became the carrier of the new national culture, and the language and the culture together became the identifying marks of the nation.

France, for example, experienced in the sixteenth century the rise of an absolute royal state, as well as the emergence of one French language and one French culture. Throughout the feudal era, France underwent a continuous struggle for power between the king and the families of the powerful feudal lords who refused to see the king as more than *primus inter pares*. Finally, in the sixteenth and seventeenth centuries the House of Bourbon succeeded in establishing its supremacy, and then the administration of the monarch reached the lives of even those people living in such distant provinces as Bretagne, Provence, and the Basque lands. This expansion of political power was accompanied by an economic integration of the country, which was furthered by the government and which in turn affected governmental integration. Then, for both political and economic reasons, more and more people had to learn the language in which the government conducted its business, the language of the seat of government, the Ile de France, of which Paris was the center. Gradually such tongues as Provençal or Breton disappeared, and for more than two hundred years people living under the government of France have spoken one single language. Territory and language in France became virtually coextensive.

The disappearance of some provincial tongues was hastened by their lack of a written form and hence of an established litera-ture.[13] If there had existed a written vernacular and a literature as a focus for the various provincial cultures (as was the case with the various Slavic nationalities of the Austro-Hungarian mon-archy), the process of French unification into one nation with one language and culture would have been more tumultuous and im-perfect than in fact it was.

In addition, the spread of literacy, which in Europe was reach-ing major proportions at that time, favored the domination of a single major language. By the time of the French Revolution, the French people defined themselves largely in terms of their lan-guage. This fact underlies a major shift in political parlance. While the Bourbon monarchs called themselves "Kings of France," Napoleon was given the title "Emperor of the French." This implies an entirely new identification; now the language and culture group constitutes the "nation."

European history since the sixteenth century can be viewed in these terms: those who speak a similar language and have a simi-lar culture demand their "one" government. The Nazi policy of expansion (under Hitler), for instance, was justified by the belief that all German-speaking people with a similar culture, regardless of their geographical location, should be united under one govern-ment. The Austro-Hungarian monarchy disintegrated into small ethnic states, on the one hand, because it tried to incorporate into one political structure such diverse groups as the Czechs, Croats, Hungarians, and Austrians, after that point in history at which language differences, signifying ethnic and cultural differences, had become politically hardened. The current attempts of the South Tyrolean minority in Italy to achieve autonomy are moti-vated by a feeling of cultural distinctness. The student of social history may find this a rewarding approach in the study of other European countries as well. England, Italy, Spain, Belgium, and the unique case of Switzerland deserve special attention.

In summation, we may say that the particular European type of nationalism resulted from the growth of a kind of "consciousness" that led all people who shared a single language and the various cultural characteristics it transmitted to unite into a single inde-pendent state, ruled and administered by a single government, conducted in that particular language. The nationalism that pre-vails today, however, and which so dramatically accompanies the emergence of new states in Africa and Asia, is directed by different social and historical constellations of forces, although its product may eventually prove to be similar.

These countries, in general, have not yet undergone the economic and political integration processes that create pressure for the adoption of a single language. Politically, they have been under colonial rule for a long time; from their colonial rulers they have inherited their territorial boundaries, in which oftentimes a wide variety of tribal cultures and languages exist side-by-side. Economically, these countries are underdeveloped and, in some instances, are still arrested at a subsistence level. Almost always, the more backward a country is economically, the greater the number of languages spoken within its geographical area. For instance, in New Guinea (one of the most untouched areas in the world today), which has about 1,750,000 native inhabitants, more than 500 spoken languages have been distinguished.

As we have already explained, in the absence of a common language, culture, or religion, the chief problem of such countries is to find a common element that can provide a basis for political unity and can serve to fuse the diverse people into a sociopolitical group, conscious of a common task and destiny. This element is usually their common history of subjection to colonial rule. This anticolonialist nationalism is most effective. Anticolonialist nationalism unifies the people in their common desire to be free of alien rulers and form an indigenous government, as well as to oppose their backward economic status under the colonial period. A remarkable unity exists among the people of new nations in their anticolonialist feeling, which cuts across tribal, cultural, religious, and class lines. The routine processes essential to daily life in the modern state are established after independence and a national consciousness have been achieved.[14] And only then the questions of who is to rule, and how, and by what means become relevant. For this reason, the future of many such countries will be marked by internal conflict. The governments, after having come to power proclaiming a nationalistic ideology, must "invent" their nations. Here, again, the need for a common language that can carry a common culture moves to the foreground. The governments must struggle to impose upon their multilingual populations a unifying language, although this may be met by heavy opposition and even bloodshed, as the recent history of India shows. A common language is necessary not only for the creation of a com-

*The Role of Traditionalism in the Political
Modernization of Uganda and Ghana*

The newly established nations of Uganda and Ghana—like all the new nations of Africa—are engaged in an effort to build new national societies out of the various tribes living within their geographical boundaries. The immediate task is to develop overarching governmental forms, with a party system as well as voluntary organizations, to bridge the traditional parochial loyalties. The special nature of the traditional loyalties in these countries is shaping the process of modernization differently in each country. David E. Apter has examined the influence of the dominant forms of traditional political organizations on the development of more modern forms of government in the Kingdom of Buganda and the Ashanti Federacy that respectively make up parts of present-day Uganda and Ghana.

Buganda, one of the most important kingdom states in the lake area of Eastern Africa, was ruled by a succession of despotic kings, the *Kabakas,* who had more than 1,000 local representatives, all directly dependent on the whims and wishes of the Kabaka. Any change that was made in this hierarchical system—the establishment of a civil-service chieftaincy, a parliament and council of ministers, modern education, free-hold tenure—was absorbed into the existing system. In fact, the innovations attempted under colonial rule did not lead to a break-down of the traditional system, but actually helped to further strengthen it. Because there was little resistance to these innovations, the hierarchy remained relatively undisturbed, and therefore traditional political and administrative patterns continued much as they had before. The form of nationalism that emerged was that of a modernizing autocracy in which the government of the Kabaka and the Kabaka himself came to represent the nation. Modernization here tends to be a prolonged drawn-out process that is grappling with the problem of replacing hierarchical authority with representative authority. Modernization also confronts, as a colonial legacy, a situation in which the more important sectors of the economy and the civil service are still monopolized by non-Africans.

In traditional Ashanti, political organization had for its prototype village chieftaincies based on the extended family. An elaborate system of check and controls stretched from the village level to the "division," the largest political unit, which was ruled by the highest chief, the Asantehene. The Ashanti chief was invested with a complex set of religious restraints that specifically served to regulate his behavior. Under colonial rule, the authority of the chiefs was fundamentally weakened by the political dominance of the British, Christianity, education, and the consequences of urbanization. The important role of religion in traditional society has been replaced by the fervor of modern nationalism which has led to active African participation in the political and economic processes of modernization. Ghana succeeded in establishing a national government with parliamentary institutions and was able to achieve political independence at a relatively early date in 1950.

Source: David E. Apter, "The Role of Traditionalism in the Political Modernization of Ghana and Uganda," *World Politics* 12 (October 1960): 45–68.

mon culture, but also for the rational administration of political and economic matters. Obviously, a modern governmental and financial enterprise cannot be carried on without a high degree of linguistic standardization.

One important point we have to bring out here is that the ideology of nationalism can and does dominate over other types of ideology which have been used for the rational purpose of creating a modern state. The history of Soviet Russia, especially during the Stalin era, gives ample evidence. Soviet Russia, originally proclaimed as a communist state inimical to nationalistic principles, was redefined by Stalin in Russian nationalistic terms in the late 1930s and during the 1940s.[15]

Clearly, critically defined anticolonial nationalism is not the rebirth of the classical nationalism of Europe. However, its sociopolitical results are similar. The impact of this novel force in history upon almost every aspect of human society is far-reaching and revolutionary.[16]

At this point we wish to reiterate the general principle behind our analyses. We are concerned with isolating the broad social processes that are rather similar in different countries at comparable stages of development. However, each of these societies has a unique history, and, in every case, this history and the patterns of behavior it creates give to the general process a unique shape. For instance, the influence of the past on the emerging structure of authority has been well brought out by the various research enterprises of Reinhard Bendix, especially in his comparative study of the structure of authority in industry in England and Russia.[17] Without wishing to oversimplify his work, we may for our purposes simply note that the emergence of the Soviet Communist type of authority was facilitated to a considerable degree by the preexistence of an authoritarian structure under the Czars. There are many studies that show the role of the traditional political structure in the modernization of newly emerging countries.

The Bureaucratic Form of Political Administration in the Modern State

We have said that the modern constitutional state is characterized by the legal-rational form of power. To run such a state, the most appropriate and, indeed, necessary system of administration is a "rational" one. And, as Weber has shown, the most rational form of administration is the bureaucratic one.[18]

Among scholars and political thinkers a controversy exists as to the nature, the role, the consequences, as well as the desirability of bureaucracy, but this need not concern us here.[19] Our interest is merely to show how the legal-rational form of authority, which characterizes government today, is exercised effectively through a bureaucratic system of administration. To understand the relation between legal-rational authority and bureaucracy, we will examine the structure of each in turn and together, guided by the various writings of Weber.[20] Rational-legal authority has these characteristics: [21]

1. "A continuous organization of official functions bound by rules."
2. The unit exercising authority is called an "administrative organ," that is, an elected president, a cabinet of ministers, or a body of elected representatives.
3. "A specific sphere of competence. This involves
    a. a sphere of obligations to perform functions which has been marked off as a part of a systematic division of labor;
    b. the provision of the incumbent with the necessary authority to carry out these functions;
    c. that the necessary means of compulsion are clearly defined and their use is subject to definied conditions."
4. A hierarchical organization of offices, with a "right of appeal and of statement of grievances from the lower to the higher."

5. A distinct written set of rules "which regulate the conduct of an officer."

6. Absence of appropriation of his official position by the incumbent—no "rights" to a position.

What we have here, as Bendix describes it, is a substantial separation between the social structure and the exercise of judicial and administrative functions. Major functions of government such as the adjudication of legal disputes, the collection of revenue, the control of currency, military recruitment, the organization of the postal system, the construction of public facilities, and others have been removed from the political struggle in the sense that they cannot be appropriated on a hereditary basis by privileged estates and on this basis parceled out among competing jurisdictions.[22]

In other words, the legal-rational form of authority gives shape to a government oriented primarily toward the efficiency of its own operations and relatively unencumbered by considerations irrelevant to this efficiency. At least in principle, positions of political authority are occupied by individuals with the required competence rather than with a hereditary right to these jobs. To conduct governmental business in accordance with generally known rules serves to minimize arbitrary decisions by powerful individuals, just as the division of labor among different functionaries undercuts individual assumptions of power. Needless to say, there will always be violations of these characteristics in practice, both deliberately (as in cases of corruption) and through faulty execution. But, the *tendency* in this type of governmental system is toward an increasingly pervasive rationality.

The development of a bureaucratic system of administration generally attends the emergence of this type of authority. This point is illuminated by the closeness with which Weber's definition of bureaucracy parallels his definition of legal-rational authority:

1. Defined rights and duties prescribed in written regulations
2. The organization of offices matching the principle of hierarchy
3. Appointment and promotion regulated and based on contractual agreement
4. Technical training (or experience) as a prerequisite for employment
5. Fixed monetary salaries
6. A complete separation between office and office-holder, in that

Bureaucracy and Nation Building
in Transitional Societies

The development and maintenance of a rational, functioning bureaucracy is one of the chief tasks of newly rising and developing nations. Under colonial rule a minute, highly articulate, and adaptable segment of the native society was recruited and trained by the colonial authority to carry out its policies. The function of this small, indigenous bureaucracy was to serve as a bridge between the dependent people and the ruling, nonindigenous power.

In the change of power at independence, the general change in political climate called for some significant adjustment on the part of the trained and experienced administrators, if they were to continue their work under the new government. They were faced with the necessity of having to adapt themselves to the new ethos of independent rule. A great number of problems had to be faced. S. C. Dube describes some special features of these bureaucracies, as they emerged and crystallized during the colonial phase.

1. Bureaucracy constituted a special subcultural segment—the high-prestige stratum of the society. Entrance to it was theoretically not barred to any section of the community, although in actual practice only the traditionally privileged could provide the necessary general background and the expensive education required for success in the stiff tests prescribed for entry into its higher echelons. In limited numbers others also gained entrance into the relatively closed group of higher civil servants. Middle-level and lower positions attracted the less privileged. Bureaucracy had a class bias and it tended to have a stratification of its own; its upper crust functioned as a privileged class. On the whole it symbolized achievement rather than ascription. Over time, it came to have distinct vested interests, and was sensitive to all threats to its position and privilege which it guarded jealously against encroachment from any quarter.

2. It existed largely in the twilight zone of cultures. Partly traditional and partly modern, it could and did in fact choose from the elements of both. In several ways it was alienated from the masses and uprooted from the native cultural traditions; significant differences in styles of living and in modes of thought separated the two. The Western rulers, on the other hand, never conceded equality to it. In consequence, bureaucracy maintained dual identification and was characterized by a dual ambivalence.

3. Besides offering security of tenure and relatively higher emoluments, bureaucratic positions carried vast powers which made them additionally attractive and important. The powers vested in a minor functionary gave him prestige, perquisites, and privileges far beyond those justified by his emoluments and position in the hierarchy. Formally the role and status of functionaries at different levels were defined, but in actual practice the system of expectation and obligation between them tended to be diffused rather than specific.

4. Within the framework of the overall policy laid down by the imperial power, in day-to-day administration the bureaucratic machine enjoyed considerable freedom from interference. Thus there were few hindrances to its exercise of power, which was often authoritarian in tone and content. Bureaucracy had, in general, a paternalistic attitude to the masses. The masses, on their part, accepted the position and looked to the administration for a wide variety of small favors.

5. Administration was concerned mainly with collection of land revenue and with maintenance of law and order. The general administrator under these conditions enjoyed supremacy. Subject-matter specialists of welfare and nation-building departments were relegated to secondary positions and functioned under the guidance and control of the generalist.

6. Bureaucracy was carefully trained in formal administrative procedure and routine. Stereotypes in this sphere were well developed and were scrupulously observed.

7. In the limited framework of its functions and set procedures bureaucracy found a self-contained system. It resented and resisted innovations.

8. Its attitude to the nationalist forces within was most ambivalent. Few within the bureaucracy were devoid of patriotic sentiments and aspirations, but only in rare exceptions could they openly side with the forces of nationalism. Requirements of their official position made them an instrument for the execution of imperialist policies. This naturally aroused in the nationalist leadership feelings of anger and distrust against them. This rejection by the leaders of the nationalist forces as well as by the politically conscious masses was largely at the root of their ambivalent attitude toward the nationalist forces.

Source: S. C. Dube, "Bureaucracy and Nation Building in Traditional Societies," *International Social Science Journal* 16:229–236.

the office-holder cannot own the means of production or administration and cannot appropriate the position

7. Administrative work as a full-time occupation.[23]

Each of these conditions of employment is found in modern government administrations, and, as Bendix notes, the process of bureaucratization has been the manifold, cumulative, and more or less successful imposition of these employment conditions since the nineteenth century.[24]

Wherever there are modern states, there are bureaucracies that resemble each other in their essential features. For example, the problem of transporting large quantities of mail as quickly, safely, and economically as possible is similar in every country. The tasks of the postal minister in Sweden and in Tanzania are much the same. Furthermore, since the activities are similar, the positions will attract similar types of individuals; and the various individual holders of these offices will be further influenced and formed into similar patterns by their similar type work. As a consequence, the bureaucrats of different countries with diverging or even opposing ideologies are better able to talk with each other than are, for instance, the political leaders who are not yet bureaucrats. Therefore, many social scientists have argued that the general and universal process of bureaucratization may have a leveling effect. We will consider this possibility at greater length later in this chapter. Here, however, let us note only that when we talk about the leveling effect of bureaucratization, we do not mean it will bring about peace and concord among nations. One of the things that this implies is that governmental machines will resemble each other in their social and structural characteristics.

The bureaucratizing of political authority in the newly emerging states—which until recently had no opportunity to build a modern, rational, stable, and efficient governmental administration of their own—can be problematical. In Europe, the transformation from traditional types of authority has been long and oftentimes painful. The developing nations, however, cannot afford to do it gradually, because the revolution of rising expectations leads them to want to be competitive in a world already dominated by modern, legal-rational types of states; therefore, they must develop a rationally functioning bureaucracy *at once*. But, studies on the relationship between bureaucracy and nation-building in transitional societies show that, in general, this causes problems. Premature or too rapid expansion of the bureaucracy when the political system (parties, electorates, formation of interest groups) lags behind tends to inhibit the development of effective politics.[25] It is generally held that democratic political institutions have a better chance to grow where bureaucratic institutions are relatively weak.[26]

The problematic question of the role of bureaucratization of the political sector and its effects upon the state takes us back to our main argument. On the one hand, the modern constitutional state which is characterized by the legal-rational exercise of power demands a rational form of organization of this power. This need is met by a bureaucratic organization of governmental activities. On the other hand, the existing bureaucratic governmental apparatus in turn now influences the conception of the state. The movement toward universal bureaucratization, which Max Weber envisaged, must be seen as a sociological process affecting modern societies in all their phases of development. The consequences of this transformation are only now becoming fully apparent.

The Growing Influence of the State

It has been generally observed that the emergence of the modern nation-state is accompanied by the growth of a large-scale governmental structure which is inclined to extend its influence to almost all spheres of social life. The degree of control and influence varies from one political system to the other. When all social activities and institutions are controlled by a state bureaucracy, then we have what is commonly called a totalitarian situation. This is obviously not the case in most societies. Even in those countries in which the government has had a totalitarian character, there are recent indications that the state is withdrawing its control from a number of social spheres. On the other hand, in countries with long traditions of opposition to the expansion of the state, the role of the state has, nevertheless, increased significantly in recent years. This modification toward uniformity is one aspect of the bureaucratic leveling alluded to earlier. It seems, then, that political rationalization involves an impulse toward totalitarianism, as well as certain resistances to the full realization of this tendency. Why this is so is no great mystery.

Let us illustrate this briefly. It is necessary for the modern state to have an important voice in, if not control of, economic planning. It can no longer afford to adhere to the *laissez faire, laissez aller* policy of the early period of industrialization; it cannot rely upon what Adam Smith so aptly called the "finger of God." The risks and dangers inherent in such a policy are too great. The assurance of the rights and the welfare of *all* its subjects, which the modern state has taken on, does not allow it to disregard one of the fundamental bases of society. Therefore, the state must play a major role in economic planning and economic control. On the other hand, it is not necessary for the state to be concerned with the religious beliefs of her subjects, because spirituality no longer moves many men to public behavior of consequence. In the United States, for example, the ideology underlying the growth of capitalism restrained, and at times precluded, the state's interference in the economic sphere. Nevertheless, in the last twenty years the government has increasingly assumed (or been forced to assume) a hand in economic matters. On the other side, the Soviet Union was, in its early years, an ideological state, and therefore had to limit and control adherence to competing religious ideologies. However, as rationalization and nationalism have come to the fore, the government has found it increasingly unnecessary to control strictly the religious activities of its population, and the tendency has been to grant more freedom in this area. The structural necessities of political rationalization have a way of overcoming ideological resistances.

The Correlation between the Economic and Political Structures

Whatever one's theory about the nature of causal connections in history, the correlation between rational economic and rational political developments is very high. The modern industrial economy seems to require a state that functions rationally.

The modern industrial economy—regardless of whether the system of ownership is capitalistic, socialistic, or mixed—has to make certain specific requirements of the political institutions of the state. Above all, it must require a continuous and stable government which can guarantee the constitutional rights of individuals and the legal framework of economic institutions and relations. It is on the basis of the governmental administration of laws and codes that a reliable, predictable situation exists in which economic plans can be made and outcomes calculated. In other words, regardless of whether an economic enterprise operates under capitalism or socialism, it is important to know that the rules of the game will not be switched.

Let us consider the positions of a producer of light machinery in the United States and in Soviet Russia. In all likelihood the American plant is administered by a professional manager, as is the Soviet plant. In both cases, the successful operation of the plant requires, among other factors, of course, a steady supply of raw materials. In both cases, the manager needs assurance that the raw materials upon which production depends can be obtained and will be delivered in a rationally predictable manner. This, in both cases, involves the government, although the communist government plays a much more direct role than does the capitalist one. In the United States the government stands behind the rational-legal system which ensures that purchase and delivery contracts are maintained. In Russia the government, at least in theory, guarantees the supply of raw material directly through its own planning and control agencies, in this case, the Commissariat of Light Industry.

Either system may, of course, break down: capitalism is subject to bankruptcy or corruption, communism to faulty planning, deceptive reporting, corruption, and the like. But we are not interested in analyzing the relative efficiency of the two systems. Obviously, in both cases there are various ways in which the rationality of economic operations is disrupted. Our point is that in both cases a rationally functioning governmental and legal order is required to support the modern economic system.

In general, it can be said that so long as a movement toward a modern industrial economy is not initiated and the society is kept in isolation, then the governmental form can maintain its traditional, that is, nonlegal, nonrational lines. For instance, Russia began the development of a modern economy very late in the history of European industrialization, and thus was also able to maintain its traditional, Czarist form of government for a long time. However, the argument can be turned around, to claim that delayed industrialization and late economic development in Russia were due to the stably traditional political structure. Again, how-ever, whatever one may believe in regard to this historical ques-tion of cause and effect, there can be no doubt about the close *correlation* between the two spheres. From the sociohistorical point of view we have always to emphasize and grasp the interre-lation of all the institutional levels that compose the social struc-ture. It is always true that change in one important institutional area, for instance, in the economy, is likely to lead to political and other changes, and vice versa.[27] What the decisive variable is will depend upon the specific constellation of forces in the given so-ciety at a certain point in its history.

One major variable force we have not considered so far is the degree to which the people are conscious of change. This force can lead in two opposite directions. On the one hand, a situation may arise where one sector of a society, let us say the economic, progresses rapidly, while other sectors are lagging behind. This is typical of societies undergoing a rapid period of transition. The people caught in the throes of this transformation may not be aware of the degree of change going on around them and, there-fore, may fail to work toward change in the other traditional sec-tors of their social life. The problems ensuing from this lack of consciousness of change may be far-reaching and have a dramatic effect. On the other hand, a completely different situation may take place, if, for instance, in an economically backward country, where there has been very little modernization, people become aware of the drastic changes occurring in other societies around them. This awareness may lead to disaffection from tradition and to the formation of potentially rebellious groups. The recent his-tory of underdeveloped countries in Asia, Africa, and South America abounds with examples that demonstrates the importance of consciousness of change. It is this consciousness of a different kind of life that makes for potential restlessness. That this was true of the Bolshevist revolution in Russia also demonstrates this point.

We can go even further in this observation and say that the *speed* of change is of significant importance. Where change is very rapid, the likelihood is that there is going to be a kind of cata-strophic appearance of what is happening and that, therefore, tra-ditional attitudes, including political traditionalism, may collapse in a catastrophic manner. This may lead to the rise of revolutionary movements and, at times, the successful establishment of radical regimes.

The history of Europe during the eighteenth and nineteenth centuries illustrates this argument. Whenever the economic sector advanced with extreme rapidity while other institutional sectors, primarily the political, failed to keep pace with this development, then violence and political disruption occurred. Revolutionary France is a familiar example of the violent disruption that will ensue when a government blinds itself to the socioeconomic demands of a changing society. The "bourgeois revolution" has, in the final analysis, to be understood as the consequence of the traditional government's failure to provide fundamental political changes that could accommodate the formation of an historically novel socioeconomic grouping.[28] English history, on the other hand, has commonly been advanced as a good example for the quiet, nonradical political transformation of a peasant society into a modern, democratic, industrial state. However, recent studies show that this transformation was far from being smooth and nonviolent.[29] Although no open revolutionary break with the old order resulted, England, along with France, had, to use Veblen's terms, to "take the penalty of taking the lead" in transforming a society. However, the relative absence of political radicalism accompanying the socioeconomic transformation of Germany and Japan may be explained in terms of what Veblen called the "advantage of the late-comer." [30]

The transformation of American society into a democracy is generally considered by social scientists and philosophers to show the closest relationship possible between the economic and political sectors of society in the initial period of nascence. The American example, it has been suggested, bears out Weber's notion that modern democracy can be achieved most fully under a system of capitalist industrialization.[31]

The relationship between the political nature and stability of a country and its state of economic development and wealth has been the subject of many studies. A stimulating theory, based upon a wide range of data obtained from many countries, has been advanced by S. M. Lipset in *Political Man*.[32] Lipset's discussion of the relationship between economic development and democracy is of special relevance here.

The Correlation between Class Structure
and Political Structure

In every society we can observe some system by which different groups are ranked. The criteria upon which this ranking is based differ greatly from society to society: it may be money, race, color, or birth, bravery, beauty in another, intelligence, or even age grading in yet another. The system of ranking is known as stratification. Stratification always has been significantly related to political power. Different strata have different interests, which relate in various ways to the power system of a given society. Frequently, the power conflicts in a given society reflect the conflicting interests of the various strata.

For instance, the political problems of Malaysia are, to an important degree, manifested in the racial conflict between Malays and Chinese, which, in turn, is triggered primarily by the differential position of the two groups within the social stratification system of Malaysia. Or, if we wish to understand the political problems of modern India, we must turn to the criterion of birth or caste that underlies the traditional Hindu caste system of stratification; Indian politics dramatically reflects this background, especially in the novel political role that the former "untouchables" play in the Congress Party in India.[33] Finally, intelligence and education were required for admittance to the bureaucracy of the Imperial Chinese government, which held a crucial political position.[34]

In modern societies, the most important form of stratification is social class in correlation with authority and status. This implies that the criteria according to which the ranking of individuals is effected are determined by factors of economic possession as well as the possession of power and status.[35] This means that individuals who have similar "life chances" in terms of these criteria make up a given social class. The class system of modern societies is, therefore, characterized by considerable mobility. This is to say that, while in a class society one cannot stop being a Chinese or an Indian "untouchable," one still has the potential chance of changing one's class position. The degree of mobility varies with the society, but in general it can be observed that with increasing prosperity the degree of mobility also tends to increase, regardless

The Case of Malaysia

The situation of Malaysia can best be described in racial terms, as the table below demonstrates:

MALAYSIA, INCLUDING SINGAPORE: PERCENTAGE OF POPULATION BY RACE (1961)

	MALAYA	SINGAPORE	SARAWAK	SABAH	TOTAL IN MALAYSIA
Malays	50.1	14.0	17.5	—	39.2
Other indigenous	—	—	50.3	67.2	7.0
Chinese	36.9	75.2	31.1	23.3	41.2
Indian/Pakistani	11.2	8.3	—	—	9.4
Others	1.8	2.5	1.1	9.5	2.2

Before the exclusion of Singapore from the Federation, Malaysia could be divided into three geopolitical parts:

FIRST: Mainland Malaya, with 87 per cent of the Malays in rural occupations and 62 per cent of the urban population Chinese; ruled by Malays politically, whereas the Chinese dominate in the economic sector.

SECOND: Singapore, the greatest Chinese city in South-East Asia, where the wealth and the power is concentrated in Chinese hands.

THIRD: Sabah and Sarawak, democratically ruled by its indigenous majority (although many of the administrative positions are still in English and Chinese hands), with Chinese dominating the economic life.

Politically, Malaysia was and still is faced by a number of serious problems centering around its racial relationships and the hostility of Indonesia. The racial difficulties, unquestionably, arise out of the poorer and more rural Malayan population's fear of Chinese wealth, power, and higher rate of education. The tensions arising out of this fear led to Singapore's leaving the Federation, retaining only economic links. Even though Singapore is no longer a part of the Federation, the racial tensions still persist, as the radical, young, competent Malaysian Chinese have little reverence for the dignified, religiously sanctioned Malay traditions.

Source: Guy Hunter, *South-East Asia* (New York: Oxford University Press for the Institute of Race Relations, 1966).

of the society's historical background.[36] This process of increasing mobility can be taken to indicate the growth of the principle of rationality, as we will show in a later chapter.

The close relationship between economic class and the political structure in modern societies is clear when considered from an historical perspective. As numerous studies have shown, the rise of the modern state in the West both created and was created by the emergence of two new social classes: the new middle class of "bourgeoisie," and the new class of the industrial worker or "proletariat." At times this process was accompanied by a catastrophic disruption of the traditional stratification system. For instance, the rise of the bourgeoisie in France in the seventeenth and eighteenth centuries resulted largely from the disintegration of the aristocracy, and it hastened further decline of the once powerful ruling strata under the centralized monarchy of the Bourbon kings. The French Revolution of 1789 must be seen as the final consequence of this process of social transformation.[37] On the other hand, the rise of a new class need not always culminate in revolutionary upheaval, as the history of England shows. The relatively violent and coercive measures that the English peasantry suffered in the seventeenth and eighteenth century at the hands of the upper classes made for its ultimate disappearance. As the peasants were forced to leave and at times were even evicted from the land they had cultivated, they aggregated around the emerging industrial centers where in the early part of the nineteenth century they became a new class of industrial workers. Throughout the nineteenth century a relatively strong and independent Parliament searched for ways and means to incorporate the industrial worker into the democratic process. Thus a relatively peaceful transition of the social order was brought about.[38]

It is plausible to conceive of politics in societies at a certain stage of industrial development as a great struggle between these two new classes, the bourgeoisie and the proletariat (that is, the middle class and the working class). The sociological and historical writings of Karl Marx serve as the most famous example here. Marx's "miseration" theory is that the working class becomes constantly larger and poorer, while the bourgeoisie which exploits the working class becomes smaller in number, and richer, as various middle groups sink down to the proletariat. He believed that the whole process would tend toward a violent confrontation, which, given certain conditions, would ultimately lead to revolution and to a total transformation of society.[39] What actually seems to have happened is the reversal of Marx's "miseration" theory: in the West there has been continuous growth of the middle class and a relatively successful integration of the working class into the new social order, as education, political participation, and general opportunities were extended to the working class. Recent Marxist theorists have revised Marx's basic tenet, envisioning the industrialized and nonindustrialized countries in a global class confrontation.

We have seen that political conflict between classes tends to diminish as the general prosperity of a country increases, as then there are available greater opportunities for the people of the lower class to enter the middle stratum.[40] If this is true, political stability can be envisaged.[41] However, whenever industrialization, or any economic-technological change, for that matter, occurs rapidly, it introduces sharp discontinuities between the pre- and post-industrial situations, and then extremist political movements crop up in the working class.[42] The Russian Revolution of 1917 is the most significant illustration of this. Leon Trotsky, in *My Life,*[43] describes the abundant political opportunities that were created, as if especially for the revolutionary leaders of Russia, by the rapid growth of industry during the early part of the twentieth century. New economic demands overwhelmed the inflexible governmental bureaucracy, and the consequent disorientation of policy caused unrest and dissatisfaction among industrial workers. Comparable developments in other industrializing nations indicate how significant for political stability is the length of time involved in industrialization.[44]

It seems that stable, nontotalitarian political regimes in industrial societies depend for their existence on there being a stable and open middle class. Only in a society where class antagonism has been minimized by the reduction of class differences can the paralyzing threat of revolutionary cataclysm be avoided. In Soviet Russia, where class antagonism has been forcefully eliminated by a totalitarian regime, the "dictatorship of the workers," class differences—while still existing—have been reduced when compared to prerevolutionary times. In general, many sociologists believe that the absence of a middle class makes it difficult for any country to build a stable political structure. The Latin American countries furnish excellent evidence for this insight, as do the newly rising states of Africa and Asia. In these countries the road is open for dictatorships of an increasingly military character, as no strong middle class can serve to balance and mediate the ruling groups and the masses.

On the other hand, the United States has been used as an example of the deterioration of radical political movements to the roles of politically irrelevant sects, due to the general growth of the middle classes and their relative openness. We also find evidence for this in immediate post-World War II Europe, where a general decline in radical political movements seems to have resulted from increased prosperity and a new awareness of expanding social mobility.[45] Of course, this general pattern is subject to the peculiar social forces active at any particular time in history, as well as to the historical and cultural traditions of each society. (The tumultuous politics in the United States and Western European countries in recent years gives reason to question this thesis. However, as yet there are no reliable data that connect the unrest expressed internationally by many students to an imaginary or real blocking up of the class system. It is possible, though, that future studies will reveal that rapidly multiplying numbers of students in institutions of higher learning are beginning to feel that what they call "the system" has no room in it to accept and make effective use of them.)

We will conclude this chapter by briefly pointing to the significant role of what is generally called the "ruling elite" or "ruling class." In recent years the need has been recognized for sociological studies of the background of old and new political elites, of the grouping of class factors that cause the emergence of one type of elite and the disappearance of another, and of the way in which class interests are personified in individual leaders. It is hoped that the study of the role of political elites in the past and the present will uncover key factors in the arena of power, helping us to analyze the political events around us today and those still in the making.

Ruling elites achieve power by various means—at times by the use of sheer force in the furtherance of their own interests, at times by traditional rights, at other times by representing the interests of the dominant social classes, and at other times by their superior knowledge. Since ruling elites hold an instrumental position in the advancement of their countries—whether industrial or underdeveloped—social scientists interested in political sociology have tried to forecast future patterns by looking at past ones. A consensus is that a new pattern of political elites is developing. Political authority, vested in traditional elite groups, is being replaced by a ruling intelligentsia, military as well as civilian intellectuals, especially in those non-Western countries that have not yet established parliamentary political structures. Here, for the first time in history, we seem to find a political elite that wields power, as it were, independently. That is, intellectuals wield it as an "intelligentsia" concerned with society as a whole, rather than as spokesmen for particular entrenched social forces.[46]

NOTES

1. Lucian W. Pye, "The Concept of Political Development," in Jason L. Finkle and Richard W. Gable, eds., *Political Development and Social Change* (New York: John Wiley, 1966).

2. Franz Altheim, *Der Niedergang der Alten Welt* (Frankfurt/Main: Vittorie Klostermann, 1952).

3. Karl Marx, *Capital and Other Writings* (New York: Modern Library, 1932).

4. For instance, Edward Gibbon, *The Decline and Fall of the Roman Empire,* Bury's Edition (London: Oxford University Press, 1926–1929).

5. The sociological usage of the term "modern" with reference to the state should be compared to the tight definition given by Weber in H. H. Gerth and C. Wright Mills, eds., *From Max Weber: Essays in Sociology* (New York: Oxford University Press, 1958), pp. 196–240.

6. Max Weber, *Wirtschaft und Gesellschaft,* 4th ed. (Tuebingen: J. C. B. Mohr, 1956), pp. 122–125. On the abstract nature of Weber's concepts, see Reinhard Bendix, *Nation-Building and Citizenship* (New York: John Wiley, 1964), p. 109.

7. For general reference on the various aspects of authority and the transformation of authority in the modern state, see *ibid.*

8. Reinhard Bendix, in *Work and Authority in Industry* (New York: John Wiley, 1956), has convincingly shown that, despite the similarities imposed by the overall sociological processes, ideological factors make a difference.

9. See A. Hourani, "Syria and Lebanon," in I. Wallerstein, ed., *Social Change: The Colonial Situation* (New York: John Wiley, 1966).

10. For general reference on the rise of nationalist movements, see Wallerstein, *ibid.,* and John H. Kautsky, *Political Change in Underdeveloped Countries: Nationalism and Communism* (New York: John Wiley, 1962).

11. Hans Kohn, *The Idea of Nationalism: A Study in Origins and Background* (New York: Macmillan, 1945) and *Nationalism, Its Meaning and History* (Princeton: Van Nostrand, 1955).

12. See Kautsky, *op. cit.,* and Louis L. Snyder, *The Meaning of Nationalism* (New Brunswick: Rutgers University Press, 1954). Also Rupert Emerson, "Ideology and Nationalism," in Finkle and Gable, *op. cit.*

13. Kautsky, *op. cit.,* p. 30 ff. Also, see Karl W. Deutsch, *Nationalism and Social Communication* (Cambridge: M. I. T. Press, 1966), p. 43.

14. The concept of "routinization" has been developed by Max Weber, *Wirtschaft und Gesellschaft,* with special reference to the transformation of charismatic authority due to the influences of everyday life in which personal and material interests demand a body to administer legal and rational measures.

15. Klaus Mehnert, *Stalin versus Marx* (New York: Praeger, 1953).

16. The various references on nationalism cited above attempt to point to the significant influence of the new nationalism on the world in general.

17. Bendix, *Work and Authority in Industry.*

18. Max Weber, *Law in Economy and Society* (Cambridge: Harvard University Press, 1954) and *Wirtschaft und Gesellschaft.* A good summary of Weber's theory of the bureaucratic form of administration can be found in Bendix, *Nation-Building and Citizenship;* see especially the chapter "Transformation of Western Societies."

19. For a general reference on the role of bureaucracy in political development, see Fred W. Riggs, "Bureaucrats and Political Development: A Paradoxical View," in Finkle and Gable, *op. cit.*

20. Special reference is taken from Weber's *Wirtschaft und Gesellschaft.*

21. The quoted passages are from Max Weber, *The Theory of Social and Economic Organization* (New York: Oxford University Press, 1946), pp. 330–332. Also see Weber, *Wirtschaft und Gesellschaft.*

22. Bendix, *Nation-Building and Citizenship.*

23. Gerth and Mills, *op. cit.,* pp. 196–198.

24. Bendix, *Nation-Building and Citizenship,* p. 109.

25. Karl A. Wittfogel, *Oriental Despotism* (New Haven: Yale University Press, 1957). Wittfogel examines in an exemplary manner the history and dynamics of Oriental bureaucratic systems.

26. Riggs, *op. cit.*

27. Compare, for instance, Theodore Geiger, *The Conflicted Relationship* (New York: McGraw-Hill, 1967), pp. 132 ff.

28. For a general discussion, see Alexis de Tocqueville, *The Old Regime and the French Revolution* (New York: Doubleday, 1955); Georges Lefebvre, *The Coming of the French Revolution* (Princeton: Princeton University Press, 1947); Hippolyte Taine, *The Ancient Regime* (London: Peter Smith, 1931); Jeffry Kaplow, *New Perspectives on the French Revolution* (New York: John Wiley, 1965).

29. Barrington Moore, Jr., *Social Origins of Dictatorship and Democracy* (Boston: Beacon Press, 1966), and Bendix, *Nation-Building and Citizenship.*

30. Thorstein Veblen, "On the Penalty of Taking the Lead," in *The Portable Veblen* (New York: Viking Press, 1948).

31. S. M. Lipset, *Political Man* (New York: Doubleday Anchor, 1963), p. 29.

32. *Ibid.*

33. See George Rosen, *Democracy and Economic Change in India* (Berkeley: University of California Press, 1966), pp. 74 ff.

34. Shu-Ching Lee, *Administration and Bureaucracy: The Power Structure in Chinese Society* (London: International Sociological Association, 1954), vol. 2.

35. This conceptualization of "class" is based on Weber's *Wirtschaft und Gesellschaft.*

36. For general reference, see S. M. Lipset and Reinhard Bendix, *Social*

Mobility in Industrial Society (Berkeley: University of California Press, 1963).

37. See Albert Salomon, "Louis Duc de Saint-Simon: The Class Consciousness of the Defeated," in *In Praise of Enlightenment* (New York: Meridian, 1962).

38. See Moore, *op. cit.,* Chapter I.

39. Marx, *op. cit.*

40. Recent studies, summarized by T. B. Bottomore, *Classes in Modern Society* (New York: Pantheon Books, 1966), forcefully argue that the gradual disappearance of class antagonism seems to be due to the spreading notion and ideology of equal opportunities for high social mobility.

41. Lipset, *op. cit.*

42. *Ibid.*

43. Leon Trotsky, *My Life* (New York: Scribners, 1930).

44. Lipset, *op. cit.,* p. 53 ff.

45. Bottomore, *op. cit.*

46. See, for example, Edward Shils, "The Intellectuals in the Political Development of the New States," in Kautsky, *op. cit.;* Harry J. Benda, "Non-Western Intelligentsias as Political Elites" in Kautsky, *op. cit.;* H. D. Lasswell and Daniel Lerner, *World Revolutionary Elites* (Cambridge: M. I. T. Press, 1966); and S. M. Lipset and Aldo Solari, *Elites in Latin America* (New York: Oxford University Press, 1967).

[3] The Economic Structure

THE development of the economic sector is one of the chief concerns of every nation in the world today. Not only are individual nations passionately engaged in attempts to further their economic progress, but also an increasing part of the activities of the United Nations is directed toward fostering the general economic development of the various countries. The tremendously important role that the economic structure plays in the overall society is widely recognized as the primary concern, regardless of whether the country is regarded as highly industrialized or economically underdeveloped. It has become apparent that the conditions and peculiarities of the economic structure reverberate in all other sectors of society. And there is little doubt that no goal—be it political, humanitarian, or cultural—can be achieved in contemporary society unless there is a viable economic structure that can initiate and sustain the efforts toward the realization of such goals. One cannot hope to develop a democratic political system if the people are starving; one cannot hope for cultural achievement if the people have no work and no income. This has been true to some extent throughout history. However, today this is so to a much greater extent due to the unprecedented rise in the world's population, which makes economic development not only a desirable but a necessary condition for survival.

The spread of communication systems throughout the world has made the world smaller at the same time, so that the events in one part of the world are known in other, quite remote, parts. This is of great significance; because of this broadened communication people can compare themselves with other people, producing what has been called the "revolution of rising expectations." And so economic achievements, primarily those in the consumer sector, which once had been a distant dream or not even known of, are now passionately demanded.[1] It is for this reason that some social scientists believe that the split between the economically highly developed countries and the economically less developed ones may be more crucial, in the long run, than the split between capitalist and socialist nations.

Comparative Economics

There are four basic problems that confront the student of comparative economic development. The first problem involves the determination of the *economic level* of a given society. It is presupposed that there exists a continuous scale of economic development whose measurement ranges from primitive economies on the one end to highly industrialized economies on the other. The problem for the economist concerned with patterns of development or growth is to develop a unified theory that will permit him to classify the growth of an economy on a continuous scale, regardless of where it is geographically and historically located, and regardless of its degree of complexity. So, for instance, Walt W. Rostow's much discussed "stages of economic growth" tries to do precisely this, by treating economic growth as a general process that occurs in step-by-step development.[2] He distinguishes five stages of growth, of which the "take-off" stage is the crucial one. Other so-called growth economists, although differing on many technical points, are in general agreement with the basic tenets of Rostow to the extent of applying certain typical characteristics to each individual stage. For example, S. Kuznets, an outstanding theorist of economic growth, defines a modern economy in terms of the following measurable criteria: the application of scientific thought and technology to industry, transportation, and agriculture; a sustained and rapid rise in real product per capita, combined with high rates of population growth; a high rate of transformation of the industrial structure; and the presence of international contacts.[3]

The second basic problem for the economist is how to determine, on the continuum of his scale, the *moments of significant*

TABLE 3-1

"Stages" of Economic and Political Development
Summary Table

STAGE	N =		GROSS NATIONAL PRODUCT PER CAPITA	PERCENTAGE URBAN (20,000)	PERCENTAGE ADULT LITERACY	HIGHER EDUCATION PER 100,000	INHABITANTS PER PHYSICIAN	RADIOS PER 1,000	PERCENTAGE VOTING	PERCENTAGE MILITARY (15-64)	PERCENTAGE EXPERIENCE OF CENTRAL GOVT.
I	11	Range:	45-64	0-18	3-48	5-63	5,800-117,000	1-63	0-55	.20-2.52	8-29
II	15	Mean:	56	5.8	12.9	27.3	46,073	11.7	29.9	.84	18.9
		Range:	70-105	0-19	1-68	4-251	5,200-95,000	3-78	0-83	.15-2.00	12-27
III	31	Mean:	87	9.6	23.9	86.3	22,160	20.2	49.4	.79	16.9
		Range:	108-239	6-72	3-91	3-976	1,394-48,000	7-161	0-95	.05-11.11	9-48
IV	36	Mean:	173	20.6	41.6	165.3	5,362	56.5	41.1	1.68	26.2
		Range:	262-794	7-82	38-99	42-1,192	400-6,400	37-348	0-100	0-4.84	14-38
V	14	Mean:	445	34.3	76.8	385.8	1,630	157.5	69.4	1.40	27.8
		Range:	836-2577	30-70	96-99	36-1,983	765-1,089	215-948	28-92	.15-3.62	15-40
		Mean:	1,330	45.3	98.0	650.0	875	351.9	77.8	1.52	29.6

I "Traditional Primitive" Societies

COUNTRY	GROSS NATIONAL PRODUCT PER CAPITA	PERCENTAGE URBAN (20,000)	PERCENTAGE ADULT LITERACY	HIGHER EDUCATION PER 100,000	INHABITANTS PER PHYSICIAN	RADIOS PER 1,000	PERCENTAGE VOTING	PERCENTAGE MILITARY (15-64)	PERCENTAGE EXPERIENCE OF CENTRAL GOVT. +
Nepal	45	4.4	5.0	56	72,000	1.7		0.86	
Afghanistan	50	7.5	2.5	12	41,000	8.0		0.81	8.0
Laos	50	4.0	17.5	4	100,000	4.3		2.52	
Togo	50	4.5	7.5		58,000	4.5			
Ethiopia	55	1.7	2.5	5	117,000	5.6		0.28	
Burma	57	10.0	47.5	63	15,000	11.4	54.5	0.49	29.1
Angola	60	4.7	2.5		14,000				
Libya	60	18.4	13.0	49	5,800	63.1		0.69	
Sudan	60	5.0	9.0	34	40,000	.9	0.0	0.20	
Tanganyika	61	3.3	7.5	9	18,000	3.6	33.8		17.6
Uganda	64	.1	27.5	14	15,000	13.8	31.0		20.9

II "Traditional Civilizations"

COUNTRY	GROSS NATIONAL PRODUCT PER CAPITA	PERCENTAGE URBAN (20,000)	PERCENTAGE ADULT LITERACY	HIGHER EDUCATION PER 100,000	INHABITANTS PER PHYSICIAN	RADIOS PER 1,000	PERCENTAGE VOTING	PERCENTAGE MILITARY (15-64)	PERCENTAGE EXPERIENCE OF CENTRAL GOVT. +
Mozambique	70	13.9	1.0		20,000	5.7			
Pakistan	70	11.8	13.0	165	8,670	3.0		0.37	12.3
China (Mainland)	73	10.0	47.5	69	8,700		0.0	0.57	
India	73	12.0	19.3	220	5,200	5.0	52.6	0.15	13.9
South Vietnam	76		17.5	83	29,000	8.9		2.00	
Nigeria	78	10.5	10.0	4	32,000	4.0	40.4		
Kenya	87	3.8	22.5	5	10,000	8.0	28.9		
Madagascar	88	7.6	33.5	21	8,427	22.4	64.8		26.9
Congo (Leopoldville)	92	9.1	37.5	4	63,000	2.5			
Thailand	96	7.7	68.0	251	7,500	6.2		0.90	15.2
Bolivia	99	19.4	32.1	166	3,900	72.7	51.4	0.47	16.1
Cambodia	99	16.0	17.5	18	95,000	6.5		1.49	
Liberia	100	0.0	7.5		16,000	77.5	82.9	0.88	
Sarawak	100	7.0	21.0		15,000	55.3			
Haiti	105	5.1	10.5	29	10,000	4.9	74.2	0.29	

TABLE 3-1 (continued)

III "Transitional" Societies

COUNTRY	GROSS NATIONAL PRODUCT PER CAPITA	PERCENTAGE URBAN (20,000)	PERCENTAGE ADULT LITERACY	HIGHER EDUCATION PER 100,000	INHABITANTS PER PHYSICIAN	RADIOS PER 1,000	PERCENT VOTING	PERCENTAGE MILITARY (15-64)	PERCENTAGE EXPERIENCE OF CENTRAL GOVT.
Iran	108	21.0	15.0	90	3,800	65.3		1.94	
Paraguay	114	15.2	65.8	188	1,800	60.8	29.1	0.96	
Ceylon	129	11.4	63.0	56	4,500	38.4	58.8	0.05	
Jordan	129	25.5	17.5		5,800	37.7		4.34	47.5
Indonesia	131	9.1	17.5	62	48,000	7.4	92.0	0.24	
Rhodesia & Nyasaland	135	9.2	16.1	3	7,400	17.6	1.9		
Egypt	142	29.1	19.9	399	2,600	65.8	0.0	0.67	36.1
Morocco	142	24.2	12.5	40	9,400	45.5		0.48	
Surinam	142	72.4	72.5	109	2,000	129.9			
South Korea	144	18.5	77.0	397	3,700		31.3	4.58	
Iraq	156	23.6	10.0	173	5,600	21.2	0.0	2.02	32.5
Nicaragua	160	20.1	38.4	110	2,800	65.5	92.7	0.43	
Taiwan	161	24.0	54.0	329	1,500	69.5		11.11	
Saudi Arabia	170	9.5	2.5	6	13,000	12.1	0.0	0.81	
Ghana	172	6.4	22.5	29	21,000	22.2	43.9	0.20	
Syria	173	38.8	27.5	223	4,600	57.3	27.6	1.71	
Tunisia	173	19.9	17.5	64	8,200	63.5	49.9	0.54	
Albania	175		60.0	145	3,500	33.6	94.6	4.12	
Algeria	178	14.1	19.0	70	6,096	54.1			
Peru	179	13.9	47.5	253	2,100	77.9	39.2	0.24	13.1
Ecuador	189	17.8	55.7	193	2,600	40.6	28.4	0.69	

Guatemala	189	11.2	29.4	135	6,400	54.3	27.5	0.37	
Honduras	194	11.5	44.0	78	4,800	66.1	36.5	0.27	
Barbados	200	54.7	91.1	24	3,000	161.0			
El Salvador	219	12.9	39.4	89	5,400	92.0	29.3	0.21	9.2
Philippines	220	12.7	75.0	976	5,555	22.3	55.1	0.28	23.8
Turkey	220	18.2	39.0	255	2,800	52.5	72.5	3.06	21.2
Portugal	224	16.5	55.9	272	1,394	98.1	18.5	1.35	
Mauritius	225	27.4	51.8	14	4,500				
British Guiana	235	17.9	74.0	27		72.2	52.1	1.12	
Dominican Republic	239	12.2	59.9	149	3,900	33.8	63.6		

IV "Industrial Revolution" Societies

Mexico	262	24.0	50.0	258	1,700	96.9	34.6	1.92	
Colombia	263	22.4	62.0	296	2,400	139.5	40.2	0.27	
Yugoslavia	265	18.6	77.0	524	1,637	98.6	91.4	3.48	
Hong Kong	272	81.9	57.5	176	3,300	55.3			
Brazil	293	28.1	49.4	132	2,100	64.3	34.4	0.71	13.7
Spain	293	39.8	87.0	258	1,000	90.0	0.0	2.39	16.5
Japan	306	43.1	98.0	750	930	106.7	71.2	0.39	34.5
Jamaica	316		77.0	42	4,300	87.9	70.6		
Panama	329	33.1	65.7	371	3,200	159.0	56.2	0.00	
Greece	340	38.4	80.0	320	800	89.9	73.3	2.52	23.6
Malaya	356	22.7	38.4	475	6,400	36.5	54.8	1.37	
Costa Rica	357	15.4	79.4	326	2,600	66.1	57.6	0.00	
Romania	360	18.0	89.0	226	788	117.0	97.9	1.79	
Lebanon	362	23.0	47.5	345	1,100	60.8	48.0	0.15	
Bulgaria	365	15.3	85.0	456	740	202.0	99.2	3.07	
Malta	377	7.3	57.6	142	980	222.0			
Chile	379	46.3	80.1	257	1,700	130.2	37.4	1.06	
South Africa	395	32.9	42.5	189	2,000	66.2	10.4	0.11	31.1
Singapore	400	75.1	50.0	437	2,400	88.3	82.3		
Trinidad & Tobago	423	13.6	73.8	61	2,300	84.1			
Cyprus	467	31.9	60.5	78	1,400	178.0	92.8	1.67	
Poland	475		95.0	351	1,100	183.0	58.3	0.45	
Uruguay	478	48.3	80.9	541	870	286.0	61.8	0.81	17.0
Argentina	490	37.0	86.4	827	660	175.0	93.5	1.14	
Hungary	490		97.0	258	650	231.0			

TABLE 3-1 (continued)

IV "Industrial Revolution" Societies

COUNTRY	GROSS NATIONAL PRODUCT PER CAPITA	PERCENTAGE URBAN (20,000)	PERCENTAGE ADULT LITERACY	HIGHER EDUCATION PER 100,000	INHABITANTS PER PHYSICIAN	RADIOS PER 1,000	PERCENTAGE VOTING	PERCENTAGE MILITARY (15-64)	PERCENTAGE EXPERIENCE OF CENTRAL GOVT.
Italy	516	30.3	87.5	362	746	170.0	92.9	1.42	34.2
Ireland	550	35.6	98.5	362	1,000	176.0	71.6	0.77	31.1
Puerto Rico	563	32.0	81.0	1,192	2,200		73.3		
Iceland	572	40.5	98.5	445	840	279.0	86.6	0.95	
East Germany	600	36.2	98.5	395		348.0	97.3	3.02	
U.S.S.R.	600	35.5	95.0	539	578	205.0	99.6	0.49	27.2
Venezuela	648	47.2	52.2	355	1,300	186.0	83.8	0.32	36.4
Austria	670	39.8	98.5	546	695	288.0	90.4	2.54	
Czechoslovakia	680	25.3	97.5	398	620	263.0	98.1	4.84	38.2
Israel	726	60.9	93.7	668	400	194.0	88.0		
Finland	794	31.2	98.5	529	1,600	289.0	72.8	1.51	30.1

V "High Mass-Consumption" Societies

COUNTRY	GROSS NATIONAL PRODUCT PER CAPITA	PERCENTAGE URBAN (20,000)	PERCENTAGE ADULT LITERACY	HIGHER EDUCATION PER 100,000	INHABITANTS PER PHYSICIAN	RADIOS PER 1,000	PERCENTAGE VOTING	PERCENTAGE MILITARY (15-64)	PERCENTAGE EXPERIENCE OF CENTRAL GOVT.
Netherlands	836	49.8	98.5	923	900	263.0	92.1	2.00	37.0
West Germany	927	55.1	98.5	528	798	319.0	86.9	0.90	30.6
France	943	29.8	96.4	667	1,014	282.0	89.4	3.62	40.0
Denmark	1,057	48.5	98.5	570	830	365.0	84.0	1.46	21.4
Norway	1,130	32.8	98.5	258	946	286.0	78.8	1.62	28.6
United Kingdom	1,189	66.9	98.5	460	935	289.0	78.0	1.86	38.8
Belgium	1,196	32.0	96.7	536	819	298.0	87.6	1.46	34.6
New Zealand	1,310	69.7	98.5	839	700	242.0	86.4	1.05	39.8
Australia	1,316	57.3	98.5	856	860	215.0	85.3	0.79	18.0
Sweden	1,380	40.8	98.5	401	1,089	378.0	83.1	1.52	39.1
Luxembourg	1,388	30.6	96.5	36	910	319.0	71.1	1.32	
Switzerland	1,428	29.9	98.5	398	765	272.0	28.0	0.15	15.2
Canada	1,947	39.4	97.5	645	900	451.0	74.2	1.16	21.3
United States	2,577	52.0	98.0	1,983	780	948.0	64.4	2.36	21.0

Source: Bruce Russett, et al. World Handbook of Political and Social Indicators (New Haven: Yale University Press, 1964).
Copyright © 1964 by Yale University.

The Main Characteristics of Industrialism

In contemporary society, economic growth is largely equated with the development of industrialization; this brief sketch of the distinguishing characteristics of industrialism is based on Herbert Blumer's "Industrialization and Race Relations."

> Industrialization is conceived to be the process which brings into being a distinctive type of economy, usually identified as "industrialism." The distinguishing mark of this economy is the use of power-driven machinery for the production of goods. A vastly differentiated system may develop from this distinguishing kernel. The compositional features which we wish to note are:
>   1. the production of manufactured products, usually in large quantity, at low cost;
>   2. the assembling of workers and other industrial personnel around the producing enterprises;
>   3. the formation of structures of diversified jobs and positions within the enterprises;
>   4. the development of an auxiliary apparatus providing for the procurement of materials and disposition of products; and
>   5. the domination of the productive system by motifs of efficiency and profitability (in the accounting sense).

Source: Herbert Blumer, "Industrialization and Race Relations," in Guy Hunter, ed., *Industrialization and Race Relations* (New York: Oxford University Press, 1965).

---

change in the nature of the economy or in the process of growth. For instance, Rostow's description of the stage of "take-off" is based on the idea that modern economic growth is the result of certain very specific conditions and changes occurring within a traditional economy. One of Rostow's conditions is a 10 per cent investment rate. This implies that sufficient capital on a large scale has to be amassed to permit economic expansion. As Rostow says:

"It is . . . useful to regard as a necessary but not sufficient condition for the take-off the fact that the proportion of net investment to national income (or net national product) rises from, say, 5 per cent to over 10 per cent, definitely outstripping the likely population pressure (since under the assumed take-off circumstances the capital/output ratio is low), and yielding a distinct rise in real output per capita." [4]

Economic Factors in Economic Development

The strictly economic factors affecting economic development are classified into the following three major areas:

1. The main physical agents of production:
   labor force;
   reproducible wealth or capital;
   provisionally nonreproducible wealth (land and natural resources).
2. Allocative mechanisms and other circumstances which dominate the allocation of agents of production and of finished goods and services:
   price system;
   extent of market;
   division of labor;
   intersector balance and aggregate demand.
3. a. Major economic decision makers.
   b. The environment of economic decision.

The roles played by factors in these categories vary with the degree of backwardness of economics. In backward countries, exogenous or noneconomic factors exercise relatively most influence; the autonomy of an economic system as such increases as the society including it progresses, and therewith the applicability of economic theory.

Source: Joseph Spengler, "The Economic Factors in Economic Development," *American Economic Review* 48 (May 1957): 243.

The third basic problem is *causation,* the discovery of how and why development takes place. For Rostow and others, this means the determination of the factors, both economic and social, that are necessary or decisive for the onset of economic development.

The fourth basic problem is that of *planned economic growth.* It can be expressed in the following question: In the absence of "natural" (unplanned) economic growth, what can be done to bring a relatively backward country out of its stage of arrested growth to make it, effectively and quickly, a modern economy? Different answers, of course, are given to this question by different economists. In terms of economic processes proper, some advocate an initial emphasis on heavy industry, others on cottage and light industry, and yet others on "balanced" economic growth.

The first two problems of comparative economics lie outside the frame of reference of this book, as well as outside the competence of the sociologist.[5] The last two problems, however, can be viewed profitably from the sociological perspective without infringing on the proper "territory" of the economist, and thereby the phenomenon of economic modernization is placed in the broader context of social and political change.

The Sociological Perspective on Economic Growth

The central problem for the sociologist interested in comparative economic development is: why has economic development been so spectacular in the West, so relatively slow, and even nonexistent, in other areas? This is the classical question Max Weber asked himself.

Weber's starting point was his observation of the unique economic development of the West—especially in the industrial and capitalist nations of Europe and North America—which has led directly to its world-dominant economic and political position. In these countries there has been an almost total transformation of traditional society into what today is called "modern society," characterized by advanced technology, industrial production, economic prosperity, as well as the numerous social and political patterns that develop from these.

From our comparative point of view the puzzling question is: why did such ancient civilizations as China and India, which had achieved a high degree of civilization long before the West started to emerge from the darkness of prehistory, never produce a "modern" society, but, on the contrary, become arrested in traditional forms? The question becomes even more complex and puzzling when we realize that the economic development of industrialization and the "modern" forms of society took place in the West, in precisely those countries that were inhabited by "barbarians" during a period when culture, politics, economies, and intellectual life flourished in ancient Greece and Rome.

Weber was preoccupied all his life with understanding the various factors that led to the transformation of Western society. At the same time, he wanted to discover those features which distinguished Western society from others. In the course of his search he threw light on the role of the rational element in science, which had its origin in ancient Greece, as well as on demythologization, the gradual liberation from magic, which had its roots in ancient Judaism. He analyzed the role of the new urban centers in Europe and their growing independence, as well as the historical transformation by which power became located in the constitutional state, culminating in the rational bureaucratic form of the state.[6] And all of his study of these phenomena peculiar to the West grew out of his one basic question: why did modern capitalism emerge only in the West?

THE WESTERN MODEL: THE PROTESTANT ETHIC
AND THE RISE OF CAPITALISM

Weber recognized, of course, that in this complex historical development all kinds of geographical, economical, political, and cultural factors were involved. Finally, though, he emphasized, as the one crucial factor, the ethics of Protestantism. He did not claim that Protestantism was the only cause, that "Protestantism caused capitalism," but rather that Protestantism provided certain values and attitudes that were conducive to the development of the capitalist mentality, what Weber called the "spirit of capitalism." Weber first had this idea when studying economic statistics for Germany, in which he noticed that Protestants tended to play an important part in business activities even in those parts of Germany where they were a minority; he attempted to find the reason for this by "pushing back" the question historically.[7]

In regard to the Protestant ethic, one phrase is crucial: "Inner-worldly asceticism." "Inner-worldly" implies that religiously motivated activities are oriented not toward another world (salvation after death or mystical illumination in this life) but toward goals that can be empirically achieved in this world. "Ascetic" suggests a moral-ethical orientation that emphasizes self-discipline and self-denial. Certainly, neither of these elements is unique to Protestantism. Rabbinical Judaism is inner-worldly, underemphasizing expectations for the hereafter and frowning on mysticism or magic, and emphasizing behavior in *this* life; but despite its piety and righteousness, it is *not* ascetic. On the other hand, Catholic

Christianity developed a great tradition of asceticism, particularly in the monastic movement, but its orientation was other-worldly. The combination of the two elements is peculiar to Protestantism.

The inner-worldly emphasis of Protestantism involved the rejection of the double standard of medieval Catholic ethics by which the monk and nun were the only ones living a truly religious life (the word "religious" still has monastic implications for the Catholic), while people living "in the world" were in a different and *lesser* ethical dispensation. Protestantism denied this dichotomy. It insisted that any lawful occupation could have the character of a religious "vocation." In this way, quite literally, Protestantism opened a completely new perspective on economic activity. This revolution in Christian ethics was accomplished by Luther and continued by both the Lutheran and Calvinist reformation movements.

The ascetic element in Protestantism was the particular contribution of Calvinism. Weber related it to the Calvinist doctrine of law and predestination, according to which the salvation of each individual has been predetermined by God. Therefore the individual can do nothing to accomplish his salvation, which is an arbitrary and undeserved gift of grace. If that had been accepted by the people, however, Calvinism might well have lead to a paralysis of activity in all spheres of secular life. What Weber tried to show, though, was that the acceptance of this terrifying doctrine in its original form was psychologically unbearable. The individual was under great psychological pressure to find out whether he was among the elect (those who have been predestined to salvation). Therefore, the search for "proofs of election" became preeminent. Partly because Calvinism is so dependent on the Old Testament, which strongly emphasizes that worldly blessings are a sign of God's grace, economic activity became a plausible place in which to look for such proofs of grace. The implication was that the person who prospered in this world could hardly be under sentence of damnation. Needless to say, this implication tremendously vulgarizes the harsh grandeur of the original Calvinist conception, but, as Weber showed in his comparative sociology of religion, religious ideas almost always become historically important only as a result of their vulgarization.

This is not, however, the entire story yet. Under the shadow of Calvinist damnation it was not enough to prosper—after all, it is

Islam and Economic Development

Subsequent to his book *The Protestant Ethic and the Spirit of Capitalism,* Weber further documented the uniqueness of Western development by studying such various religions as Hinduism, Confucianism, and Judaism and their influence on man and society. He concluded that these religions prevented their followers from becoming modernized in the Western sense of the term. Many present-day students of developing areas agree with Weber that traditional belief systems were, on the whole, "dysfunctional" in the process of modernization. Ali A. Mazrui, in a highly provocative essay "Islam, Political Leadership, and Economic Radicalism in Africa," looks at the influence of the Muslim religion on the economic and social values of Islamic countries and raises a number of challenging questions about the future.

> Of all the charges against Islam which Westerners made in the nineteenth century, perhaps the one which hurt Muslim intellectuals most deeply was the accusation that Islam was incompatible with modernity. In politics modernity was associated with liberal individualism. In economics it was linked with the entrepreneurial skills and spirit of private achievement characteristic of the new ethos of industrial capitalism. By both criteria of modernity Islam in the Middle East was found wanting.

The Islamic equivalent of the Protestant ethic, Ali Mazrui argues, while encouraging and sanctioning commercial activities, fell short of developing into capitalism because of a variety of factors in Islam which inhibited an economic development similar to the West.

One factor was the *communalistic* nature of Islamic loyalties that presented a serious barrier to the development of economic individualism and accumulation. Although Islam encouraged commercial activities among its followers, the foremost obligation of a good Muslim was to meet a host of responsibilities toward relatives and coreligionists. These responsibilities hampered accumulation. The Islamic laws of inheritance made sure these obligations were met, and thus they were "almost calculated to thwart intergenerational capital formation."

Intimately related to the "distributive concept of social justice" was the *equalitarian* aspect of Islam. A relative equalitarianism—having more to do with intention than with achievement—based on a common faith of rich and poor alike, emerged quite early as a precept of religion. Equalitarianism, according to Mazrui, is to be distinguished from democracy, the former being more collectivistic, the latter more individualistic.

A third factor that may have been anti-accumulative was the Islamic attitude toward certain forms of risk-taking. In Weber's words: "The restriction against gambling (in Islam) obviously had important consequences for the religion's attitude toward speculative business enterprises." [a]

Mazrui concludes:

> All these factors in Islam, which were, from the outset, at once communalistic and anticumulative, came to look "antimodern" by nineteenth century standards. Modernity had come to be conceptualized in vigorous individualistic terms. The "dead weight of Islam" seemed to be stifling the individual initiative of its followers.

Consequently it can be argued that the communalistic, equalitarian aspects of social life served to prevent the emergence of a spirit congenial to the formation of capital on the Western scale. It is Ali Mazrui's challenging contention, however, that in the twentieth century the broad contours of the social and economic situation has changed to the extent that, on the whole, the ethic of individualism is being replaced by the ethic of social fellowship and welfare. "Modernity has retreated a little from the rugged liberalism back to some form of communalistic fervor." Islam, whose tradition it is to set standards of public behavior and to create a certain readiness in the population for collective sacrifices, may come to terms with the new demands of modernism much more easily and thus may become congenial to the new forms of modernization.

[a] Max Weber, *Sociology of Religion* (Boston: Beacon Press, 1964), p. 264.
Source: Ali A. Mazrui, "Islam, Political Leadership, and Economic Radicalism in Africa," *Comparative Studies in Society and History* 9 (1967): 269–281.

obvious even to a vulgar mind that wicked men can be rich—but this prosperity had to be part and parcel of a total life lived in obedience to God's commandments. Therefore, prosperity could not be religiously "valid" if it resulted from luck or crime, but only from hard work, honesty, and sacrifice. What is more, because an individual was *either* elected *or* damned, his life had to be all of one piece; Calvinism eliminated the ethical calculus of good and bad deeds which characterized both Judaism and Catholicism. A man had to be *all* good. Because any slight deviation from the moral standard produced the suspicion that a man did not belong among the elect, these highly peculiar Calvinist ideas resulted in a morality that demanded unrelenting discipline and self-denial. Very simply, it demanded that men work hard, but also that they do not enjoy the fruits of their work. It is precisely because Protestantism simultaneously encourages productivity and saving, and thus is highly conducive to capital formation, that the modern economic forms developed first in Western, Protestant societies: England, the Netherlands, North America, parts of Germany and France.

To repeat, Weber did not claim that Protestantism was the sole factor that led to capitalism nor that capitalism could not also develop in non-Protestant areas, but that Protestantism, particularly in its Calvinist form, greatly facilitated its development. He did not deny, furthermore, that once capitalist development was under way it produced its own orientations and values that were no longer directly linked to any particular religious ideas. Nevertheless, Weber seems to have been correct that the early linking of religious and economic factors produced the Western economic development. Capitalism is, historically, the precursor of industrialization, which until recently was not achieved in any noncapitalist society. Even though there are today other paths to it, nevertheless, every road to industrialization requires the cultivation of certain orientations, attitudes, and values that encourage capital formation. Every transformation of a traditional into an industrial economy requires discipline, hard work, and sacrifice. Weber's theory is important, therefore, not only as an historical explanation of Western development, but because it alerts us to the fact that some kind of "functional equivalent" to the Protestant ethic is necessary if people are to be motivated to act in the manner required to create industrialization.

THE RUSSIAN MODEL

Russia was a relative late-comer on the industrial scene.[8] At the outbreak of the Russian Revolution in 1917, more than 80 per cent of the population lived in villages and farms, and 75 per cent of the population was engaged in agriculture—as compared with 25 per cent in the United States at that time. Since then, as we will detail below, they have industrialized at a spectacular rate. However, lest their rate of growth seem even greater than in fact it has been, we must keep in mind that the stage for industrialization had already been prepared under the rule of the Czars. As far back as the reign of Peter the Great (1689–1725), industrialization was initiated: several state enterprises, especially in mining and in arms production, were founded, and factories were built. Incidentally, in this we should not underestimate the role of Protestantism, especially of Germany and France; craftsmen and traders were invited to Russia by the Czar and Russians were encouraged to go to these countries for purposes of study. Directly and indirectly, ideas and sentiments peculiar to Protestantism were transplanted. Later, under Catherine II (1762–1796) and throughout the nineteenth century, the government played a direct hand in industrialization. In the 1880s, after the emancipation of the serfs in 1861 (and more specifically after 1880), the Russian economy began to develop rapidly, particularly around Moscow, St. Petersburg, and in the area of the Donetz. For instance, between 1890 and 1900 the number of industrial workers increased from 1,425,000 to 2,373,000. Nevertheless, the pre-Communist transformation to modern industrial processes was still much slower than in the United States. For our purposes, the significant point is that in the Western model the emerging social class of entrepreneurs set the tone for the changeover, but in the Russian model, the government, Czarist and communist alike, took the initiative and control in the early unfolding of industrialization. Even after the emancipation of the serfs, even when private entrepreneurship was encouraged by the government, while the government's control over economic enterprises declined, and even though there was the nucleus for a small industrializing class, despite all this the governmental influence remained crucial. This was primarily due to the autocratic rule of the Czar, established and maintained during the eighteenth and nineteenth centuries, which, with special "ukases" and decrees, regulated rigidly the relationships between the various social classes and helped to prevent the unfolding of an independent, enterprising social class which could have become the carrier of the new process.[9]

After the revolution of 1917, the new regime was not faced with having to initiate an industrial take-off, for the necessary basis had been established: a transportation system existed (the trans-Siberian railroad had been built in the 1890s); textile mills, coal, iron, and oil industries had been developed. The problem of the revolutionary government was to *speed up* industrialization to ultimately bridge the production gap between Russia and the Western industrialized nations, which were all relatively hostile to the communist state.

Nevertheless, the leap into modernity did not begin immediately. During the period of "War Communism," introduced by Lenin, when all energy was directed toward establishing firmly the new regime and reorganizing the system of ownership, Russian industrial production fell disastrously—to 21 per cent of the pre-World War I level. By 1921, Lenin was forced to halt this disintegration of the economy. The NEP (New Economic Policy), introduced by Lenin, gave some small freedoms to the hard-pressed Russian people, allowing a certain amount of free enterprise into economic activities. The ruling party in Russia claimed that NEP was "two steps backward, one step forward," in an attempt to explain the deviation from the strict theory of communism, as Lenin had described it in *The State and Revolution*. Under the NEP, the economic machine began to move forward, mainly because private initiative had stepped in where the government had failed. However, the NEP was always considered merely a transitory stage.

By 1926, two years after Lenin's death, prewar quotas of production had again been achieved, and in 1928, Stalin began the complete transformation of Russian society and economy with the first Five Year Plan. The unfree, noncapitalistic, non-Protestant development of industry had now begun for the first time in history. As we have just seen, it started as a modified form of capitalism—state capitalism.

Since 1928, the Russian economy has expanded at a spectacular rate, although the actual rate of growth is under dispute. By Soviet claims, national production between 1928 and 1937 grew at a rate of 15.7 per cent a year, and between 1945 and 1950 at the even more astounding pace of 20 per cent annually. Western analysts estimate the Russian rate of growth, as measured in terms of their gross national product, at between 6 and 7 per cent a year. It constitutes, in any case, an extraordinary and unique model, unmatched by any other country (the historical rate of growth in the West ranged between 3 and 4 per cent; the Japanese rate has been calculated between 4 and 5 per cent). Economists believe they understand which features of the Russian economy account for this astounding rate of growth. Some argue against the possibility that the Russian economy will exceed the Western, and especially the

FIGURE 3-1

Rate of Growth of Total Industrial Production in the U.S.S.R. for the Period 1913-1956.

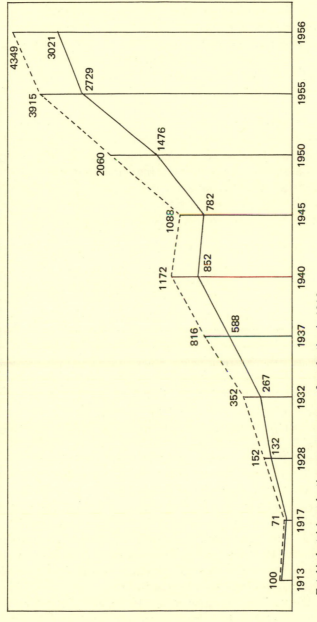

___ Total industrial production, as percentage of production in 1913.
----- Heavy industry production, as percentage of production in 1913.
Source: Robert Maxwell, ed., *Information U.S.S.R.* (New York: Pergamon Press, 1962). Reprinted by permission.

American, economy.[10] However, these questions are not for us to answer; our interest is in the detection of those *sociological* features that may have influenced this process.

The Soviet system had to manage to accumulate the huge sums of capital necessary for industrialization; this was not done freely but was instituted and controlled by the central government. (In this sense, as Bendix has pointed out, there can be observed a continuity between the Czarist handling of authority and that of the Soviets.) Popular consumption patterns were maintained at a very low level over a relatively long period of time. Production in all areas of consumer goods as well as housing has been kept forcefully at a low level by the central planning agencies, so that capital was invested primarily in heavy industry, which underwent an unprecedented boom. The Russian argument is that only when basic industries have outpaced the Western level can efforts be directed into other areas.

This is not the place to discuss the great sacrifices forced on the Russian people for the sake of this speeding-up process, nor to judge the cruelties perpetrated in the name of "economic progress," nor to evaluate the efficiency of these methods. What interests us here is that in the Russian experience we have a model, quite different from the Western one, for rapid industrialization. Whereas industrialization in the West resulted largely from the autonomous struggles of a newly emerging social class, in Russia it has been a planned process imposed upon the population autocratically, both in the Czarist times and the communist era. The difference is that the Soviet leaders pushed more forcefully than had the Czarist governments for this transition from a basically agricultural to a modern industrial society. The sociological question about the Russian method pertains to the question of motivation and values. In the Western model, as we have seen, the Protestant ethic, as Weber showed, was instrumental in providing a basis of conduct, a style of life, a set of secular values congenial to the development of an industrial economy. This spread gradually to all layers of society, eventually making for a total transformation of society. What, however, in the absence of a Protestant ethic in Russia, could provide the motivations and values that would support their tremendous industrial activity?

As Bendix tried to show in his *Work and Authority in Industry,* the communist ideology derived from Marxist doctrines served a purpose similar to that of the Protestant ethic. It fostered, on a national scale, a high valuation of hard work, thrift, and competitive achievement. In this sense, communism was an integrating and propelling force, and like a religion, made a total claim upon the individual. Yet we still must ask *why,* in the absence of the incentive of *private* gains, an individual should exert himself and regiment his desires for a pleasurable life. What goal can be offered to him, for which he will continuously labor and sweat, and for which he will give all the potentialities and abilities he has at his disposal?

Only one goal is offered to the individual as the ground for increasing his exertion: that he perform his work out of loyalty to the cause. All the people are said to work for themselves (rather than for an exploiter), because they own the means of production and hence work for their own society. . . . As the individual's right of citizenship imposes on him the duty to do military service, so in Soviet Russia the rights of citizenship impose on everyone the duty of labor. Hence, increase in productivity is rewarded as courage is in battle: . . . by material benefits and honorific distinctions. Everything is done to make every individual a full participant in the crusade to increase production and prepare for the coming struggle with the enemy. And all distinctions of material and honorific rewards are made to serve the solidarity of a society organized on the model of a combat unit. Thus, the nation is put on the basis of a continuous, military emergency, wherein the masses bear the brunt of a nearly unparalleled extinction of privacy and personal freedom, not only in the formal political sense but also in terms of an absence of material well-being.[11]

If we study the writings in which Soviet leaders themselves analyzed the Russian situation and explored the ways of infusing into the Russian peasant a spirit of work that would transform him into a Westernized industrial worker, we shall be struck again and again by the quasi-religious qualities attributed to communist doctrines.[12] The sociologically interesting aspect is how successfully this feeling seems to have been transmitted to the people. Of course, Western writers always point to the defects of this ideology, insisting that even today the Soviets are forced to take into account the materialistic instincts of individuals, who fifty years after the Revolution still have not completely lost their "capitalist" tendencies. These may be correct observations, but they must not be placed in the context of Russia's overall success with a model of industrialization so unlike that of the West. Russia has succeeded in an unprecedented way.

THE JAPANESE MODEL

When Commodore Matthew C. Perry forcefully opened Japan for the West in 1854, a period of more than two hundred years of isolation from outside influence was put to its end. With this cataclysm, the reign of the Tokugawa-Shogunate (1603–1868) was undermined. And with this political fall, there began an economic development that has been next to miraculous. The Meiji Restoration (1868) put Japan on the "high road to modernity" and to becoming the most economically advanced country in Asia.

When the Meiji Restoration began, Japan's economy presented a typical picture of an underdeveloped or traditional economy. Probably between 75 and 80 per cent of the labor force was engaged in agriculture and the amount of arable land which could be brought under cultivation was minimal. Furthermore, Japan was critically deficient in the basic mineral resources which are supposed to be a prerequisite for industrialization. The few manufacturing activities that existed were mainly in the areas of textiles and food processing.[13] Yet, despite these unpropitious conditions, Japan underwent a transition from a poor peasant society to a modern, highly industrialized one in a short time, without outside help and without such governmental controls as the imposition of protective tariffs (which played so significant a role in the initial capital accumulation and industrialization of continental Europe).

Various explanations and theories have been advanced to account for the rise of Japan, the first (and, so far, only) modern power in Asia. Clearly the rise to a modern state is based upon the highly developed economy. Edwin Reischauer, an expert in Japanese history, has emphasized the feudal tradition that provided Japan with a class and political structure similar to that of Europe. He believes that this explains Japan's receptivity to Western influences.[14] Walt W. Rostow has tried to show that economic conditions in Japan had already developed in the Tokugawa period to the stage where all the preconditions for an economic "takeoff" to industrialization were established.[15] There is, of course, no one answer, but a variety of factors, all peculiar to Japanese society at the time of the Meiji Restoration (1868), all put to intelligent use by the new elite, have aided in shaping the future of the country. Let us consider those factors in the social structure of Japan that facilitated the process of economic change.[16]

Japan entered its new political and economic era (1868) under the leadership of a demilitarized aristocracy. This aristocracy took over the leadership in almost all spheres of social life—political, economic, educational, cultural—and assumed responsibility for Japan's new course.[17] To understand what they accomplished, we must examine the social situation and the values of this modernizing elite.

Under the Tokugawa Shogunate, the *samurai*—originally a warrior class of overlords who administered justice, kept peace, and levied taxes—were removed from their positions. This process was essentially complete by the end of the seventeenth century. Under the Shoguns the administration of the country was vested in about two hundred *daimyos*, "great lords," who resided in newly erected castles, governing their own provinces.[18] The *daimyos* were bound to the Shoguns by the *kotau* system, which forced them to maintain residence at the court for a certain period of the year. (This *kotau* system is comparable to the manner in which Louis XIV forced the French aristocracy to a life at the Court of Versailles toward the end of the seventeenth century.)

The Shoguns, through these measures, caused a genuine class division within the aristocracy: a few thousand families of superior lineage monopolized the important offices of government, while several hundred thousand families of *samurai* (6 per cent of the population) were cut off from the privileges associated with their rank. The *samurai* were held as military retainers by the *daimyos* at extremely low rewards, with little opportunity to become useful as officials in the provincial or central bureaucracies. Most of the *samurai* lived in real poverty, in constant conflict with the merchant class, and were forced to seek "degrading" employment such as spinning and handicraft.[19] But, while as a *class* the *samurai* were reduced to an insignificant social role, their *ideology* was not affected. They still abided by the tradition of loyalty to the lord and maintained a military posture, though it was oddly out of touch with their social reality (some Japanese films depict this period very convincingly). The discrepancy between pretended social position and actual social reality seems to have been very wide indeed, especially for the lower *samurai*.

During the Tokugawa period a clear distinction seems to have emerged within the *samurai* class between an upper and a lower stratum. While both abided by the official *samurai* ideology—encouraged by the Shoguns and *daimyos*—the upper *samurai* could afford to adjust this ideology to their social reality. They were mainly educated in the "polite accomplishments," use of weapons, and other aristocratic skills of that time. The lower ranks were forced to turn to other activities, which prepared them for occupations where they could gain employment. They were now educated mainly in writing and arithmetic, skills much despised by the upper *samurai*. On the basis of these skills they increasingly found employment in the growing bureaucracy of the central administration.[20] Smith and Bendix argue that gradually a new ideology and a new set of aspirations developed among the lower *samurai,* and Bellah, in his study of Tokugawa religion, tries to show the link between their new ethics and the religion of Shinto, which reinforced them.[21] These lower *samurai* were responsible for the Restoration of 1868. It was largely from their ranks that the new Meiji government was formed, and "they provided the leadership for many innovations, economic and cultural as well as governmental, of the new era." [22]

The modernization of Japan, it is clear, was led not by an emerging social class, like the bourgeoisie in Europe, but by the efforts of certain elements in the old nobility. The source of their strength was not economic but political. "Thus both the Restoration and the subsequent modernization of Japan must be seen first in political terms and only secondarily in economic terms." [23] The motivation behind the drive toward modernization was largely derived from the Tokugawa religion, which supplied the *samurai* with inspiration and legitimation for certain necessary political innovations, and it was this religion that "reinforced an ethic of innerworldly asceticism which stressed diligence and economy." [24] Their Shintoism also gave a peculiarly nationalistic cast to their motivation, by reinforcing their commitment to the central values of Japanese life—the family and the nation. In Shintoism, the family and the country are viewed not merely as secular collectivities, but also as religious entities. This latent nationalism behind the drive toward rationalization and modernization in Japan should be contrasted to the antinationalistic ideology of communism in Russia—at least in its early stage—and to the individual-centered modernization of capitalistic societies.

SUMMARY: THREE PATHS

Our discussion of these three well-known models of economic growth shows how diverse are the possible routes to industrialization. Clearly, no two routes can be exactly alike, and it is quite possible that additional paths to industrialization may be developed in the future. For instance, the Dutch sociologist W. F. Wertheim maintains that the general situation of the newly developing countries is complicated today by the co-existence of developed and underdeveloped societies in the same historical era; this, he thinks, may lead to new, different, and more patterns of development.[25]

The foregoing analyses must have made it clear that all attempts to deal with the causes of social change and of the transformation of societies on a broad scale must be sensitive to a wide range of historical and social conditions. The student of comparative societies must keep his mind open to all of the factors at work in a given society at a particular point in its historical development. Above all, he must be able to conceive of the possible economic efficacy of courses of economic development that do not follow the pattern of the society in which he himself has been placed by the accident of birth. Arguments for the universal preferability of any one pattern are inappropriate to a sociohistorical frame of study.

It has become clear by now that from a sociological perspective the problem of economic development posits different problems from the ones commonly recognized by economic theorists. While recognizing the importance of the availability of natural resources, economic constellations, political leadership, ecological factors as necessary preconditions for the growth and development of any society, it becomes obvious that in societies in economic transition —and, as we have pointed out before, because of the opening-up of communication channels, almost all contemporary societies are transition-oriented—the habits, the customs, the beliefs and the institutions of traditional societies must undergo profound changes, if the new aspirations are to be fulfilled.

We will now turn to a study of those social elements that have a direct bearing upon the initiation and the realization of economic growth.

The process of industrialization and economic growth cannot, as we have seen, develop simply as a consequence of a question of decision. Two fundamental sociological factors must be present: there must be a sufficient number of individuals who are eager and able to seize the opportunity to engage in those activities that lead to economic development, and there must be a sufficient number of people in the society who can carry out those activities that make for and sustain large-scale economic growth. In other words, there must be an industrializing elite, a group of individuals who can and will take the lead in these novel forms of economic activities. They must be able to create and recruit a labor force that will make the economic process initiated by the industrializing elite a reality and a permanent, if not a dominant, feature of social life.

The Industrial Elite

The search for entrepreneurs, willing and able to lead in the development of a modernized economic system, is particularly crucial today in the underdeveloped countries. In the absence of conditions that have made for the "natural" growth of an entrepreneurial class, and faced with the pressure of a need for rapid industrialization, these nations are under pressure to find or produce individuals who are motivated to undertake entrepreneurial activities. How can this be done? There are a number of theories worth consideration.

One of the classical theories about economic development was formulated by Joseph Schumpeter, who believes the key factor for economic growth is the availability and the activation of entrepreneurial talents.[26] Even though he holds a dim view of the role of entrepreneurs in highly industrialized economies, he recognizes their crucial role in the original development of capitalism and argues that without entrepreneurs an economy reposes in a state of equilibrium. Although Schumpeter does not specify the conditions that cultivate a nation's entrepreneurial talents, he makes it quite clear that traditional *laissez faire* policies, which give room to and provide incentives for individual talents, are conducive to the emergence of enterprising individuals. Schumpeter's view thus implies the desirability of "free enterprise": the desire for profit produces the (private) accumulation of capital, which, in turn,

produces (general) capital accumulation, and eventually, industrialization.

A different line of argumentation has been advanced by David
McClelland, the psychologist, who supplies a great variety of examples from which he deduces that a strong, deeply rooted need
for "achievement orientation" is the motivating element in "entrepreneurial man." His contention is that this drive, which he tries
to measure in a number of ways empirically, seems to be "underdeveloped" in economically backward countries. In these nations
men seem motivated more by other desires, chiefly by a desire for
power. Because achievement-orientation seems to McClelland the
product of a specific type of socialization, he cautiously advo-
cates developing an overall plan for standardizing socialization
processes to build in the necessary drives and form the character
type that will be conducive to economic development.[27]

The economist Everett E. Hagen, after years of experience as
an economist in Asian countries, basically agrees with McClelland's social-psychological approach.[28] In an attempt to formulate
a general theory of economic and social change, Hagen explains
that different personality structures appear under different social
conditions. He conceives of a four-stage development from backward and stagnant economical systems to dynamic and modern
ones, and emphasizes the essential role played by what he calls
"subordinated" groups in economically backward countries.
Young wives in traditional Chinese households, "unclassifiable"
(having no place in the rigidly structured social, political, and economic hierarchy) merchants in Tokugawa Japan, "untouchables"
in the Indian caste system, younger sons in societies where male
primogeniture regulates socioeconomic and political status—these
are a few of the many subordinated groups cited by Hagen, all of
whom are in one way or another alienated from their society and
must search for creative outlets on the margins of the traditional
worlds. In other words, the outsider, the marginal person who
cannot achieve status and general success if he follows the usual
paths to power and privilege, becomes the innovator of change.
Since Hagen believes character structure is formed early in socialization, he concludes that several generations at the least must go
by in the underdeveloped and backward countries before there
will exist the general conditions necessary to change the society's
character types and produce the needed innovators.

The McClelland-Hagen approach to the problem has met with

much criticism. Arthur Lewis, while recognizing the importance of the general value system of a society, has commented that underdeveloped countries have no shortage of commercial talents and that a great reservoir of entrepreneurial talent exists in these countries, but economic rather than psychological factors have prevented their utilization.[29] Wilbert Moore, the sociologist, warns against an easy acceptance of the McClelland-Hagen argument, because it is "exclusively preoccupied with character formation in early socialization. Since that in turn is mainly the responsibility of parents and particularly of mothers, how do mothers come by their orientation to achievement? . . . The other warning is practical. Within a given country, the circumstance that innovation is perpetrated by marginal groups may precisely inhibit general acceptance. The real or imagined benefits must sooner or later have a wider appeal if development is to continue." [30] Both points are well taken, but they do not constitute a total challenge to the argument.

The importance of character structure and the social value system is analyzed in a rather different context by the Dutch economist J. H. Boeke.[31] Boeke argues that in Indonesia today there are two co-existent economic systems and, corresponding to these, two differing personality types: a precapitalist economy and a high-capitalist one, which are mutually influencing each other. However, in contrast to Western societies, he contends that Eastern and Western men are motivated by quite different social values. For instance, he feels that Indonesians value commodities for their social value and not for their economic use—a cow has significance primarily as a symbol and not as a commodity. He also claims that Indonesians, like Orientals in general, have an aversion to taking risks, and, therefore, enterprising individuals who will play the role of creative innovators in the economy remain scarce. He expects this to continue for quite some time to come. Hence, Boeke argues that we cannot expect the spontaneous rise in the East of an economic system similar to the Western model of capitalism. He is led to this pessimistic conclusion about the future economic development of the East not only by the analysis discussed above, but also by the tremendous population explosion and the consequent emergence of a regressive process called "involution." [32]

The foregoing discussion suggests that creative economic development depends upon the existence of a dynamic elite, to intro-

"Involution": A Different Form of Change

There are different forms of change and development. Not all development is progressive; quite often change may lead a society in an opposite direction. The term "involution," used by Clifford Geertz—who borrowed it from A. Goldenweiser—seems appropriate to describe this type of development.

In rural Javanese society, Geertz describes a process of increasing complexity and refinement in all kinds of relationships, as a response to a growing ecological pressure. The Javanese society is characterized by:

> increasing tenacity of basic pattern, internal elaboration and ornateness, technical hairsplitting and unending virtuosity. And this "late Gothic" quality of agriculture increasingly pervaded the whole economy: tenure systems grew more intricate; tenancy relationships more complicated; cooperative labor arrangements more complex —all in an effort to provide everyone with some niche, however small, in the overall system.

The social arrangements have been dictated largely by a concern for social justice: in a society with a low level of *per capita* production, near the subsistence margin, there is a strong tendency to develop social arrangements and institutions intended to guarantee that nobody will need to starve. Geertz calls this a "shared poverty" system.

Since the growing complexity of the social system leads the society away from true technological progress with its ensuing rise in *per capita* productivity, Geertz calls this type of development "involution," which is the reverse of evolution.

Source: Clifford Geertz, *Agricultural Involution* (Berkeley: University of California Press, 1963).

duce and extend new forms of economic activity into a previously traditional economic system. These creative innovators do not simply emerge upon demand. Sociologically, we have to assume that certain social conditions are more conducive than others for producing such individuals. As we have shown, there are different theories as to which social conditions better serve to produce economically enterprising individuals. Rather than trying to prescribe the most fruitful theory, we will briefly describe the various types of elites which have throughout history served as leaders in the process of economic development and industrialization.

1. The middle class: the typical Western model, dominant in the history of European and North American capitalism
2. Dynastic leaders: the *samurai* in Japan in the period after the Meiji Restoration
3. Colonial administrators: a transitory phenomenon, but one which nonetheless had an important impact on such countries as Algeria and South Africa
4. Revolutionary intellectuals: for instance, in Russian model, which we find repeated frequently today in underdeveloped countries
5. Nationalist leaders: for instance, in Turkey, Egypt, and India; and often closely related to revolutionary intellectuals today

In those modern countries where the social conditions do not produce a "natural" emergence of an entrepreneurial class, the revolutionary intellectuals and the military officers (whose powers derive from antithetical factors) are the most likely agents to decide on, initiate, and impose economic development. Recent history has shown that military leaders often fulfill this function most effectively. This is because all rational systems, like the modern industrial economy, require rational methods as well as rationally operating individuals to ensure their success. In addition to the power of the military elite commands in many underdeveloped countries, it also is a uniquely rational institution to accept discipline of a rational type, to make decisions, and to use power effectively. Furthermore, the military elite stands for law and order, and will try to eliminate disturbing elements that might impede their program.

While the importance of an elite that will indeed lead is widely recognized, even by traditional economists, sociologists have warned against a doctrine of "entrepreneurial determinism." [33] While recognizing the importance of innovative leadership, they have argued that economic development entails more than that. One of the important requirements is the creation of a committed industrial labor force.

THE INDUSTRIAL LABOR FORCE

Regardless of who takes over the role of the economic innovator in a given country, another requirement remains similar:

An Integrated View of Social and
Economic Development

The developmental process requires complex planning, for it involves
the interrelation of many factors. J. A. Ponsioen argues that development can not be viewed in terms of spontaneous growth, but requires
a policy fully formulated by the governmental machinery. Yet the
government must interact with, rather than simply try to manage the
many interdependent factors. It must have flexibility in its planning,
and must consider the sociological factors in the process.

> Too often the assumption is made that development can be made by
> governments solely by allocating money resources for certain pro-
> grammes or projects. This assumption is as wrong as the opposite
> one, that people should start their development without assistance
> and promotion by the government. Under the first assumption com-
> plaints are often raised that everything was all right but the human
> factor failed. Under the second assumption—and this complaint is
> often raised by community development promoters—the people are
> judged to be energetic enough and willing, but that the social struc-
> tures, red tape, or conservative administration kill all initiatives.
> Both assumptions are indeed wrong. Development cannot be made
> by the government, because real development happens in the minds
> of people. It happens by them and with them. To reach change in
> the minds governments cannot restrict themselves to providing only
> the material facilities, they have also to act as the principal agents.
> They have to set social structures, institutions, incentive systems
> which are able to produce development attitudes, which when sup-
> plemented with aptitudes, such as literacy, technical skills, knowl-
> edge and training, can produce development.

Source: J. S. Ponsioen, *National Development* (Geneva: Mouton, The Hague, 1968).

namely, the recruitment, the development, the maintenance, and
the direction of a large and diversified industrial labor force. The
members of this working force "must learn to accept the authority
of managers in place of the family, tribe or village. They must
conform to a pace of work established by the dictates of new
masters rather than by their own inclinations or traditional
standards." [34] In other words, modern forms of production de-

mand from the industrializing elite the ability to introduce and spread new forms of work and work relationships. Although the norms governing work in an industrial society are aspects of more general norms in a society (such norms as punctuality, steady working habits, achievement), the success of the venture of industrialization depends in particular on making these norms a part of the workers' attitudes to and participation in the industrial process.

Work in industry is essentially different from work in traditional and peasant societies. Above all, now that the worker is "expropriated" from ownership of most tools of production, he must accept the "impersonality" of his product as well as of his relationship to work and the industrial system in general. The enormity of the necessary reorientation, of socialization into industrial life, should be more than evident. There is an abundance of data describing the barriers and problems that have to be overcome in individual societies in order to socialize traditionally oriented men so they will fit into the new kind of society.[35] Anthropologists are right to emphasize the significance of being acquainted with the traditional cultural and normative system of the individual society, in order to find the ways of overcoming resistance to change. We must, first of all, know how all the various institutions of the society (ranging from the political and economic to the ethical and religious) function and influence each other. In this chapter we will examine, in this manner, how societies recruit, develop, maintain, and organize an industrial labor force.

THE RECRUITMENT OF THE
INDUSTRIAL LABOR FORCE

The history of recruiting industrial workers begins with the various involuntary measures used to coerce unwilling workers to become involved in the new economic structure. These measures range from blatant enslavement, indenture, and military conscription to the levying of taxes, payable not in goods but only in money (which nonindustrial laborers could not gain access to) and to the forceful removal of the peasant from the land, as in Russia, or in England where peasants were removed from the land through "enclosure," and thus had no alternative to industrial work in the developing urban areas.

Today there is no longer a problem of attracting workers to the factories and mines in most industrializing countries. The world-wide appeal of consumer goods and urban life is felt even by people in the remotest corners of the globe, and it motivates large numbers to drift to the industrial centers where they can earn the money to purchase these goods. Indeed, the problem today is quite often the oversupply of men and women seeking employment in industrial enterprises. This demand for consumer power has produced a curious situation in Western European countries: due to the uneven boom of industrial activities large groups of workers who cannot find employment in industry in their own countries (as in Turkey, Greece, Spain, Portugal, and southern Italy) migrate to those highly industrialized countries where manual labor is scarce (as in Holland, Belgium, Western Germany, France, and Switzerland). In these advanced countries all aspects of work are clearly organized, and there is legislative control over the activities of the worker as well as the employer. However, in underindustrialized nations where industrial positions are sought by overabundant numbers, there is much discrimination: for instance against Africans in the Union of South Africa, against certain castes in India and Ceylon, against whites in some black African countries. That any such form of discrimination is contrary to the rational principles that govern work and work relationships in industrial society has not diminished its reality, and it is this reality that produces much of the tension in the world today.

The basic point, however, is that recruitment of workers for industrial enterprises no longer requires any compulsory methods. Even in the Soviet Union, where there was a traditional lack of volunteers for work in the government-initiated industrial centers in Siberia and where the government was forced to apply compulsory methods, this problem seems to be disappearing. Opportunities, which are not available in already industrialized areas of the country, provide ample challenge to people to move to developing areas.

THE COMMITMENT OF WORKERS TO
INDUSTRIAL WORK AND LIFE

Although the recruitment of workers today poses no insurmountable problems, it is still not perfectly clear how to develop in them a sense of commitment to their new kind of life and work. Clark Kerr and his associates differentiate four attitudes toward

Industrialization and Industrial Conflict in Lebanon

In comparison to what has occurred in other developing countries, industrialization in Lebanon has been relatively slow and gradual.
Moreover, its sociocultural environment—in contrast to that in other
societies undergoing this transformation—has been relatively receptive
to the changes brought about by industrialization. However, the process of industrialization inevitably involves conflict, as the traditional
system of social values and the cultural milieu attempt to build a new
value-system more in line with the demands of the emerging industrial
order. Thus, in every case an established order must be disrupted or
even lost so that a new order may be created. On the basis of empirical data, Samir Khalaf tries to show how this process operates in regard to Lebanon. Khalaf believes that continuous industrial unrest may
result from the failure of the industrial community to provide agencies
to mitigate some of the strains brought about by disruption to individual and community life.

1. LOSS OF SOCIALLY RECOGNIZED SKILLS
Some of the most pervasive effects of industrialization result from
the loss of traditional forms of livelihood that formerly provided the
main sources of prestige and security. Prior to the establishment of
the factory system a skill hierarchy dominated the lives of independent artisans and helped establish their prestige in the community.
The introduction of the machine into most parts of the production
process largely destroyed the skill hierarchy.

Previously, Lebanese craftsmen not only found physical security
in their domestic system of production, but also psychological security because of the close integration of the work life with the rest of
their social life. Within his work the craftsman acquired virtue,
prestige, and respect. As he aged he climbed upward, and having
reached the top, he taught those who were younger. The young as-
pirants for skill looked up to him as he had previously looked up to
his own teachers.

Slowly this way of life has been degenerating in Lebanon as machine and factory employment have usurped the virtue and respect
once held by the particularized independent craftsman. At the same
time the traditional skill hierarchy has become obsolete, but this occurs long before the actual skill hierarchy has been abandoned. The
result is considerable and widespread personalized resentment of the

demands of mechanization throughout the young industrial community. This resentment finds little or no constructive outlet and expresses itself impotently, largely in the form of absenteeism and an unstable labor market.

2. LOSS OF FREEDOM AND SPONTANEITY

At heart, the average Lebanese still pursues his daily activity at leisure and with an attitude of ease. In his work he seems disengaged and unoccupied, which gives one the feeling that he is generally uncommitted to a life of activity or effort. Compared to the West, the tempo and pace of life, especially in traditional communities, is still much slower. Even to the casual observer, the Lebanese, as no doubt elsewhere in the Middle East, appears to indulge in the pleasures of repose all too often. The so-called dignified calmness and being at peace or in tranquility are states of being which are sought and highly valued.

The Westerner often grows impatient and is frequently irritated by the Lebanese's lack of concern for time and his failure to be prompt, unaware perhaps that the Arab in general has a lot of time at hand and does not seem to be in too much of a hurry. In fact, a classical and commonly quoted proverb "Hurry is the Devil's work," still decorates the walls of many a business office. So pervasive is the leisure-orientation that it is often singled out as another form of lapse into fatalism, which constitutes the very reverse of the "Protestant Ethic."

Not only has the Lebanese craftsman lost part of his freedom as an independent producer, but with the advent of mechanization the industrial worker has found it increasingly difficult to adjust to the rationalized and disciplined requirements of industrial organizations. Partly because of their leisure-orientation and continued attachment to nonindustrial pursuits, many of Lebanon's native workers still find it difficult to fit into the time-discipline pattern and impersonal authority more or less inherent in the complex organization of the rising industrial system. And although they differ in no innate quality compared with Western workers, the traditional Lebanese social system contained few complex institutions in which the people themselves were given specialized responsibility. Thus the type of experience they have had provides little background for punctuality and precise interdepartmental coordination.

3. FAILURE TO APPRECIATE THE NEW STATUS SYSTEM

As was implied earlier, the Lebanese social structure still contains some ascriptive and particularistic traits for evaluating skill and status in society. The persistence of such traits has not only been instrumental in creating differential and biased attitudes among industrialists, but has also acted as barriers to the acceptance of the more universalistic and achievement-oriented status system inherent in the industrial order.

Not only is this status system inherently concomitant with an industrial system not appreciated by the workers in Lebanon, it often lies at the root of much that passes as negative political nationalism and "anti-Westernism." The powerful and prestigious classes, as no doubt elsewhere, cry out for the benefits they assume will come with industrialization while at the same time condemning any tendency it may have to upset the traditional status structure. If the presumably educated managerial classes have not yet learned that "they can't have their cake and eat it too," it is little wonder that the laboring classes remain bewildered and resentful of a revolution in their work life that leaves them in a more depressed status than before.

4. PARTIAL COMMITMENT OF THE LABOR FORCE

A serious obstacle to the spread of industrialization in Lebanon has been the workers' continuous demonstration that they are not as yet firmly committed to the industrial system.

Industrialists in Lebanon all hasten to decry the high incidence of absenteeism, labor turnover, damages to equipment, indiscipline, poor performance, and other evidences of noncommitment, but very few indeed have taken the necessary steps to reduce such tendencies. They haven't even realized that the push from the land can create a discontented industrial labor force, if nothing is done to adapt it to factory and urban requirements. As in other industrializing societies, the development of a stable and committed industrial labor force in Lebanon is much more a function of "pulls" from rather than "pushes" toward the impoverished rural regions. As long as this is lacking, let alone the deficiencies in the roles of the government and labor unions, it is little wonder that the industrial labor force remains uncommitted to a way of life that provides little security or promise.

Some of the economic and ecological factors which constitute major blocks to commitment are: a.) the ecological proximity of rural to urban areas, along with the seasonal fluctuation of employment, are inclined to render the industrial worker more accessible to his village and family ties. Thus his industrial employment is viewed as a temporary interlude only; b.) the relatively poor status of urban housing and living conditions, the anonymity and impersonality of city life in general, also account for much of the pull that urban life exerts on the industrial worker to return to his village. Since union organizations are still relatively weak to offer any solid basis of allegiance, the divided loyalty is more between the worker's commitment to his village and kin and his commitment to

the industrial system in general. This situation reflects in part the
failure of management and other agencies in the industrial community to provide the appropriate conditions for commitment.

Source: Samir Khalaf, "Industrialization and Industrial Conflict in Lebanon, *International Journal of
Comparative Sociology* 7, 1 (May 1967).

work among laborers whose societies are changing from a traditional to an industrial way of life: the uncommitted worker, the
semicommitted worker, the generally committed worker, and the
specifically committed worker.[36] Here we will only briefly describe
these four attitudes that individuals have toward industrial labor.

The Uncommitted Worker: he enters industrial work for an immediate purpose, usually to procure a certain sum of money
needed to live in his village or tribe. He has no wish to settle
down to industrial life as he will return home once his fixed goal
has been met. Good examples of this are the "target" workers in
South African mines, or the seasonal migrant workers in Sierra
Leone, who annually come to Freetown from the provinces after
the harvest has been gathered but return to their villages after several months of work in the factories.

The Semicommitted Worker: the semicommitted worker is the
one who, for a variety of reasons, tries to "keep one foot" in the
tribe or the village. He works more or less regularly in industry
but has not yet severed his ties to the land, the tribe, the village.[37]
He lives between two worlds and does not really belong to either.
Often, his wife and the family remain on the land where they grow
their own food while he labors in the city to meet the money requirements of the family. A certain security is provided, as he is
not completely dependent on the fluctuations of the industrial
work situation. A good example is what has been called the "industrial bachelors" in some African countries.

The Generally Committed Worker: he has become a permanent
part of the industrial world. He no longer has strong ties to the
tribe or village, as his family lives with him in the urban center
and depends totally on his industrial income. He may change one
job for another, but he is not drawn back to the country, being
committed to remaining in factory labor.

The Specifically Committed Worker: he is usually a permanent,
specialized worker in a particular branch of industry, and often

has earned seniority, pension, and welfare rights with a particular factory. Quite often he is committed personally to a particular employer as well, as is the case in many Japanese factories, but also in Germany (Krupp workers), Italy (Fiat and Olivetti), and France (Renault), where sometimes generations of specifically committed workers stay with the particular enterprise whose welfare has become for them a matter of personal pride.

It has been observed that in general the worker's degree of commitment is related to the stage of industrial development. From the point of view of substantial and continual industrialization, a committed labor force is essential. Costly labor turnover and absenteeism are usually high with the semicommitted and the uncommitted workers and can be rationally controlled only when a body of committed workers is available. However, for countries setting out to industrialize and still in the first stages of the process, semicommitment may be preferable, as it cuts the expense of providing for the needs of the laborers' families. When these families become urbanized, the costs of providing for educational, welfare, health, and other needs become very great.

THE DEVELOPMENT OF A COMMITTED LABOR FORCE

Since committed workers have a kind of motivation that is essential for the growth of industrialization, it becomes increasingly important not to rely primarily on the workers' own initiative to develop his industrial skills, versatility, and what could be called an "industrial consciousness." The development of an industrial consciousness accompanies the development of industrial skills, general industrial versatility, and orientation to industrial achievement.

The important questions, therefore, are who is to develop, to train and educate the industrial worker, and what methods best serve the purpose. The solution of these problems vary from country to country. In some societies the initiative rests solely with the worker. It is up to him to learn how to select the most appropriate training for the achievement of his goal. For instance, in Sierra Leone, a man, living in his village, may be lured into the city (Freetown) for different reasons (chief among them to escape the boredom of village life). But, upon arriving in the city he finds that his lack of skills bars him from finding satisfactory employment. So he casts about and if he is fortunate, he may become apprenticed as a "motor boy" to the driver of a lorry. His job will be to service the vehicle and give general assistance. In return, the driver of the lorry will teach him how to drive, provide lodging and food, and perhaps even pay him a small daily wage. Often, though, he will go, uncomplaining, without wages—there are opportunities to earn small tips or trade spare vehicle parts—because the prospect of promotion to driver is so attractive (even some literate men are enticed).[38] In all of this, though, there is no formal or established path for the prospective laborer to follow.

This tradition of the individual carving out his own way is inherited from the colonial administrators, who rarely concerned themselves with education, leaving it instead to the missionaries; exceptions were the government schools of Dutch Indonesia, British India, and British Africa.

But today no state is willing to rely wholly on individual initiative. All states, without exception, try to create some educational, if not vocational, opportunities, even though the fulfillment of even modest educational goals can consume a relatively great proportion of the gross national product of a developing country.[39] Therefore, it is a matter of the greatest concern for these nations to decide who should do the teaching and what should be taught first. In certain countries, educating is done not by the conventional agent, trained teachers, but by military men and the army, as in Pakistan, Egypt, China, and the Sudan. In most other states, however, the civilian government has undertaken to establish educational systems. For them the paramount issue is whether industrial development is best served by province- or nation-wide compulsory general education or by the vocational training of skilled labor.

Our own view is that literacy and general knowledge of industrial life ultimately make for a more efficient worker, who can become committed to the view that industrial life is best for his future. Today there is the debate whether developing nations should give primary consideration to the development of universal education or to providing training in labor skills. It has been argued that newly emerging nations cannot yet afford the expense of universal education, and economists like P. N. Rosenstein-Rodan have gone so far as to maintain that "the first task of industrialization is to provide for the training and skilling of labour." [40] But, it has been argued that general education should assume top

When an African Chooses to Become a Miner

Today a young man does not go through a life cycle which, formerly, was much the same for all men. He makes a choice. If he is born in a village and decides not to remain to farm, or fish, or tend his cattle, he can come to a town. A large number of Africans in this area came to a mining community. Formerly the young men traveled on foot, later by bicycle, and now usually by bus or train. If the men are married, there was an increasing tendency for wives to come with them or to follow shortly afterward. According to Mitchell's survey of 1951,[a] 66.9 per cent of the men were married and had wives with them. As of 1961, eighty per cent of the Africans had wives and children with them (the proportion for Europeans was about the same). "Wives" in this context included those who had come from the villages, others who had married in the township and, probably, some who did not have the benefit of a marriage ritual.

When unskilled Africans first came to the mine, it appeared to be quite easy for them to learn how to handle the tools and the new techniques. An induction class for new miners, in which an experienced African taught them the names and functions of the new tools, provided a good beginning; and it took relatively little time to gain the necessary familiarity with the implements. It took longer to get used to working underground.

(As Powdermaker points out, many Africans doing hard manual work, which often involves underground dangers, were really perplexed by a system which pays more to men, Europeans and Africans, who sit in offices on a job which requires no physical strength and has no unusual hazards.)

The hierarchy of labor is differentiated according to the skill, responsibility, and education required for the job. At the bottom are the unskilled laborers: the lashers, the underground men who shovel and load the rock after blasting, "handle boys," "spanner boys," and surface workers such as compound sweepers and night-soil collectors. In the semiskilled groups we find: boiler attendants and stokers in the power plant, mine police, watchmen, painters, plumbers, tinsmiths. In the highest group we find the skilled and supervisory employees (boos boys, skilled mine workers, supervisors, clerks, social workers, record keepers, storekeepers).

[a] J. C. Mitchell, *African Urbanization in Ndola and Luanshya* (Lusaka: Rhodes Livingston Communications No. 6, 1954).

Source: Hortense Powdermaker, *Copper Town: Changing Africa* (New York: Harper and Row, 1965), p. 88.

priority, not only for economic reasons but also for political ones.[41] Since there is not yet any basis for calculating which model of development works best under particular conditions, we must simply note the question and say that both types of education are needed and that each country has to take inventory of its educational resources and potentials in weighing priorities. Individual industries themselves have been active in many countries, training men on the job (in a number of countries this seems to have been the most successful way) and in developing basic training schools in order to guarantee their supply of qualified workmen. But in highly industrialized countries all avenues to the creation of an industrial labor force are interdependent, and in the long run, it will be more efficient to make a similarly concerted effort in the industrialization of underdeveloped nations. For this the state, however, will probably have to take the lead.

THE MAINTENANCE OF A COMMITTED LABOR FORCE

As Kerr and his associates have pointed out, the establishment of a general welfare and security system is the final step in building an industrial labor force.[42] In modernized countries a whole network of laws has emerged to define the welfare of the individual as a specific responsibility of society. Nonetheless, there are still some neglected areas, even in such highly industrialized countries as Japan, where the maintenance of the retired worker is largely left to his family: recent data show that the aged in Japan constitute the poor. Even in the United States there is still debate on the question of health-care and adequate social security for the aged. But, in countries like Argentina and Chile, the government programs for the security and maintenance of the citizens are apparently too costly for their stage of industrial development. In newly developing economies these questions are urgent and highly problematic, especially as the role of the state and its responsibility is often not clearly defined. However, as industrialization progresses, committed workers will organize to demand that the state and the enterprise together share the responsibility for security and maintenance of the laborers' families.

THE BUREAUCRATIZATION OF INDUSTRY

While industrialization is a major problem to large parts of the world, those countries that already have progressed on the road of industrialization are also facing a new stage, termed among other things, the "managerial revolution"—the "new Leviathan," the rise of the organizations, of the executives, or of the "organization man." [43] Regardless of what labels are attached to this process, they all refer to the same basic development, the rise of mass-production plants employing thousands of people, highly organized according to the insights of specialized technology and of "scientific" management, guided by strictly "rational" economic principles, and managed by professional managers who have no stake in ownership.

While the early phase of industrialization was characterized by a struggle between a new and an old way of life that marked a total break with the past, there is no such struggle observed in the second revolutionary stage in industrial development. The development today is self-understood and expected as a necessary step in the industrial process. Peter Drucker has aptly described the essential features of this mass-production society by a social principle, "a principle of *human* organization" [44] that dramatically determines a man's relationship not only to his work but to society in general. In industrial mass-production man is divorced from the product he helps to produce and from the means of production: this level of alienation Marx so gloomily described during the early stages of industrialization. But what is more decisive today in the industrial system is that the individual is no longer the decisive element, but the organization. The industrial organization then makes for a new order of things. The industrial organization creates the patterns not only of the economy, but of society in general. And, in very general terms it can be said that the industrial enterprise is the mirror of society, as it is the most representative institution of an industrial era.

The salient characteristic of all industrial organization is its *systematic* structuring and coordination of functions. This systematic organization is commonly called bureaucracy; Weber believed bureaucracy to be the most purely rational organization of behavior.[45] In it the rights and duties of positions rather than individuals are clearly defined and prescribed in written regulations, and the priority of authority and the relations between positions are systematically ordered. Appointments to positions and promotions are regulated and based on contractual agreement. Technical training or knowledge (that is, competence) are a formal condition of employment, and are affixed to the position. Furthermore, there is a strict separation of office and office-holder in that the office-holder does not own the "means of administration" and cannot appropriate the position as a personal property. Finally, administrative work is a full-time occupation. Although Weber established an "ideal type" of bureaucracy, a general model, there are in reality a large variety of bureaucratic forms, as the bureaucratic structure is highly flexible. Nonetheless, common to all industrial societies is the rise of some bureaucratic order in every sphere of life, most obviously in the economic and political ones.

The growing bureaucratization of economic life may be viewed from many perspectives; we will consider three:

1. Measurement of the growing bureaucratization of economic life
2. The way economic enterprises mold the individuals within them, the "organization men"
3. The influence of the individual in shaping these industrial enterprises—the origin, the roles, and the values of the managers

AN INDEX OF THE BUREAUCRATIZATION
OF ECONOMIC LIFE

Sociologists generally agree with Bendix that the most useful single index of the growing bureaucratization of economic enterprises is "the proportion of salaried employees in the occupational structure of a country." [46] He has shown that as industrialization progresses the number of independent proprietors and entrepreneurs becomes proportionately smaller while that of dependent employees increases. And, similarly, as production plants increase

FIGURE 3-2

Ratios of administrative and production employees for five countries in selected years

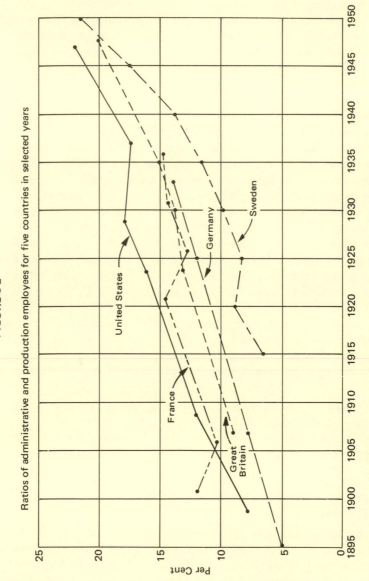

Source: Reinhard Bendix, *Work and Authority in Industry* (New York: John Wiley, 1956), p. 216. Reprinted by permission.

(individual countries differ here in the speed with which the process progresses), the proportion of salaried workers to manual workers increases faster. In certain types of industry (for example, in the chemical industry) the proportion of salaried workers—administrators, as well as technicians and marketing personnel—increases faster than it does in others (for example, in mining). Professor Bendix has statistically established some major differences in the patterns of growth and speed of bureaucratization in such countries as the United States, Great Britain, France, Germany, and Sweden. (Although he was unable to get figures on the bureaucratization of industry in Russia, it is generally assumed that the process is similar to that in Western industrial countries.)

The kind of historical data that Bendix has gathered will not serve well as a model for the economy of the newly developing countries because they are confronting a special situation, which may be called "negative bureaucratization." [47] This can occur when the number of administrative employees is out of proportion to the number of production employees, [48] or when the number of administrative employees increases too rapidly if contrasted with the increase in the number of production employees.

THE INFLUENCE OF ECONOMIC ENTERPRISES
ON THE INDIVIDUAL

Since the publication of William H. Whyte's *The Organization Man,* the attention of laymen, social scientists, and social philosophers has been directed to the effects of the organizational structure on the men within it, and, less directly, on society in general. [49] Whyte's particular focus is on the problems facing American society, which is a leader in the growth of industry and large-scale economic enterprises. Using Whyte's findings, we can generalize to the extent of stating that all societies which undergo similar processes will be confronted with similar problems.

Whyte believes that the organization man, the man employed in some administrative or technical capacity by the large-scale organization, is the man of the future. He is destined to shape the future development of America. Not only is he the keystone of the economic life, but also of our religious, intellectual, medical, and legal institutions. Whyte claims that on the basis of the information he has organization men are growing more and more alike, since they all function within an organization ethos that is independent of the particular purposes of the organization. He calls this ethos the "social ethic," which he views as diametrically opposed to the "Protestant ethic" that is commonly considered instrumental in America's rise from a British colony to the foremost industrial nation in the world—all in the amazingly short time of two hundred years.

The analyses by Whyte and others of the organization man in America have opened up the significant question of what his effect is and will be on the general culture and values of society. We will return to these considerations more elaborately at the appropriate time.

THE INFLUENCE OF THE INDIVIDUAL
ON THE INDUSTRIAL ENTERPRISE

In sociological literature, a prime subject is the role played by those individuals who are influential in shaping industrial activities: the managers.

The peculiar and novel feature of industrial enterprises in economically advanced societies is that management has become bureaucratized. In the early stages of industrialization the entrepreneur played the decisive role, but in recent decades the bureaucrat has taken over.[50] This means that the career patterns of the business and industrial elite follow the criteria of bureaucracy outlined earlier. The bureaucrats in industrial enterprises are appointed to their positions on the basis of their technical training and basic managerial competence; at least in principle, they do not get their positions by inheritance, nepotism, or other irrational considerations. They are salaried employees, employed by a contractual agreement. Their careers are characterized by gradual, step-by-step advancements within an administrative hierarchy. In fact, in American enterprises these careers usually begin and end within one firm. Data on West German industrial practices indicate, on the other hand, that a manager rarely reaches a top-level position within the firm in which he began his career.

While bureaucratization of career patterns in industry is a general feature in all industrially advanced countries, whether capitalist or communist, the criteria that actually determine success and failure differ from nation to nation. That is, management, as a profession, has become a typical feature of industrial societies, but in each society, different value is placed on different kinds of education and general orientation as a basis for entering management. Bendix has tried to define the features common to and different in the American and the Russian manager; David Granick is concerned with the same question.[51] In both countries in recent decades a college or a specialized education has become an absolute requirement for managerial positions. Although Granick argues that a larger proportion in Russia has formal college training, the trend in America is certainly in the same direction. This trend reflects the universal imperatives of large-scale enterprises and highly complex technology, regardless of political and ideological differences. However, the type of education is not the same in the two countries: there is a greater emphasis on technical training in Russia, whereas in America business training now seems to be considered most significant.

Granick has tried to uncover the career patterns of industrial managers in Germany, Great Britain, France, and Belgium.[52] He points to some of the elements antedating modern industrialization in Europe, which are still powerful and provide a class basis and a set of social values radically different from those which are dominant in the United States. In Western Europe, bureaucratization is taking place within an older structure of society that influences this process.

NOTES

1. Compare Paul Hoffman, *World without Want* (New York: Harper and Row, 1962).
2. W. W. Rostow, *The Stages of Economic Growth* (New York: Cambridge University Press, 1960).
3. S. Kuznets, *Economic Growth: Brazil, India, Japan* (Durham: Duke University Press, 1955).
4. Rostow, *op. cit.,* p. 37.
5. Students interested in these questions may turn to the works of Rostow, Kuznets, Gerschenkron, Rosovsky, and others.
6. Max Weber's works are gradually finding their way into English. To list all the English translations would take too much space, so here we will refer only to those that represent his essential interests. *The Methodology of the Social Sciences* (Glencoe: Free Press, 1949); *The Theory of Social and Economic Organization* (New York: Oxford University Press, 1947); *Ancient Judaism* (Glencoe: Free Press, 1951); *The Religion of India* (Glencoe: Free Press, 1958); *The Religion of China* (Glencoe: Free Press, 1951); *The Protestant Ethic and the Spirit of Capitalism* (New York: Scribner,

1930); *General Economic History* (Glencoe: Free Press, 1950); and *The City* (Glencoe: Free Press, 1958).

7. Max Weber, *The Protestant Ethic.*

8. General information on the Russian model can be found in the following: Rostow, *op. cit.;* Reinhard Bendix, *Work and Authority in Industry* (New York: John Wiley, 1956); Alex Inkeles and Kent Geiger, *Soviet Society* (Boston: Houghton Mifflin, 1961); and William McCord, *The Springtime of Freedom* (New York: Oxford University Press, 1965).

9. Bendix, *op. cit.,* pp. 117 ff.

10. See especially Rostow, *op. cit.,* pp. 93 ff.; G. Warren Nutter, "Soviet Economic Developments: Some Observations on Soviet Industrial Growth," *The American Economic Review* (May 1957); and Robert Campbell, *Soviet Economic Power* (Evanston: Row Peterson, 1953).

11. Bendix, *op. cit.,* p. 12.

12. See, for example, V. I. Lenin, *Selected Works* (English trans., Moscow), 7: 332–333.

13. See J. W. Hall and R. K. Beardsley, *Twelve Doors to Japan* (New York: McGraw-Hill, 1965), pp. 538–586.

14. Edwin Reischauer, *Japan, Past and Present,* rev. ed. (New York: Knopf, 1970).

15. Rostow, *op. cit.*

16. In our summary of these features, we will be guided mainly by the analyses of Robert N. Bellah, *Tokugawa Religion* (Glencoe: Free Press, 1957); Reinhard Bendix, *Nation-Building and Citizenship* (New York: John Wiley, 1964); Barrington Moore, Jr., *Social Origins of Dictatorship and Democracy* (Boston: Beacon Press, 1966), and Byron K. Marshall, *Capitalism and Nationalism in Prewar Japan* (Stanford: Stanford University Press, 1967). The bibliography in Marshall's book is excellent.

17. Cf. Thomas Smith, "Japan's Aristocratic Revolution," *Yale Review,* 50 (1961): 370–383.

18. *Ibid.*

19. Moore, *op. cit.,* pp. 235 ff.

20. Bellah, *op. cit.,* p. 45.

21. Cf. above quoted works of Smith, Bendix, and Bellah.

22. Bellah, *op. cit.* p. 45.

23. *Ibid.,* p. 185.

24. *Ibid.,* p. 194.

25. W. F. Wertheim, *East-West Parallels* (Chicago: Quadrangle Books, 1965).

26. Joseph Schumpeter, *Capitalism, Socialism and Democracy* (New York: Harper, 1950).

27. David McClelland, *The Achieving Society* (Princeton: Van Nostrand, 1961).

28. Everett E. Hagen, *On the Theory of Social Change: How Economic Growth Begins* (Homewood, Ill.: Dorsey Press, 1962).

29. Arthur Lewis, "Economic Problems of Development," in Council on World Tensions, *Restless Nations* (New York: Dodd, Mead, 1962), p. 83.

30. W. Moore, *Impact of Industry* (Englewood Cliffs, N.J.: Prentice-Hall, 1965), p. 42.

31. J. H. Boeke, *Economics and Economic Policy of Dual Societies as Exemplified by Indonesia* (Haarlem, 1961).

32. Cf. Wertheim, *op. cit.,* pp. 12 ff.

33. Cf. Arnold Feldman and Wilbert Moore, eds., *Labor Commitment*

and *Social Change in Developing Areas* (New York: Social Science Research Council, 1960), p. 45.

34. Clark Kerr, John T. Dunlop, Frederick Harbison, and Charles A. Myers, *Industrialism and Industrial Man* (New York: Oxford Galaxy Books, 1964), p. 140.

35. See the essay by Max Gluckman in A. Southall, ed., *Social Change in Modern Africa* (New York: Oxford University Press, 1961), and E. H. Spicer, ed., *Human Problems in Technological Change: A Case Book* (New York: Russell Sage Foundation, 1952).

36. Kerr, *op. cit.,* p. 145.

37. See Melville Herskovits and Mitchell Harwitz, eds., *Economic Transition in Africa* (Evanston: Northwestern University Press, 1964).

38. Michael Banton, *West African City: A Study of Tribal Life in Freetown* (New York: Oxford University Press, 1957), p. 55.

39. Arthur Lewis, *The Theory of Economic Growth* (Homewood, Ill.: Richard D. Irwin, 1955).

40. P. N. Rosenstein-Rodan, "Problems of Industrialization of Eastern and South-Eastern Europe," in A. N. Agarawala and S. P. Singh, eds., *The Economics of Underdevelopment* (New York: Oxford University Press, 1958), p. 248.

41. Albert Hirschman, *The Strategy of Economic Development* (New Haven: Yale University Press, 1958).

42. Kerr, *op. cit.*

43. See James Burnham, *The Managerial Revolution* (Bloomington: Indiana University Press, 1960); Peter F. Drucker, *The New Society* (New York: Harper, 1949); and William H. Whyte, *The Organization Man* (New York: Doubleday, 1957).

44. Drucker, *op. cit.,* p. 4.

45. See Chapter 3, note 16, for references.

46. Bendix, *Work and Authority in Industry,* p. 211.

47. See Fred W. Riggs, "Bureaucrats and Political Development: A Paradoxical View," in Jason L. Finkle and Richard W. Gable, eds., *Political Development and Social Change* (New York: John Wiley, 1966).

48. For instance, Justus van der Kroef, in his study of Indonesian entrepreneurs, maintains that the growth of a bureaucratic structure in government and industry has made a peculiar situation in Indonesia, whereby individuals seek for security primarily at the expense of taking risks and engaging in innovatory activities. Cf. J. van der Kroef, "The Indonesian Entrepreneur: Images, Potentialities and Problems," *American Journal of Economics and Sociology* 19 (1959–1960): 413–425.

49. Whyte, *op. cit.*

50. William Miller, ed., *Men in Business* (Cambridge: Harvard University Press, 1952), and Bendix, *Work and Authority in Industry,* p. 229.

51. David Granick, *The Red Executive—A Study of the Organization Man in Russian Industry* (New York: Doubleday Anchor, 1961).

52. David Granick, *The European Executive* (New York: Doubleday Anchor, 1964).

[4] Stratification: Caste, Estate, Class

IN the chapters on the political and economic structures of society, we have become aware of the importance of class. For example, we have seen how it is impossible to discuss political and economic changes without taking into account what effect they have on the ranking systems in society. Indeed, we have seen that the emergence of new classes and changes in class mobility are of crucial importance in the modernization of societies. In this chapter, we will examine these developments in more detail. Although it is impossible to discuss all the various theories and approaches that sociologists have employed in dealing with stratification, we can indicate the broad features of the problem.[1]

In different societies stratification occurs in quite different forms and it differs in the way it influences everyday life. This is apparent even to a traveler within the Western nations. For example, an American traveling in England or in Germany will encounter class in everyday situations in ways quite different from those he has been accustomed to in America. He will find that Englishmen are alert to the class indicators in people's speech in a manner unthinkable, and indeed impossible, in America; it will seem to him that an Englishman can barely say "good morning" without thereby giving a full account of his position and history in the class system, at least to the ears of other Englishmen. In Germany he will find people conscious of honorific titles to a degree that would be regarded as ridiculous in America: one must even know who merits an address as Herr Doktor or Herr Professor and even whose wives should be addressed as Frau Doktor or Frau Professor. (Omitting such honorifics may be more perilous socially with the wives than with the husbands.) If a traveler moves beyond the boundaries of Western civilization, the differences in stratification naturally become much more baffling and, at times, shocking. It is difficult, for example, for an American or other Westerner traveling in some Asian countries to come to terms with the indifference felt toward the misery of people in the lower strata by upper-strata individuals, an indifference likely to strike him as both callous and foolish. Thus we may encounter different systems of stratification even on the level of ordinary, everyday experience, and these differences may be so striking that the sociologically unsophisticated person will be led to ask what they mean and how they have come about. Stratification has naturally been an area of acute interest for sociologists since the beginnings of the discipline, though their approaches to it have varied greatly.

In recent American sociology a good deal of work on stratification has been done in the context of community studies [2] and the approach developed here has been applied to other societies as well.[3] The widespread preference for this microcosmic approach is because the limited size of a small town or a neighborhood in a larger city allows the sociologist a controlled overview somewhat similar to that which is available to an anthropologist studying a primitive tribe; it is easier to hold in mind the data about a small group than about a modern society as a whole. Furthermore, data from community studies have an empirical solidity and down-to-earth quality that make them attractive: there is rarely any doubt that such data refer to real life and to real people. On the other hand, however, there are global structures in modern society that are not readily visible from the vantage point of the local community: for example, the network of influence that exists on a national level in the uppermost stratum of the economic system. For another thing, community studies of both the sociologist and the anthropologist tend to neglect historical backgrounds; the community is studied as it appears here and now, without much regard as to how it came to be as it is. And, such an approach, in turn, often leads to the omission of important factors in the present situation.

Work of great relevance to stratification has also been accomplished in survey research, sometimes operating with national samples.[4] The Kinsey studies in the sexual conduct of Americans are probably the most famous of these and have yielded interesting information on the workings of the class system. But, in such

Language and Class Membership

Sociologists and general observers of social life are in agreement that language is a basic clue to class differences. Nancy Mitford's essay on the "English Aristocracy"[a] has given rise to much heated discussion on whether, today, social classes still can be distinguished from each other. The discussion is based on a paper written by Professor Alan Ross of Birmingham University.[b] Professor Ross points out that today the upper classes are distinguished solely by their language, since they are neither cleaner, richer, nor better educated than anybody else. "Nor, in general, is he [a member of the upper class] likely to play a greater part in public affairs, be supported by other trades or professions, or engage in other pursuits or pastimes than his fellow of another class."[c] In his search for languages differences, A. Ross invented the formula: "U" (for upper-class speaker) versus "non-U." Here are a few examples of U and non-U usage.

1. Non-U, "They have a lovely home," versus U, "They have a very nice house."
2. Non-U, "I was ill," versus U, "I was sick."
3. Non-U, dentures, versus U, false teeth.
4. Pardon! is used by the non-U in three main ways: (1) if the hearer does not hear the speaker properly; (2) as an apology (for example, on brushing by someone in a passage); (3) after hiccupping or belching. The corresponding U-terms are more curt: (1) what? (2) sorry! (3) silence. In the first two cases, U-parents and U-governesses are always trying to make children say something "politer": "What did you say?" and "I'm frightfully sorry."
5. "Pleased to meet you!" This is a very frequent non-U response to the greeting "How d'you do?" U-speakers normally just repeat the greeting; to reply to the greeting with "Quite well, thank you," for example, is non-U.

In addition to such "give-away" phrases, pronunciation as well as intonation play a similar role. Nancy Mitford describes behavior patterns of English upper-class members. For instance, "Silence is the only possible U-response to many embarrassing modern situations: the ejaculation of 'cheers' before drinking, for example, or 'it was so nice seeing you,' after saying 'goodbye.' "

Digby Baltzell views the language of social class difference in a similar manner:

In addition to accent, word usage also differentiates the members of the upper class from the rest of the population. They avoid carefully certain common words and expressions which are standard speech among the middle classes. The Proper Philadelphian, Bostonian, or New Yorker, for instance, never refers to "living-room or bedroom suites," "davenports," "divans," or "drapes," and unlike almost all Americans (and like his British cousins), he makes the "a" in "tomato" always short. Such word usage is sure to betray one's middle-class origins.[d]

[a] Nancy Mitford, ed., *Noblesse Oblige* (New York: Harper & Row, 1956).
[b] Ross, A. S. C., "U and Non-U" in Mitford, *ibid.*
[c] Ross, A. S. C., *ibid.*, p. 55.
[d] Digby Baltzell, *Philadelphia Gentleman* (New York: Free Press, 1958).

surveys, even more than in the case of community studies, both social structure and history tend to disappear, leaving only "socio-economic" status (the "SES" in research terminology) seemingly operating in a mechanical fashion in conjunction with other factors. However, in contrast to the community sociologists and survey researchers, those sociologists who have tried to analyze modern stratification systems as a whole (C. Wright Mills' studies of American middle classes and "power elite" are cases in point[5]) have been criticized, with some justification, for a lack of empirical validity in their analyses. There are real limitations to all sociological techniques, but we contend that a comparative approach is most likely to yield meaningful results nevertheless.

Stratification is not a modern interest exclusively, for it was a central concern during the "classical" period of sociology. Karl Marx was the first to assert the prime importance of class in social events.[6] Class was, for Marx, essentially an economic fact, and the approaches to stratification in the Marxist tradition have always emphasized the economic foundation of class phenomena. The political aspect of stratification was emphasized by classical sociologists in Italy, especially by Vilfredo Pareto and Gaetano Mosca.[7] It was the great achievement of Max Weber to develop a concept of stratification that integrated all the various factors, economic, political, and social (in its narrower sense).[8] Weber's approach interests us because it opens the issue to historical contexts and sociological comparativism. Weber's theory of stratification is quite complex, and it would serve no useful purpose to give a detailed explanation here. However, we will rely heavily on Weber's concept, although simplified and modified for our purposes.

Basic Concepts

We know of no society without stratification. Different societies, though, have quite different types of stratification. Put differently, all societies *rank* their members, but they do not all use the same criteria to determine who belongs to which rank. Three principle types of stratification may be distinguished: *caste, estate,* and *class.*[9] These types may be seen as on a continuum both in terms of mobility and rationality, with class on the high pole on both counts, caste on the low one, and estate in an intermediate position.

A caste system is one in which each stratum is so perfectly closed—in theory and often in practice as well—that there is no mobility: the individual is born into his particular caste and remains in it all of his life. Caste position is inalienable, be it for better or for worse. Thus, the high-caste individual cannot lose his position by economic misfortune or by conduct unbecoming to a member of his group, and the low-caste individual cannot improve his position by becoming wealthy, getting a first-rate education, or by any means. In a caste system there are strict rules concerning marriage and social relations generally; typically, the individual can marry only within his caste and have social relations with other members of his caste only. The latter is defined by "rules of commensality," that is, who may eat with whom, and so forth. Thus, caste systems are marked by rigid prescriptions and proscriptions, usually with the quality of religious taboos, which minimize their capacity for easy rationalization.

The prototypical caste system is, of course, that of traditional India, where the term was originally applied. (There the system was legitimated by an elaborate religious theory.) The term is applied by sociologists to other cases as well, in which stratification takes a similarly rigid form. Typically, it is applied to stratification based on racial or ethnic criteria; the notion of caste has been widely used by sociologists to describe the racial system in the United States.[10]

Caste systems, in their rigidity and their permeation with quasi-magical taboos, are inimical to rationality, particularly economic rationality. It has been observed, consequently, that caste systems are modified as social and economic modernization proceeds. This

Caste in Everyday Life

Caste reveals itself most conspicuously and most rigidly in everyday life, as in the concept of pollution that is fundamental to the Hindu social system. At one end of the scale, to flay dead animals is polluting because it is an unclean occupation; at the other end of the scale, a high-caste Hindu is polluted (and must therefore undergo ritual purification) if his shadow is crossed by that of an Untouchable.

A few examples will illustrate some aspects of life in a caste society today.[a]

High-caste members can be polluted by the proximity of men of castes lower than their own, whether their shadows mix or not, and there are elaborate prescribed distances for each rung of the ladder. Thus in Kerala, according to the rules, the Thiyas (toddy-tappers) are Untouchable to the Nayars (soldier caste). To a Pattar Brahmin a Thiya is Unapproachable by 20 paces, and to a Namboodiri Brahmin by 25. The Pulayas, Cherumars, and Parayas (all of them Untouchable castes) are Untouchable to one another, each one claiming superiority over the other and indulging in a wash when touched and defiled. A member of anyone of these communities is Unapproachable to a Thiya by 10 paces, to a Nayar by 20, to a Pattar Brahmin by 40, and to a Namboodiri Brahmin by 60. So that everyone should know where to stand, when a Namboodiri Brahmin walked in the street he was preceded by a Nayar runner who shouted "Ha-ha" as a warning.

Some things that are polluting for a particular caste or sub-caste are not polluting for another. Fasting meat is considered polluting, yet all Kshatryas, and they come next to the Brahmins, eat meat. There are even Brahmins, the Pandits of Kashmir, who not only eat meat but eat it in the company of Muslims; they continue to be Brahmins and remain entitled to look upon all non-Brahmins as inferior. But Brahmins who observe vegetarianism look on Kashmiri Pandits with a disgust reminiscent of what many Britons would feel if a frog was served on their plate. The late Sir Girja Shankar Bajpai, Secretary General for Foreign Affairs, once told me that it was only because he was truly westernised that he could bring himself to eat at the same table as the Prime Minister. 'But you are both Brahmins,' I ventured, 'so what is the difficulty?' 'He is a Kashmiri Pandit. I am a Kanya Khubha, I belong to the highest hierarchy of Brahmins, the ones who are Chaturvedis (of the four Vedas), we are strict vegetarians by caste, at least at home; but

Nehru is a Kashmiri Pandit, his ancestors were reared on meat and fish . . . I would not wish a girl of my family to marry into his although I have the highest regard for him as Prime Minister.' This may sound reactionary but nevertheless it must be realised that had one of his daughters married a Nehru she would have had to make adjustments in the way the home was run in some ways deeper than those necessary for a Daughter of the [American] Revolution marrying a Southern Negro.

It is always important to remember that the essential characteristic of a caste is that one can not decide to no longer be a Hindu—there is no procedure by which one can cease to be a Hindu. However, it can happen, and indeed, it has happened, that one is thrown out of one's caste and sub-caste if one's behavior flaunts custom. Custom has become ritual, and this ritual is enforced rigidly by means of ostracism, excommunication in the true sense of the word, and outcasting. This is the most terrible thing that can happen to a Hindu. For when one is no longer a member of his caste, nobody will talk to, eat, drink or sit with, marry, or help with the funeral rites of the person who has been so excommunicated: the penalty for breaking this boycott of the outcaste is itself excommunication. The fear of this ruthless penalty explains why few Hindus have dared to risk ostracism, and how the institution of caste has become so pervasive a phenomenon.

[a] Source: Taya Zinkin, *Caste Today* (New York: Oxford University Press under the auspices of the Institute of Race Relations, 1962).

can readily be seen both in the Indian and the American cases. In India the pattern of modification already appeared when the British began to build railroads. The caste system, in principle, would have demanded, at the least, a four- or even five-fold segregation of passengers both on trains and in stations. Obviously, it was impossible to construct four or five types of coaches, waiting rooms, toilet facilities, and so on. Willy-nilly, the castes had to associate with each other on the railroads. The same rational imperatives served to modify the system as industrialization and modern urbanization began to affect Indian society. Since the Indian caste system was based on occupation, industrialization particularly threatened it. The racial caste system in America, though less complex in structure (there being only two castes), is similarly irrational in terms of modern economic processes. It has been retained most successfully in rural and semirural sections of the country, particularly in the South, while being subjected to severe shocks in the fully industrialized sections. A subjugated caste population (whether legally enslaved or not) can be effectively used as a labor force for nonindustrial production, as in the old southern plantation economy. Such a labor force, however, is irrational in modern industry, where productivity requires positive incentives rather than brute coercion. Such incentives, however, presuppose a measure of social mobility—a process tending toward the disintegration of caste.

An estate system is one in which social position is determined by birth and is retained by allegiance to what Weber aptly called a "code of honor." Like caste systems, estate systems typically define occupational hierarchies, institute rigid rules governing marriage and social relations (that is, they proscribe and prescribe connubium and commensality), and are not conducive to mobility. Unlike caste systems, however, the inhibition of mobility is less total: it is possible to improve one's position to some extent by a "good marriage," or to lose one's position by conduct that outrages the traditions of the group.

The feudal system in Europe was a typical estate system, permitting little mobility, but it was nevertheless far less rigid than a caste system in its regulation of the individual's life course. Feudal estate patterns survive in contemporary European aristocracies and are, at least superficially, emulated in the older groups within the American upper class. Marriage is, logically, of crucial importance in these groups. And there is always the possibility of loss of estate status as a result of specific malfeasances—for instance, not paying one's debts (particularly gambling debts), or not avenging an offence against one's family honor. In the early stages of bourgeois capitalism in Europe, the bourgeoisie itself emulated the aristocratic patterns by constituting itself an estate of this kind. This, however, changed with the acceleration of modernization brought on by the industrial revolution. Economic criteria became progressively more important than traditions, codes of conduct, and ultimately, even birth, family, and marriage. Thus the typical development in stratification in Western countries has been from the estate to the class type.

A class system is one in which social position is determined by essentially economic criteria of ownership of or of power over goods and services. This does not mean that there are not also important noneconomic factors, those which may be broadly called

Estate in Feudal France

In the estate system of stratification that was typical of European feudalism, the various structures of society were closely interconnected. The political system was characterized by an independent nobility, loosely bound to a relatively weak royalty that was "primus inter pares," one among equals; economically, there was an agrarian system based on barter, instead of salary, since services were paid for in land, lodging, and food; social relations were based on servitude, or vassalage, with punishments for those who left the fief that served to tightly group men into a stable society in which each individual had a clearly defined political, economic, and social role. The following is a description of the structure of society in the feudal period of France.

Each individual is born into it with his hereditary rank, his local post, his pay in landed property, with the certainty of never being abandoned by his chieftain, and with the obligation of giving his life for his chieftain in time of need. In this epoch of perpetual warfare only one regimen is suitable, that of a body of men confronting the enemy, and such is the feudal system; we can judge by this trait alone of the perils which it wards off, and of the service which it enjoins. 'In those days,' says the Spanish general-chronicle, 'kings, counts, nobles, and knights, in order to be ready at all hours, kept their horses in the rooms in which they slept with their wives.' The viscount in his tower defending the entrance to a valley or the passage of a ford, the marquis thrown as a forlorn hope on the burning frontier, sleeps with his hand on his weapon, like an American lieutenant among the Sioux behind a western stockade. His dwelling is simply a camp and a refuge; . . . Every taste, every sentiment is subordinated to military service. . . . Thanks to these braves, the peasant (villanus) enjoys protection. He is no longer to be slaughtered, no longer to be led captive with his family, in herds, with his neck in a pitchfork. He ventures to plough and to sow, and to rely upon his crops; in case of danger he knows that he can find an asylum for himself, and for his grain and cattle, in the circle of palisades at the base of the fortress.

By degrees, necessity establishes a tacit contract between the military chieftain of the donjon and the early settlers of the open country, and this becomes a recognized custom. They work for him, cultivate his ground, do his carting, pay him quittances, so much for house, so much per head for cattle, so much to inherit or to sell; he is compelled to support his troop. But when these rights are discharged he errs if, through pride or greediness, he takes more than his due. As to the vagabonds, the wretched, who, in the universal disorder and devastation, seek refuge under his guardianship, their condition is harder; the soil belongs to him, because without him it would be uninhabitable; if he assigns them a plot of ground, if he permits them merely to encamp on it, if he sets them to work or furnishes them with seeds, it is on conditions which he prescribes. They are to become his serfs, his mortmains; wherever they may go he is to have the right of fetching them back, and from father to son they are his born domestics, assignable to any pursuit he pleases, taxable and workable at his discretion and not allowed to transmit anything to a child unless the latter, 'living from their pot,' can, after their death, continue their service. . . . When we clearly represent to ourselves the condition of humanity in those days, we can comprehend how men readily accepted the most obnoxious of feudal rights, even that of the *droit du seigneur*. The risks to which they were daily subject were even worse.

Source: Hippolyte A. Taine, *The Ancient Regime* (New York: P. Smith, 1931), p. 7.

"styles of life." [11] Thus each class has its own consumption patterns, values, and mores which include, for instance, sexual habits and preferences. But, in the long run, all of these can be acquired by economic means, can be bought, if not in the individual's lifetime, then in that of the next generation. In the United States, for example, there are very specific class styles, but, with a few exceptions in the very top classes, these can be acquired provided one has the economic means. Some, to be sure, cannot be bought outright but must be learned; the educational processes, however, in which one learns them, are subject to purchase, if not for oneself, then for one's children. Thus the new member of the upper middle class may have to limit himself to the physical aspects of this class's "style of life"—the type of residence, automobile, furniture, travel, and the like—being too set in his ways to learn the non-physical aspects—diction, taste, attitudes. But he can buy an education for his children that will ensure that they have not only the correct clothes and automobiles, but also the correct speech and thought.

Because a class system is geared to mobility, it has few, if any, *safe* positions. While it encourages upward mobility (varying in degree, of course, in different cases) from the lower strata, it always entails the danger of downward mobility also: just as lowly

The Class Structure of Society in
Post-industrial England

The industrial revolution radically transformed the relatively static estate system of preindustrial England into a class society. In England, it soon created two rapidly growing new strata: the "bourgeois" class of entrepreneurs and the "proletarian" class of industrial workers. There was no precedent for either; they had come into existence simultaneously, and they were closely tied to each other. Since then this new class order of English society has become increasingly complex and presents many analytical difficulties to the sociologist. The following paragraphs are the attempts of E. A. Johns to deal with it.

> Broadly speaking, the term working class refers to a large body of people chiefly characterized in occupational terms by manual jobs (such as coal miners, factory operatives, etc.), plus a substantial number of non-manual workers (such as junior clerks) who may be on the verge of entry into the lower-middle class. At the other end of the scale is the so-called upper class, perhaps no more than 2 per cent of the population, comprising the aristocracy, "society," and a few important families whose common feature is the ownership of land. Since the Industrial Revolution there has been considerable infiltration into the ranks of the upper class by those who were formerly in the senior ranks of the middle classes—indeed, the continued existence of many large estates may have depended on intermarriage with some *nouveau riche* captain of industry—until today it is scarcely possible to draw a line between the two. Equally, it is virtually out of the question to attempt a definitive barrier between the working and the lower-middle classes. However, by adopting these very broad generalizations, it should be possible to isolate the middle classes by excluding the upper and the working classes in society. This would imply that the middle classes constituted about one-third of the total population. Unfortunately, these theoretical estimates do not coincide with the estimates of the people concerned, for we must take into account the subjective aspirations of those who, objectively, belong to the working class (two-thirds of the population). In 1952, for example, the British Institute of Public Opinion conducted a Gallup Poll, in which a sample of adults throughout Great Britain was asked the question: "If you had to say what social class you belong to, which would it be?" The replies (given in the following Table) indicate that, of those who replied 49 per cent placed themselves in the middle classes and 46 per cent in the working class.

CLASS LABEL	PERCENTAGE OF THE WHOLE SAMPLE
Upper	1
Upper middle	6
Middle	27
Lower middle	16
Working	46
No reply	4

What is especially significant is that the number of people describing themselves as working class had declined appreciably since a similar inquiry carried out in 1946. Clearly a continuing trend of rising wages had enabled many more working-class people to aspire to a middle-class standard of living. If this trend were to be sustained indefinitely, there would undoubtedly be a gradual accumulation of numbers in the middle classes at the expense of the working class, but this movement could easily be halted or even reversed by economic events.

Source: E. A. Johns, *The Social Structure of Modern Britain* (Elmsford, New York: Pergamon Press, 1965), pp. 65 ff.

origins are not an insurmountable obstacle to moving up in the system, a "good background" is no ironclad guarantee against moving downward. This insecurity has rational economic consequences, as it encourages and even necessitates enterprise, there being no other surety of successful survival. Both success and failure serve "to encourage the others." The class system is thus the most viable stratification system for the development of an industrial labor force and a modern managerial elite.

We may define a class system in terms of economic criteria for social position, but this does *not* mean that economic enterprise *alone* decides class mobility. Under conditions of intense bureaucratization, as we have discussed before, education becomes increasingly a vehicle of mobility. This is true in America today and in some other industrial or industrializing societies. In other cases, political power may be an important means; for instance, in the socialist countries, a career in the political apparatus that controls the economy is the foremost determinant of class mobility.[12] It is not sufficient, therefore, to state that a particular nation's stratification system is of the class type. It is always necessary, with each society, to understand the particular nature of the class structure, and especially its patterns of class mobility. Since the factors that influence this are frequently very complex, sociological work in this area is marked by controversy.[13] In general, however, we are on safe ground in saying that modern industrial societies everywhere are characterized by the development and consolidation of class systems, even in the Marxist societies whose ideologies deny this fact. Older patterns of stratification, of the caste or of the estate type, are being progressively swept away by the dynamics of industrialization that all societies are experiencing in their individual ways.

Historical Perspective

Already we have insisted on the critical importance of a historical perspective in dealing with the problems of comparative sociology. This is particularly true in the study of stratification. We will undertake to study European class systems in this manner.[14]

Class developed in European societies with the rise of a market economy. It was through the growing influence of expanding activities that the estate society of medieval feudalism was gradually transformed. In that society there was a rigid, closed order, in which each individual was born into "his hereditary rank, his local post, his pay in landed property, with the certainty of never being abandoned by his chieftain, and with the obligation of giving his life for his chieftain in time of need." [15] This stable order was fragmented by the growing number of people engaged in new types of activity, which were not provided for in the feudal system of estates. The location of these activities was the towns, which became centers of power, as the Hansa cities in Germany, the Flemish towns of Bruegge and Ghent, and the Italian Renaissance cities of Venice and Florence. Merchants became persons of importance, such as the merchant families of the Fuggers and the Welsers. "Merchant princes" became powerful financial backers of some European monarchs who became increasingly indebted to the merchants because of the monarch's inability to raise money for military adventures. The Medici family of Florence in the fifteenth and sixteenth centuries is an illustrious example of a family of merchants, financiers, and bankers, rising to the position of a noble house with immense power, the protector of artists and the electors of kings (for instance, Catherine de Medici "made" her husband a king of France, Henry II, 1547–1559).

The late Middle Ages witnessed not only the rise of merchants, financiers, and bankers, but also of a novel social stratum, that of the clerks. Originally the clerks were the ecclesiastical descendants of the ancient profession of scribes. In an increasingly secularized world they developed and specialized this task of keeping records, largely through the study and practice of law, which made them particularly suited to meet the personnel needs created by the expanding activities of political administration. Gradually they, too, attained positions of great power and prestige.

Both merchants and clerks lived, for the most part, in the towns. The towns became the focus of this new class of people, and in this locale they could not be assimilated into the traditional estates of the feudal order: they became a stratum with uncertain social status and, *ipso facto,* with considerable latitude of action. The merchants and clerks together became known as the bourgeoisie, that is, the people who lived within the fortifications of the feudal castles (or Burghs) which had become the new town walls. These people could not be classified within either of the two feudal estates (aristocracy or "people") as they were an entirely new stratum in the middle, a "middle class," in the precise sense of the word, whose lack of belonging to the feudal order could not be disguised by calling it a "third estate." In fact, it was not a third estate like the two traditional ones, but an altogether new formation, a class, which was to become the gravedigger of the old order. The sixteenth and seventeenth centuries saw the rise of this new middle class in Central and Western Europe—the eighteenth century its consolidation and attainment of political dominance.

The rise of the middle class in Europe was facilitated by a number of political circumstances. On the one hand, the monarchs needed this class of people (clerks and financiers), trained and able to take care of the growing administration of the state. On the other hand, this class offered a good counterbalance to offset the old aristocracy, which often was at odds with the power of the kings. Skillful rulers such as Louis XIV played off the new class of political administrators, lawyers, financiers, and merchants against the troublesome aristocracy. It was to a large extent the monarchy that helped the consolidation of this middle class, and concentrated political and economic power in its hands. As long as the "absolute state," on the model of the France of Louis XIV, lasted, the monarchy was able to maintain itself precisely through this controlled balancing of aristocracy and bourgeoisie. But this balance in France, for instance, did not outlive the eighteenth century: the Revolution of 1789 ratified the rise to power of the bourgeoisie by, ironically, destroying the very monarchy that had brought about its emergence. In Russia, by contrast, "absolutism" was maintained far into the nineteenth century.

During the nineteenth century, Central and Western Europe saw the emergence of yet another new class, the industrial workers. With the rapid growth of industrial technology after the invention of the steam engine by James Watt, industrialization proceeded in parts of Europe, especially in England, with amazing speed. The masses of people flocked to work in the newly created industrial centers, forming the basis of the new class of industrial proletarians, whose plight Karl Marx and Charles Dickens, among others, described so vividly. Unprotected and exploited, uprooted from all traditional patterns of life, they conglomerated in the most disagreeable parts of the cities, giving rise to the urban slums that still exist in most industrial societies. Throughout the nineteenth century this new working class struggled to create its own economic, political, and social rights.[16] This new class had no common history. It was fused into a class by a common experience of misery and common efforts to escape this misery. The struggle was by no means peaceful, not even in the countries that succeeded in avoiding bloody revolutions. But in most of the industrial countries of Europe the growing pressures of this struggle led to increasing concessions to the demands of the new class, primarily as a result of the development of labor unions. Legal and political rights were gradually extended equally to all classes, opening the road to the "plebiscitarian" form of democracy, based on universal suffrage, which has become the established political structure in Western societies.

However, despite egalitarianism in legal and political terms, these societies have remained class societies. While there are no officially recognized differences between the various classes, economic and social inequalities have persisted. Sociological analysis of this is particularly important in societies like that of the United States, where the law and the political ideology of egalitarianism tend to obfuscate the persistent reality of class.[17]

By studying the historical development of social classes in Europe during the time since the Middle Ages, we can observe clearly the close interplay of political and other social processes. Technological and economic developments have produced new social classes, which then have a major impact on the political structure in such a way that it has, in turn, influenced new class developments. Only from a historical perspective are we able to grasp the way in which this complex interplay of forces can lead to a complete transformation of entire societies.

The Modernizing Process

All human societies are comparable, in principle, since "nothing human is alien." All human societies known to us are stratified, and so can be studied comparatively. What is peculiar to the modern situation, however, is that the *same* fundamental forces appear to be active everywhere. Modern societies, consequently, are comparable in a much more specific way. This can be readily seen in the area of stratification. It is possible to speak of specifically modern stratification processes, which closely resemble each other, irrespective of the particular character of the historical situation in which they arose. To show this, we will study three cases, representing the three types of stratification systems we have defined earlier—*caste, estate,* and *class.*

The prototypical case of a *caste system,* of course, is traditional India.[18] This system, which had been of unusual longevity and flexibility for a very long period of history, came under the impact of modernizing forces as a result of the establishment of British rule in India. Even then, it maintained itself with considerable vigor until the very recent past. Perhaps paradoxically, its most rapid disintegration has come in the wake of India's independence in 1947.

We cannot describe in great detail the traditional caste system here, but we must warn against any oversimplified views of it, as there is a common, unscholarly tendency to reduce its complexity and uniqueness in order to make it serve as an abstract, ideal-typical concept of sociology—with the result that people have tended to read the abstractions back into the empirical case. The traditional caste system was of immense complexity and varied greatly in different parts of India. The fundamental four strata of the system, already mentioned in the Vedas, are the so-called *varnas* ("colors"): the Brahmins (the top caste of priests), the Kshatryas (the military aristocracy), the Vaishyas (the stratum of merchants and ritually pure craftsmen), and the Shudras (the subordinated, ritually inferior laborers). Below even the Shudras are the Untouchables, the ritually impure people, practicing occupations that bring about pollution in terms of Hindu ritualism. They are, to all intents and purposes, outside Hinduism as a social structure. The four *varnas* are traditionally dichotomized between the "twice-born" castes—which have a ritual initiation into caste status, a "second birth" (the top three)—and the "once-born" castes, the Shudras and the Untouchables. Historians tend to believe that the "twice-born" castes derive from the Aryan conquerors—respectively, the once highly magical priesthood, the warrior leadership, and the ordinary Aryan folk—while the Shudras and the Untouchables derive from the subjugated pre-Aryan population. If this is true, the caste system would once have served as an ingenious device to integrate at least the upper portion of the subjugated population into the social structure of the conquerors. Some historians insist that the foundations of the caste system were already present in India prior to the Aryan conquest, who simply adapted them. Be this as it may, the caste system was highly successful in organizing the postinvasion society and in diffusing it throughout the subcontinent and even beyond.[19]

This system of four *varnas,* however, is only an ideological blueprint, serving, at best, to schematize a multiform structure. Traditional Hinduism consists of many hundreds of castes and subcastes, relating to each other in ways that were far from either uniform or fixed, varying greatly from one part of the country to another. The British, as a part of their effort to establish a *rational* administration, tried to "schedule" the entire system uniformly, but most Indian castes, even today, remain idiosyncratically "unscheduled." This ideal schematization must contend with the fact, moreover, that despite the theoretically absolute rigidity of the caste system, there has been, in reality, much collective and individual mobility. While individuals cannot achieve large "jumps" between strata, they can make minor adjustments in their status, most frequently through marriage. More importantly, entire castes or subcastes can change their relative positions in the system. This typically happens through the acquisition of land, often by migration, and through the adoption of a stricter ritual life; this latter is a most interesting process that has been called "Sanskriti-zation" because it entails patterning one's rituals on the Sanskrit culture of the Brahmins.[20] The decreasing amount of land availa-ble for such experiments has hindered this process, weakening the flexibility of the system (quite apart from the effects of moderniza-tion). Previously, however, these mechanisms of mobility had al-lowed the caste system to adapt itself in a complex way to a vari-ety of stresses and changes in Indian society.

Today the caste system is disintegrating. To be sure, it remains strong in rural areas, which still contain the largest part of the population. But, the fate of India, contrary to Gandhi's hopes, is being decided in and by the cities. It is here that the caste system is coming face to face with modernization.[21]

The basic factor in the disintegration of the castes in the urban situation is simply that the maintenance of ritual purity is almost impossible, as isolation does not exist. Modern urban living, al-ready beginning with the simple necessities of mass transportation, leads to the mingling of people and thus to pollution (in the tradi-tional Hindu sense). The premium on available living quarters makes it impossible to allocate it along caste lines. The rational-ized political and economic life, on which the city is based, is sim-ilarly uncongenial to caste lines. The British were forced to under-emphasize caste to meet their personal needs, both in political administration and in economic enterprise. Independent India has been compelled to do the same, as industry creates occupations that were unprovided for in the traditional caste division of labor. This necessitates a redefinition of the relative importance of tradi-tional occupations. For example, all leather work had traditionally been considered to be polluting, making leather workers corre-spondingly inferior in the caste hierarchy. However, when the leather industry became beneficial for the economy of India, there was a sudden turn of fortune for these people, as they were uniquely qualified for this work. Furthermore, as there was a greater need for leather workers than the traditional workers could provide, other castes found themselves engaged in work that was ritually taboo. Eventually, even high-caste individuals entered ad-ministrative positions in the leather industry. While this is an ex-treme example of the disintegration of traditional attitudes, it il-lustrates a much more general process.

Modern educational institutions, organized by the British (especially their missionaries), have reinforced a similar disregard

for caste divisions. And contact with Christian ideas further converted Indians to an egalitarian ideology that could not be reconciled with caste. The independence movement, spearheaded by
Gandhi and the Congress Party, appropriated this ideology, giving
it legitimation (often rather forced, if one looks at the historical
background) in terms of the "real" meaning of Hinduism. When
India became independent in 1947, it defined itself as a secular republic. Not only has caste no legal standing today, but public discrimination based on caste has been declared illegal. Thus education, political ideology, industrialization, and the legal institutions
all operate as democratic forces inimical to the caste system.

In several ways the position of caste in contemporary India is
comparable to that of race in America. Here, as there, the modernizing forces in the society—democratic ideology, and the political and legal institutions animated by it—tend to make traditional patterns obsolete. All the same, here as there, the
traditional patterns have shown a considerable, if hidden, persistence. Most educated, modernized Indians are likely to deny that
caste is an important factor in their lives, or even in the country
as a whole. But a contradictory picture emerges if they are asked
about their own marriages or their marital plans. There has been
very little intermarriage across the broad caste divisions (across
contiguous caste strata intermarriage was not uncommon in traditional India); family life, and the related sphere of private social
relationships, has widely remained within the traditions of caste.
Also, certain castes will dominate in special occupations; for example, in the professions and other white-collar occupations, the
Brahmins, with their long-standing emphasis on education, have
an important headstart and are still disproportionately represented.
Vaishyas have had a similar headstart in business (though an interesting part has been played in economic activities by religious
minorities that are free of Hindu caste inhibitions, such as the
Parsees, the Sikhs, and the Christians). It is in the new occupations, especially those based on modern technology, that lower-
caste individuals have succeeded in making advances, perhaps primarily because they do not have the abhorrence of manual activity
and physical effort felt by the upper castes, particularly the Brahmins.

The most important modernizing force in India, however, has
been the emergence in the cities of a middle stratum that has the

characteristic structure of a class rather than a caste: in the upper and lower strata caste has proved a more resistant attitude.[22] This emerging middle class is still numerically small, though it is of strategic significance for the development of the nation. It is composed, on its upper levels, of professionals, technicians, administrators, and businessmen, and on its lower reaches, petty shopkeepers, schoolteachers, and the mass of clerical workers. This is the stratum with the most intense modernizing drive. It is also, even in its lower middle group, a stratum with considerable education —indeed "too much" for the immediate needs of Indian society. There are "unemployed intellectuals," drawn from this stratum, who feel intense social frustration. It is this stratum, then, that constitutes a factor of unrest and a catalyst for radical social change. One of the most serious problems for contemporary India is whether this unrest will spur development within the present structure of society or whether it will transform itself into a revolutionary upheaval inimical to the ideology upon which the independent Indian state was founded.

The nature of the *estate system* in Europe and the impact of modernization on it have already been discussed. Although estate was linked to feudalism in Europe and in many parts of the world, it is important to understand that this is not inevitable. Feudalism is a peculiar combination of economic and political patterns, not in itself a stratification system. An estate system can exist under other conditions, as it does in our contemporary world.

There are other salient characteristics of an estate system beyond the ones described above. Estate systems are, above all, typical of agricultural societies, where land ownership is of fundamental economic importance and where the size of landholdings is sufficiently variegated to create social differentiation. Furthermore, there must be sufficient basis to support a group specializing in military activities—the aristocracy of an estate system. In estate societies, political power tends to be concentrated in a combination (sometimes an amalgam) of large landowners and professional soldiers. Typically, such a situation results from military conquest: certain soldiers are given appropriate rewards of land. The conquered population provides a more or less coerced (sometimes enslaved) agricultural labor force. In such cases, the subjugated people have virtually no possibility of social mobility, although there may be some mobility among the higher estates.

Such a system is sociologically quite different from the caste system, but its fate under the impact of modernization may be markedly similar.

The estate system in Latin America offers an important case of this kind.[23] Its historical origin, of course, goes back to the Spanish and Portuguese conquests in the Americas, but its basic patterns have persisted after the independence of the Latin American republics. There are great variations among the Latin American nations, but it is, nevertheless, possible to see a general pattern.

The top estate generally consists of the landholding and commercial aristocracy, and the professional military leadership, as well as the leading politicians, are from this stratum. To a very large extent, the state functions as an "executive committee" (to use Marx's apt term) to protect the interests of this group. At the lower end of the system are the great rural masses, both the small tenants and the landless agricultural workers. In the middle, there is a very small stratum of small landowners, merchants, clerks, and craftsmen, who often are the "poor relatives" of the top group. In other words, the middle estate is, for the most part, the result of downward mobility from the aristocracy, although occasionally it contains individuals who have risen from the lower stratum. In most of Latin America there is an important racial dimension to this system. Except in Argentina, Chile, and Uruguay, the mass of the subordinated population is Indian or, in the Caribbean area, Negro. The aristocracy, proud of its "pure" Spanish or Portuguese descent, is anxious to preserve it from racial mixture.

In this system the aristocracy virtually monopolizes not only privilege and power, but also "culture"—Spanish or Portuguese culture—by the simple expedient of monopolizing access to the educational institutions and, consequently, to the professions. This has been true in great measure even with the educational institutions of the Catholic Church, meaning that the priesthood (insofar as it has not been imported from Europe) has not been an avenue of social mobility, as in other Catholic parts of the world. Instead, both the priests and the Church have been in the hands of the aristocracy. It is only the ownership of land, *per se,* not whether the land is rationally used, that legitimates the aristocracy, giving them a "patent of nobility." The entire ethos is strongly inhibitory not only of reasonable adaptation to social change, but also of modern economic activity of the capitalist type. The middle stra-

Estate and Class in Contemporary Peru

Sociologists generally agree that Peruvian society has a feudal structure deriving from Spanish colonization. Under the pressure of political modernization and economic development, it presents a complex picture. In addition to the persistence of feudal characteristics in the rural areas, mainly in the Sierras, a class society with features commonly found in transitional societies has developed in the urban centers along the coast. This dichotomy is reflected in the 1961 census data on the occupational structure of Peru.

PERCENTAGE OF PERUVIAN POPULATION ACTIVE IN VARIOUS OCCUPATIONS[a]

Employers (*patronos*)	1.9
Self-employed (including professionals, small and intermediate farmers, small businessmen, artisans, as well as a large number of those who do not have a permanent or definite employment)	38.5
Clerical and sales employees	11.0
Laborers (including plantation workers, miners and industrial workers)	31.5
Domestic help	5.6
Unpaid domestic help	9.1
Unspecified labor	2.4

[a] This data presents a number of difficulties. The student is referred to an essay by Aníbal Quijano Obregon, "Tendencies in Peruvian Development and in the Class Structure," J. Petras and M. Zeitlin, eds., *Latin America: Reform or Revolution* (Greenwich, Conn.: Fawcett, 1968), for a challenging analysis of this situation. The above 1961 census data can also be found in this essay, p. 312.

tum in this system constitutes an estate with a most tenuous economic base. It is not only small in numbers, but dependent economically and (very important) ideologically on the aristocracy. Because it faces the constant necessity to maintain its differentiation from the lower masses, it is generally conservative, resistant to social change.

This system has, however, been faced with adaptation to the typical forces of modernization, brought about by the invasion of capitalistic enterprise from the United States and from Europe. Consequently, the social structure, based on agriculture, has become increasingly obsolete as industrialization and urbanization have had effects similar to those described in earlier instances. Economic and technological changes have demanded new skills and, for those capable of meeting these demands, have opened up new opportunities. Land has become less important as the basis of social position, and with the expansion of education, there has emerged dissatisfaction with the old patterns. These forces have tended to undermine the traditional estate system, although there has been vigorous resistance, facilitated by control of the military with its means of violent repression and by alliances with foreign capitalistic interests. For these reasons, Latin America has recently been experiencing frequent and deepening turmoil, accompanied by violence.[24]

The crucial development has been the emergence of a new kind of middle stratum: a middle class. Logically, this has taken place in those countries where the development of capitalistic and industrial enterprise has proceeded most rapidly. Much of this new class is composed of European immigrants (for instance, Germans and Italians), but this class, unlike the old middle stratum, now recruits itself through social mobility from below, being less dependent on the old aristocracy, both economically and ideologically. Of especial importance to this new middle class are the intellectuals, professionals, professors, and university students. (Students in Latin America are frequently oriented toward radical social change and have a strong concern for the low stratum.)

Industrialization has brought about the creation of a new lower stratum, a working class, different in outlook from the old rural population. In several Latin American countries, this working class has been organized into revolutionary labor unions, which have become important agents of social change. And, at the same time, a new revolutionary impetus has sprung up within the old subordinated population itself, often under the direction of middle-class intellectuals who have despaired of the possibility of peaceful change.

It is impossible here to discuss these developments in individual Latin American countries, which would entail an analysis of the Mexican and Cuban revolutions. It is appropriate only to say that the traditional estate system will not be able to maintain itself. The future of the nations over which it previously held sway will be decided in a struggle between the attempt of the new middle class to modernize the social structure to bring about social justice, on the one hand, and the ability of radical political groups to mobilize the increasingly desperate low stratum in a violent assault on the present social structure. Recent events in Chile, for instance, express an attempt to bring about fundamental changes that possibly can forestall revolutionary upheaval. Cuba, of course, serves as the model for the latter alternative. The future of these nations will depend, to a large extent, on external forces, especially on the power and influence of the United States. But, in either case, the traditional estate system has no future.

Stratification by *classes* is, as we have seen, what modernization pushes traditional caste and estate systems toward. Class systems themselves, however, are also susceptible to further modernization. In other words, we can distinguish between the "less modern" and "more modern" class system, with the former typically still marked by many characteristics of the estate system from which it emerged. This means that "style of life" is a significant factor even in class systems, especially in Europe, where the remnants of estate are more visible than in the United States. The modernization of class systems may be observed not only in terms of economic and social-structural developments, such as rising income or social mobility, but also in terms of such matters of life style as consumption habits, morals, dress, demeanor, and language. England serves as a good example.[25]

Sociologically, nineteenth-century England was definitely a class society. Yet it was very different from what is termed a class society today, in England or elsewhere. All of its processes had their roots in the older estate society, as throughout the nineteenth century English society was still in transition between the two types of stratification systems. Legally, the society was open, that is, with the exception of the legal provisions of nobility, the law no longer served to maintain the traditional divisions between strata. Legal equality, however, did not fully correspond to social realities. Even though there was considerable mobility, particularly an upward movement from the middle class, the stratification structure was generally quite stable, with barriers between strata quite formidable. For most people, upward mobility from the lower class was too difficult. The discrepancies in life style among the upper, middle, and lower classes were very sharp.

The upper class was highly visible and, even where it was resented, it was widely emulated; all of England was oriented toward its upper class, not only in the sense that it commanded all privilege and power but also in terms of the values and general attitudes of the people. It was, moreover, a rather broad and diverse grouping, itself stratified into noblemen and commoners. Indeed, even the nobility itself was far from a uniform estate, as it encompassed both the old aristocratic families whose traditions harked back to feudal times and also some recently knighted families; by continuing its practice of knighting meritorious commoners, the nobility absorbed many upward-bound individuals, thereby succeeding in broadening its base. And, of course, even the unknighted upper-class commoners were drawn into an ambience whose tone was set by the formal aristocracy. These upper-class commoners, who are today called the Establishment, constitute a rare sociological phenomenon, as they come to their position from both above and below. Many of them are middle-class individuals, successful in the modern world, but a considerable proportion of them belong to a downwardly mobile segment of the nobility. Because an extreme form of primogeniture exists among the English nobility, only the eldest son inherits the family title; the "younger sons," despite their background and education, have to accept social positions in a stratum lower than the one into which they were born. So, in this peculiar English way, the upwardly mobile moderns and the downwardly mobile feudal aristocracy came to rest together in the commoner upper class.

The typical career of an upper-class male was characterized by an early "eviction" from the family home, into a boarding school (commonly called a "public school"), and followed by a term or two at Oxford or Cambridge. After this, if he was to carry on a gainful occupation, he was supposed to take up one of the three "permissible" careers: government, the military, or the Church of England. In government service, diplomacy was generally deemed the most prestigious, but for the less successful, there were always the colonies, the administration of which absorbed a considerable number of the less successful or otherwise less suitable upper class.

The most important characteristic of the three permissible occupations was that "gentlemen" looked upon them, strictly speaking, as not really work—work in the usual sense of the word (being suitable only for the avaricious middle class). If a member of the upper class were to finance with work a truly gentlemanly way of life but lacked connections to gain entry into a "suitable" career, he gravitated to those upper-middle-class occupations that were somewhat removed from the unseemly turmoil of industrial capitalism: banking, publishing, or perhaps journalism.

The middle class was, in a similar way, stratified within itself; in addition, it was divided into urban and rural types. Dickens' *Pickwick Papers* remains the most reliable guide into this world, but we cannot go into details here. We will stress again the long shadow that the upper class cast over it. The upper class was emulated, as much as possible, in middle-class life styles: the symbolic value of a country residence, the ambition to be educated at Oxford or Cambridge (where, unlike the upper class, the middle class went to get *a degree*—a crude ambition, from an upper-class viewpoint), and even manners and speech, which are to this day a sensitive barometer to class in England.

The working class developed a world quite apart from this complex hierarchy of strata—"another nation," as Disraeli so aptly called it. There was little mobility out of it, at best into the lower middle class with its depressing penury and desperate attempts for respectability. Working-class manners and mores were distinctively divorced from the higher strata, and in the course of the nineteenth century, a strong class consciousness developed, finding expression in the trade union movement and eventually in the Labour Party. With much justification, this class saw the entire structure above it as a unified class enemy, against which its social and political forces had to be mobilized.

The class system has been profoundly transformed in recent decades, particularly since World War II.[26] This change can be seen in the self-identification of people in terms of class; for example, successive public opinion polls have shown a decline in the number of people who think of themselves as part of the "working class."[27] This change in social consciousness is related to a number of objective changes in the social structure. The increasing pace of industrialization is a crucial factor, especially the rise in mass production of consumer commodities, making them available to most people. Despite periodic crises, the continuing rise in prosperity has lifted the working class from its underprivileged, oppressed position in society to relative comfort. In addition, this has been helped by the broadened social services of the new welfare state, as well as by the virtual disappearance of the British Empire, which, as we have seen, served a significant function in the old class system.

The new class system is characterized by two important structural changes. First, the old upper class has merged increasingly with a new upper middle class, more open to entry from below and correspondingly less conservative of traditional estate patterns. Existing no longer in the shadow of the aristocracy, the modern upper class is oriented toward business activities, much like its American counterpart. Second, massive social mobility has been gained for the working class, so that its members have attained middle-class status and hold middle-class occupations in large numbers. Moreover, the working class as such has changed its character as a result of increased prosperity, developing a middle-class style of life. This *embourgeoisement* of the working class, of course, has had important political consequences, as the recent history of the Labour Party clearly shows. More simply, the English class system has become increasingly middle class oriented rather than upper class, meaning that both upper-class and working-class individuals are coming into a broad middle stratum geared to a modern industrial economy. Contemporary English literature, drama, and the cinema provide evidence of the stresses and strains produced by this transformation, but it seems that there is little doubt about this basic trend.

The effect of modernization on caste, estate, and class systems of stratification has now been briefly sketched. Using three cases, we have seen the convergence of stratification systems in the modern world. This convergence has been toward a class system, regardless of the differences in the historical background of various societies. Within the new class system, two characteristics stand out: an increase in upward social mobility and the growing importance of the middle class, both numerically and in terms of cultural influence.

Contemporary Patterns

By now it should be clear that in each society different historical factors affect the patterns of stratification; for example, family background or lineage affects one's social position more in Europe than in the United States. Or, again, political power determines class position in socialist countries to a far greater degree, and more directly, than it does in capitalist societies. With this in mind, it would be a distortion of social reality to speak of stratification in industrial society as if there were a uniform, inevitable pattern everywhere. But it should be clear that there are broad global processes related to industrialization that cause societies with diverse histories to develop along increasingly similar lines. As for stratification, we can see that there are universal trends that tend to minimize historically caused differences among societies. What are these trends?

Some of these processes are directly related to industrialization. Industrialization expands the occupational structure, creating new skills and greatly increased opportunities for work. These opportunities, after a certain degree of industrialization has been attained, are *least* in the area of unskilled labor, as industrialization depreciates the work traditionally performed by lower strata. At the same time, it opens up work opportunities in higher social strata. Since people traditionally in the higher strata are not numerous enough (further limited by a disinclination to industrial work), unfilled higher-strata jobs come into being, thereby creating a surge in upward mobility.[28]

This upward social mobility is of a specific type—namely, it is mobility brought about by activity in the economic sphere. It is a type of *class* mobility, which is different from the type of mobility that might result, for instance, from military conquest. The upward social mobility induced by industrialization, therefore, pushes the stratification system in the direction of the class type, *whatever* its earlier type may have been. We have already discussed this novel process when observing the Indian, Japanese, and English cases, but it is worth restating as a general trend.

Underlying the surge in upward mobility that industrialization leads to is a significant demographic factor: there is a fertility differential between the upper and lower strata.[29] In most societies the lower strata are more fertile and populous than the upper ones. Throughout human history this differential has been one major source of human misery, but industrialization diminishes this by opening "room at the top" (or more precisely, room in the middle—at any rate, higher up) for the formerly unemployable populations of the lower strata to find work in. However, this positive demographic factor is generally offset by the upsurge in pop-

TABLE 4-1

Occupational Distribution of Employment, United States, 1900-1960
(Thousands of people, 14 years of age and older)

OCCUPATIONAL GROUP	1960	1900	CHANGE 1900-1960	PERCENT INCREASE 1900-1960
Total	66,159	29,030	+37,129	128
Total Farm Employment	5,037	10,888	−5,851	−54
Total Non-Farm Employment	61,122	18,142	+42,980	237
White Collar Workers	28,507	5,115	+23,392	457
Professional, Technical, and Kindred Workers	7,418	1,234	+6,184	501
Managers, Officials, and Proprietors	7,032	1,697	+5,335	314
Clerical and Kindred Workers	9,710	877	+8,833	1,007
Sales Workers	4,347	1,306	+3,041	233
Blue Collar Workers	24,280	10,401	+13,879	133
Craftsmen, Foremen, and Kindred Workers	8,606	3,062	+5,544	181
Operatives and Kindred Workers	11,988	3,720	+8,268	222
Laborers	3,686	3,620	+ 66	2
Service Workers	8,335	2,626	5,709	217
Service Workers Excluding Household Workers	6,134	1,047	5,087	486
Private Household Workers	2,201	1,579	622	39

By permission of C. Kerr *et al.*, *Industrialism and Industrial Man* (New York: Oxford University Press, 1964), p. 19

Source: U.S. Department of Labor, Bureau of Labor Statistics, *Employment and Earnings, 1960;* and U.S. Department of Commerce, "Occupational Trends in the United States," Bureau of the Census Working Paper No. 5 (Washington, 1958), pp. 6-7.

ulation that immediately follows the development of industrialization, mainly because of better nutrition and health. But, whether it is for better or worse, we must always remember to consider the significance of population patterns that underlie the dynamics of social structure and mobility.

As industrialization changes the occupational structure, it also changes the place of particular jobs in the system of stratification: some occupations gain status, others lose. Broadly speaking, there is a gain for all occupations related to industrial production and distribution, especially those in technology and business. Concomitantly, there is a loss of status for occupations related to the preindustrial economy, notably agriculture. This means that land ownership ceases to be the primary determinant of class position, although in some societies, it remains a prestige symbol— sometimes solely acquired for this purpose by the newly successful in industry and business.

As a consequence of technological and bureaucratic rationalization, industrial societies experience a decline in inheritable positions. In sociological terms, fewer positions are "ascribed," more and more must be "achieved," and this is the essential quality of a mobile society.[30] The necessity of achieving everything proves a great catalyst to education among all or nearly all classes, as education is the most rational way to acquire the skills, habits, and attitudes necessary to hold a position in the higher levels of the system. Even those on the upper levels must give thought to education, as birthright is rarely a guarantee for maintaining a position; there is always the threat of downward mobility. Statistics show that the number of inherited positions of leadership in American industry has been declining.[31] This may be compared to the purely political career appointments in Soviet industry.[32] In other words, the "right" family background no longer guarantees a top position in most sectors of the American economy, nor does the "right" politics in the Soviet Union. As the criteria for the occupation of economically important positions tend toward rationality, the individual intent on attaining these positions must rationalize his preparation for them by acquiring an education.

Sociologists have found that, regardless what stage of industrialization a country is in, the middle stratum makes the most effective use of the educational opportunities; the lower or working class, however, responds differently in every society. Its response is always dependent both on how mobile the society actually is, and how mobile it subjectively seems to the working-class people within it.[33] In a country such as France there persists a strong working-class consciousness with a political organization to support it, making a less subjective orientation toward mobility than there is in the United States where working-class consciousness as such has been almost nonexistent up to very recently. This means that national societies differ in the degree to which their working classes are oriented toward the middle-class style of life. Despite these differences, it is safe to say that advanced industrialization generally leads to an *embourgeoisement*—a middle-class life style—and thus to a decrease in the political militancy of the working class.[34] In effect, then, industrialization and the concomitant spread of education enhance political stability. This makes it unlikely that the working classes in industrial societies at a certain stage of their development will be actively revolutionary.

If one thinks of the stratified social ranks as forming a pyramid, as they do in most preindustrial systems, the development of industrialization tends to transform the strata into a octahedron, showing the stratification with a bulge in the middle. The middle class becomes most numerous, tending to dominate the cultural style of the society as a whole. Despite considerable national differences, the new middle-class cultural style is relatively consistent throughout all societies. This is partly due to the *newness* of middle-class status. There is a widespread social insecurity, an uncertainty about status; one expression of this is the emphasis on type and degree of consumption as a symbolization of status.[35] Also, mobility aspirations, having become an organizing principle for the individual's whole life, do not suddenly cease when a certain position has been attained. There is a tendency to remain mobility-oriented—a striving, "achieving" stratum—and the whole society, not merely the middle class, becomes a conglomeration of people permanently "on the make." [36] The values of the middle class reflect this orientation and, because of its dominance in the society, the society as a whole is influenced by these values. Interestingly enough, the dynamism of mobility has little or no political expression; on the contrary, since the mobility- and achievement-oriented individual has a stake in society as it is, his political values are conservative. Finally, because the world of the new middle classes is shaped by similar social-psychological forces, there develops a sort of global personality type. Most middle-class life today is characterized by bureaucratic forms of organization; concomitantly, there is a diffusion of what might be called a bureaucratic personality type, which will be discussed later.

We may observe the leveling force of industrialism on class structure in a comparison of the two most powerful industrial countries in the world today, the United States and the Soviet Union. This comparison is particularly interesting because, despite the differences in their historical development and the sharp antagonism between their contemporary political and ideological systems, several features in their respective stratification systems, particularly of the upper and middle strata, are strikingly similar.

THE AMERICAN CASE

Preindustrial America was a society in which small farmers, small businessmen, and small traders predominated. The opening sentence of Alexis de Tocqueville's *Democracy in America* succinctly sums up the overall impression the country made on this famous early-nineteenth-century visitor: "Among the novel objects that attracted my attention during my stay in the United States, nothing struck me more forcibly than the general equality of condition among the people." [37] This earlier America was egalitarian in sociological fact, as well as in political doctrine. Although disparities of wealth and social rank existed, they were far less extreme than those prevalent in European countries. De Tocqueville saw preindustrial America as a model of "property-owning democracy," in which the principle of equality produced few stable class divisions. He described a society in which class boundaries were easily crossed and that, therefore, were not perceived as significantly real. It was a society in which people believed in equality of opportunity and, even if this belief did not correspond fully to the social reality, it had a profound effect in minimizing the objective and subjective barriers to it. In the century and a half since then, however, monumental economic changes have delimited our equality: to one observer, at least, these changes have "destroyed most of the foundations upon which the egalitarian ideology rested." [38]

The rapid growth of industry after the Civil War led to major changes in the occupational structure. At the end of the Civil War most of the population was engaged in agriculture, forestry, and fishing. Some fifty years later, in the 1920s, by far the greater number of people was engaged in manufacturing, mining, and the building trades, as well as in the swiftly growing "tertiary industries"—trade, transportation, communications, the professions, and the service occupations.[39] And in recent years the pace of these changes in the occupational structure have accelerated even more.[40] Altogether in the past one hundred years the occupational structure of America has undergone two interrelated transformations. First, it changed from a predominantly agrarian to an industrial society, as reflected in the increasing number of persons engaged in nonagrarian occupations. Second, there has been a transformation of the industrial order through an increase in the proportion of administrative employees, a "bureaucratic revolution." Thus in 1957, for the first time, the number of administrative employees exceeded the number of manual workers in industry.[41]

These transformations have had a profound effect on the class system. Class divisions have been accentuated and crystallized. Mobility remains high, but it has become limited: it is almost impossible to "jump" more than one class in a lifetime—even more difficult to enter the highest class. The studies of Digby Baltzell have shown this crystallization of the American upper class in the twentieth century, as it has taken the character of a closed "establishment." [42] Baltzell's picture contrasts sharply with De Tocqueville's, who observed that "in America most of the rich men were formerly poor; most of those who now enjoy leisure were absorbed in business during their youth." [43] But the growing number of middle-class occupations has facilitated mobility into the middle class from below for individuals with the necessary qualifications and ambition. As a result, the total rate of upward mobility has greatly increased and the middle class has expanded, both in absolute size and in proportion to the population as a whole. American society is essentially middle class, with relatively contracted upper and lower levels of the class system. Put graphically, this is the octahedron of stratification mentioned earlier, with a bulging middle, rather than the traditional pyramid of strata.

The old dream of America as a society of equals, as a land of limitless opportunity, continues as an ideology, despite the changes in the class system, and also despite the continuing presence of poverty in certain groups of the population. The relative absence of class consciousness in America is partly due to this ideology, and to its realization in practice through the growth of education as a prime vehicle of social mobility. The absence of strong class consciousness in the past has had a politically stabilizing effect, inhibiting the growth of radicalism in the lower classes. All this, however, can only be said in abstraction from the racial situation, which cuts across, and perhaps substitutes for, the class system. But a discussion of this is beyond our present purposes.

THE SOVIET CASE

The stratification system of the Soviet Union, like that of the United States, has also undergone considerable change since the Revolution of 1917.[44] Both countries profess a democratic ideology of equal opportunity for all. The Soviet Union, however, regards itself also as a classless society, in which the struggle between classes and the exploitation of one class by another (which Marx believed was the essence of previous social history) no longer exist. In accordance with Marxist doctrine this claim is based on the outlawing of private ownership of the means of production and of private capital formation. This fact suffices to explain "classlessness" in terms of Marxist ideology, but a sociological analysis shows that the situation is actually quite complex.

Immediately after the Revolution the new Bolshevik regime tried to implement its belief in classlessness by equalizing incomes throughout the society. This policy was abandoned quite early in the history of the Soviet state and, concomitantly, the literal understanding of the ideal of equality was modified. The first decade of Soviet rule was an economic fiasco. Later, it became clear to even the staunchest supporter of Bolshevik egalitarianism that, for industrialization to succeed, there would have to be personal incentives based on differential economic rewards.

As we have shown in Chapter 3, industrialization in the Soviet Union did not begin to develop significantly until after deviation from the strict original policy of equalitarianism had become official doctrine. In the years since then, the Soviet Union has moved into the forefront of industrial countries. In 1917, 90 per cent of the Russian population was engaged in primary production—or agriculture and the allied occupations; by 1959, the majority of the population was engaged in the secondary and tertiary industries, manufacturing, and the various white-collar occupations, reflecting the character of the country.[45] To be sure, compared to America and Western Europe, Russia still has a large rural and agriculturally employed population, but the basic character of contemporary Soviet society is related to the growth of its white-collar occupations.

White-collar workers were originally referred to in Soviet writing as the "cadres"; they are now called the "intelligentsia," comprising such varied occupations as party and government officials, industrial managers, engineers and technicians, administrators of the collective and state farms, doctors, teachers, lawyers, and military officers (the military being a very special type of "intellectual"). Below this stratum is a less clearly structured one, between the "intelligentsia" and the industrial workers, comprising clerical workers in offices, hotels, railways, postal service, and the like.[46] Beneath these are the industrial workers and the agricultural workers, making up two large strata. The landworkers, now that there is little enforced labor, may be regarded as the bottom stratum of Soviet society, although this, needless to say, is contrary to the official ideological position that "workers" and "peasants" are equal partners in the U.S.S.R.

Without intending to oversimplify a development that is very complex but also difficult to assess fully because of the limited availability of data, we must note that available data clearly suggest that Soviet society has gone through the same two-stage transformation of its occupational structure that America did: first was the transformation from a peasant to an industrial society, and second is the transformation brought about by the accelerating growth of managerial, bureaucratic, and professional occupations.

Contrary to original ideological intentions ("from each according to his ability, to each according to his needs"), there is today a highly differentiated income structure in Soviet society.[47] The disparity between the higher managerial salaries and the wages of simple industrial laborers is, at the very least, equal to that in Western industrial countries. The differentiation in income has inevitably led to very different styles of life between the different levels of the occupational structure. These differences have been further accentuated by government practices (strongest during the Stalinist period, but existing today) that bestow special privileges on those whose skills are particularly valued by the state: privileges include special housing, special stores, special vacation resorts, and the like. In this way, Soviet society, if viewed sociologically, may be seen as a *de facto* class society, at least within its industrialized sectors. Their class system, to be sure, is not based on private property, but rather on differential managerial *control* of the means of production and on differential advantage in the consumption of products. In this, however, the Soviet "intelligentsia" class is not unlike the managerial elite in Western countries, which also often has economic power and privilege without having actual ownership of the means of production.[48]

Data on Russian social mobility is too sparse to permit a satisfactory comparison with mobility in other countries. However, whatever the mobility rate, it is clear that the nature of mobility in the Soviet Union has been changing.[49] Previously, the key criteria for mobility were political orthodoxy (coupled, of course, with political acumen as needed in making a career in the brutally competitive apparatus of the party or government) and a properly proletarian background—with strong discrimination against persons of bourgeois origin. Now, however, this has become secondary to the possession of rational qualifications for the particular position. Such qualifications, however, are mainly the result of education. In Soviet society, too, education has become a principal vehicle of social mobility. In the urban areas, where there exists more equality of educational opportunity (probably more so than in Western countries) mobility thus is possible.[50] For the rural population, the opportunities are far fewer, limiting their mobility into the privileged positions and strata. Compared to Western countries, the top levels of Soviet society are still relatively open, though there apparently is an increasing trend toward "internal recruitment" to these levels; this, however, is not irrational, but rather devolves from the advantages that inevitably accrue to the children of the privileged.[51]

There has been much debate about whether there is a structural convergence between Western and Soviet society.[52] Our position should be clear by now. While we do not believe the term "industrial society" is magic, nor claim a universal leveling of social structures regardless of historical, political, and ideological differences, we do nevertheless contend that there is a general movement toward convergence in the middle strata of these societies, although the historical paths to it may be quite different. For instance, in America the establishment of a middle-class, differentiated society followed the triumph of industrial capitalism, and has been maintained in its essence despite various modifications, including the modifications brought about by the growing welfare state since the 1930s. In Russia, there was at first the virtual destruction of the pre-Revolutionary class society, then a subtle reintroduction of class patterns to support the desired industrialization. Yet, regardless of their individual roads to it, their modern realities are quite similar, as we have seen. In both nations an egalitarian ideology is permanently at tension with the realities of the social structure. Both in America and in Russia the ideology is

TABLE 4-2

Comparative Indices of Upward and Downward Mobility in Percentages

	NONFARM POPULATIONS		
COUNTRY	UPWARD MOBILITY (NONMANUAL SONS OF MANUAL FATHERS)	DOWNWARD MOBILITY (MANUAL SONS OF NON-MANUAL FATHERS)	TOTAL VERTICAL MOBILITY (NON-FARM POPULA-TION MOBILE ACROSS THE LINE BETWEEN WORKING AND MIDDLE CLASS)
United States	33	26	30
Germany	29	32	31
Sweden	31	24	29
Japan	36	22	27
France	39	20	27
Switzerland	45	13	23

	POPULATIONS WITH RURAL AND URBAN OCCUPATIONS CLASSIFIED TOGETHER		
COUNTRY	HIGH PRESTIGE OCCUPATION SONS OF FATHERS IN LOW PRESTIGE OCCUPATIONS	LOW PRESTIGE OCCUPATION SONS OF FATHERS IN HIGH PRESTIGE OCCUPATIONS	PROPORTION MOBILE ACROSS HIGH AND LOW OCCUPATION PRESTIGE LINES
Denmark	22	44	31
Great Britain	20	49	29
Italy	8	34	16

Source: S. M. Lipset and R. Bendix, *Social Mobility in Industrial Society* (Berkeley: University of California Press, 1963), p. 25. Reprinted by permission of The Regents of the University of California.

official as well as a common dream. In both nations the vast financial differentiation between the upper and lower classes is not easily overcome, but in each nation the road to middle-class status is relatively open, and the education that is necessary to attain it is generally available, though less so to certain alienated classes like the peasants in Russia and the blacks in the United States.

These general patterns, moreover, are typical of other Western industrial societies. The rate and kind of mobility in America and Western Europe are rather alike, although America may still be the most mobile nation in the Western world.[53] In Western Europe, as in America, education has become a principal source of mobility. To this extent, then, we feel entitled to argue that the term "industrial society" does indeed refer to an international social reality, cutting across historical and political boundaries. There is a basic stratification pattern corresponding to industrialism: it is a relatively open, highly mobile, middle-strata-oriented class system. There may be particular modifications—such as race (or caste) in America or politics in the Soviet Union—but one might even argue that if these various idiosyncracies are irrational organizationally, there will appear a strong tendency to eliminate them, almost as if the class system had a "will" to eliminate those patterns of stratification that fail to meet its intrinsic "logic."

THE TRANSITIONAL SOCIETIES

Of particular sociological interest are those societies that are now beginning to modernize, but have no previous history of class orientation; they offer a rich "laboratory" in which to study stratification.[54] The newly independent countries of Africa are perfect subjects. There are, of course, considerable differences between these countries, some of which are rooted in the various indigenous cultures; others are due to the different policies of former colonial rulers: as an example, consider the different educational policies of the British and the Belgians, which have resulted in the British leaving behind well-educated African cadres, whereas the Belgians allowed an educational vacuum that had much to do, for instance, with the chaos in the Belgian Congo when it became independent. In terms of stratification, the crucial question for all these nations concerns the emergence of a middle class.

It is this class—relatively educated, urbanized, and detribalized —that will determine the future shape of these new nations. It is the "carrier" both of modernization and of the new national identity. The peculiar characteristic of it is that it is not the *result* of industrialization, or only so in a very limited way—in most of Africa, industrialization has barely, if at all, begun. The new middle class is also not the result of capitalistic entrepreneurship, as was the case in Europe in earlier times: in most of Africa, such capitalistic enterprise as exists is mainly the work of foreign, mostly "ex-colonial," activity. This new middle class is, rather, the result of general economic diversification, urbanization, and primarily of the growth of governmental bureaucracy. It constitutes an educated "salariate," that small part of the population which is vitally connected with the political processes at the new national centers. Because its recent history is linked closely to the struggle for inde-

The Newly Rising African Middle Class

In an essay on the African middle class. T. Hodgkin describes the contrast between the small bourgeoisie of professionals and small land-owners and the *classe moyenne,* which is a particular phenomenon of the new nations. He also presents the essential, general characteristics of the emerging middle class.

Occupational criteria: Because of diversification of the economy in growing towns, expansion of the bureaucracy in new national states, and the general spread of Western education, there has emerged a middle class. Education is the chief criterion for middle-class member-ship. However, in Africa semiliterate or self-educated farmers, con-tractors, lorry-owners, traders, and the like have to be included in this class, provided they "enjoy a relatively comfortable standard of life, with European-style furniture and equipments."

Economic criteria: Compared with the mass of the population, the members of this class are relatively rich; compared with Europeans, they are absolutely poor. In certain parts of Africa, it is estimated, white-collar officials who constitute 3 per cent of the total popula-tion receive nearly 14 per cent of the national income.

External criteria: These are rather uniform. One must live in a solid, European-style house equipped with European furnishings, wear European-style clothing (for everyday purposes, at least), eat European food, read newspapers, listen to the radio, and have membership and participation in associations of many sorts.

Attitudes: Belief in the value of education; a new individualism; preference of "progressive" ideas in relation to marriage, family, and possibly religion ("progressive" means Western): these signs of class membership are relatively difficult to assess and more research is re-quired.

Source: T. Hodgkin, "The African Middle Class," *Corona* 8, 3 (1956).

pendence, it is a class tending strongly toward radical politics. This tendency is augmented by the employment problem of any intelligentsia in any underdeveloped society, which sometimes takes the forms similar to those we described earlier in the case of India.

In these countries education is *the* vehicle of social mobility, and the educated class leads a highly distinctive way of life. It is urban and considerably divorced from the indigenous tribal cultures. It is oriented toward the West, not necessarily politically, but in language, dress, and consumption patterns, and above all in its drive toward modernization. It is understandably of interest to the sociologist to see how this peculiar class structure will change, and particularly to see how closely it will approximate the patterns of the older industrial societies, as these countries progress in modernization.

NOTES

1. Of the wealth of literature on social stratification, we will list here a few of the most comprehensive. Publications on theories of stratification: Reinhard Bendix and S. M. Lipset, *Class, Status, and Power: A Reader in Social Stratification* (New York: Free Press, 1965); Kurt B. Mayer, *Class and Society* (New York: Doubleday, 1955); Bernard Barber, *Social Stratification* (New York: Harcourt, Brace, 1957). Publications on comparative social stratification: S. M. Lipset and Reinhard Bendix, *Social Mobility in Industrial Society* (Berkeley: University of California Press, 1963); Kaare Svalastoga, *Social Differentiation* (New York: David McKay, 1965); S. M. Miller "Comparative Social Mobility," *Current Sociology* 9 (1960): 1–72.

2. A summary of American community studies can be found in Maurice R. Stein, *The Eclipse of Community* (Princeton: Princeton University Press, 1960).

3. About France: Laurence Wylie, *Village in the Vaucluse* (New York: Harper and Row, 1964); Robert and Barbara Anderson, *Bus Stop for Paris* (New York: Doubleday, 1965); Laurence Wylie, ed., *Chanzeaux, A Village in Anjou* (Cambridge: Harvard University Press, 1966). About England: Josephine Kline, *Samples from English Cultures* (London: Routledge and Kegan Paul, 1965); Madeline Kerr, *The People of Ship Street* (London: Routledge and Kegan Paul, 1958); Hilda Jennings, *Societies in the Making* (London: Allen and Unwin, 1958).

4. See the bibliographies in Harold M. Hodges, Jr., *Social Stratification—Class in America* (Cambridge: Schenkman, 1964), and Milton M. Gordon, *Social Class in American Society* (Durham: Duke University Press, 1958).

5. C. Wright Mills, *White Collar* (New York: Oxford University Press, 1951), and *The Power Elite* (New York: Oxford University Press, 1959).

6. Karl Marx, *Capital*, trans. Ernest Untermann (Chicago: Charles H. Kerr and Co., 1909), Vol. 3, Chap. 52, and Karl Marx and Friedrich Engels, *The Communist Manifesto* (New York: International Publishers, 1932).

7. Vilfredo Pareto, *Mind and Society*, 4 vols. (New York: Harcourt, Brace, 1935). Volume 4 is of special interest here.

8. Max Weber, *From Max Weber: Essays in Sociology*, eds. H. H. Gerth and C. Wright Mills (New York: Oxford University Press, 1958), Chap. 7; and Max Weber, *The Theory of Social and Economic Organization*, trans. A. M. Henderson and Talcott Parsons (New York: Oxford University Press, 1947).

9. *Ibid.*

10. See Gunnar Myrdal, *An American Dilemma* (New York: Harper and Row, 1944), and John Dollard, *Caste and Class in a Southern Town* (New Haven: Yale University Press, 1937).

11. See particularly W. Lloyd Warner et al., *Yankee City Series,* Vols. 1–4 (New Haven: Yale University Press, 1941–1947).

12. Milovan Djilas, *The New Class* (New York: Praeger, 1957).

13. Ralf Dahrendorf, *Soziale Klassen und Klassenkonflikt* (Stuttgart: Enke, 1957), and S. Ossowski, *Class Structure in the Social Consciousness* (London: Routledge and Kegan Paul, 1963).

14. For various studies of the European development, see especially the series *Main Themes in European History,* Bruce Mazlish, General Editor (New York: Macmillan). Of special interest is the volume, Bernard and Elinor Barber, eds., *European Social Class* (New York: Macmillan, 1965).

15. Cf. Illustration 4-3, from Hippolyte Taine, *The Ancient `Regime* (New York: P. Smith, 1931), p. 7.

16. For a detailed discussion of this, see Reinhard Bendix, *Nation-Building and Citizenship* (New York: John Wiley, 1964).

17. See Milton Gordon, *Social Class in American Sociology* (Durham: Duke University Press, 1958).

18. See J. H. Hutton, *Caste in India,* 3rd ed. (New York: Oxford University Press, 1961); J. A. Dubois, *Hindu Manners, Customs, and Ceremonies* (London, Victor Gollancz, 1906); Max Weber, "India: The Brahman and the Castes," in *From Weber: Essays in Sociology.*

19. Weber, "India: The Brahman and the Castes."

20. This term was introduced by M. N. Srinivas, *Religion and Society among the Coorgs of South India* (Oxford: Clarendon Press, 1952).

21. See M. N. Srinivas, "The Indian Road to Equality," *Economic Weekly* 12 (June 1960): 867–872; Roy Turner, ed., *India's Urban Future* (Berkeley: University of California Press, 1962); George Rosen, *Democracy and Economic Change in India* (Berkeley: University of California Press, 1966).

22. See, especially, Rosen, *op. cit.,* pp. 38–50.

23. For general information on Latin America, and special emphasis on its social structure: James Bryce, *South America* (New York: Macmillan, 1916); William Lytle Schurz, *This New World: The Civilization of Latin America* (New York: Dutton, 1954); Robert J. Alexander, *Today's Latin America* (New York: Doubleday Anchor, 1962).

24. "Social Change in Latin America Today," *Harper's,* April 1960, special issue; John Johnson, *Political Change in Latin America: The Emergence of the Middle Sectors* (Stanford: Stanford University Press, 1958); and Andrew H. Whiteford, *Two Cities of Latin America: A Comparative Description of Social Classes* (New York: Doubleday, 1964).

25. Lawrence Stone, "Class Divisions in England, 1540–1660," J. H. Hexter, "Myth of the Middle Class in Tudor England," and W. O. Aydelotte, "The Business Interests of the Gentry in the Parliament of 1841–47," in Barber and Barber, *op. cit.* The student should read some of the famous novels of nineteenth-century England, such as those by Dickens, the Brontës, and Thackeray.

26. E. A. Johns, *The Social Structure of Modern Britain* (Elmsford, N. Y.: Pergamon Press, 1965); M. Young and P. Willmott, *Family and Class in a London Suburb* (London: Routledge and Kegan Paul, 1960); R. Lewis and A. Maude, *The English Middle Classes,* rev. ed. (Baltimore: Penguin, 1953); T. B. Bottomore, *Classes in Modern Society* (New York: Random

House, 1966); and D. V. Glass, ed., *Social Mobility in Britain* (Glencoe: Free Press, 1955).

27. Lockwood, "The New Working Class," *European Journal of Sociology* 1 (1960): 248–259.

28. Lipset and Bendix, *Social Mobility in Industrial Society*.

29. *Ibid.*, p. 58.

30. See Ralph Linton, *The Study of Man* (New York: Appleton-Century-Crofts, 1936), pp. 115 ff.

31. Reinhard Bendix, *Work and Authority in Industry* (New York: John Wiley, 1956), pp. 226 ff.

32. David Granick, *The Red Executive* (New York: Doubleday Anchor, 1960).

33. See Bottomore, *op. cit.* and Lipset and Bendix, *Social Mobility in Industrial Society*.

34. In Bottomore, *op. cit.*, English, French, and German data are summarized in substantiation of this.

35. J. R. Seeley, R. A. Sim, and E. W. Loosley, *Crestwood Heights* (New York: Basic Books, 1956).

36. *Ibid.*

37. Alexis de Tocqueville, *Democracy in America* (New York: Knopf, 1945).

38. Bottomore, *op. cit.*, p. 49.

39. Colin Clark, *The Condition of Economic Progress* (New York: Macmillan, 1940), p. 346.

40. Lipset and Bendix, *op. cit.*, p. 85.

41. *Ibid.*

42. E. Digby Baltzell, *An American Business Aristocracy* (New York: Collier, 1962), and *Philadelphia Gentleman* (Glencoe: Free Press, 1958).

43. De Tocqueville, *op. cit.*, p. 54.

44. Alex Inkeles and Kent Geiger, *Soviet Society* (Boston: Houghton Mifflin, 1961); Klaus Mehnert, *Soviet Man and His World* (New York: Praeger, 1962); and Institute for the Study of the U.S.S.R., *Soviet Society Today: A Symposium* (Munich, 1958).

45. See Arvid Brodersen, *The Soviet Worker* (New York: Random House, 1966); Raymond Aron, et al., *The Soviet Economy* (London: Oxford University Press, 1956); Abram Bergson, ed., *Soviet Economic Growth* (Evanston: Row Peterson Co., 1953).

46. Mehnert, *op. cit.*, p. 22.

47. Alex Inkeles, "Myth and Reality of Social Classes," in Inkeles and Geiger, *op. cit.*

48. This point has been effectively made by James Burnham, *The Managerial Revolution* (Bloomington: Indiana University Press, 1960).

49. See Alex Inkeles, "Social Stratification and Mobility in the Soviet Union: 1940–1950," *American Sociological Review* 15 (1950): 465–479. Also see S. V. Utechin, "Social Stratification and Social Mobility in the U. S. S. R.," *Transactions of the Second World Congress of Sociology* (London: International Sociological Association, 1954), 2: 55–63.

50. See Nigel Grant, *Soviet Education* (Pelican, 1964); George S. Counts, *The Challenge of Soviet Education* (New York: McGraw-Hill, 1957); and Nicholas de Witt, "Recent Trends in Soviet Education," in Inkeles and Geiger, *op. cit.*

51. See Alex Inkeles, "Myth and Reality of Social Classes," in Inkeles and Geiger, *op. cit.*

52. See Bottomore, *op. cit.*; Raymond Aron, *The Industrial Society*

(New York: Praeger, 1967); and Stanislav Andreski, *The Uses of Comparative Sociology* (Berkeley: University of California Press, 1965), pp. 343–365.

53. See Lipset and Bendix, *op. cit.* and Bottomore, *op. cit.*

54. See P. Mercier, "Problems in Social Stratification in West Africa," in Immanuel Wallerstein, ed., *Social Change: The Colonial Situation* (New York, John Wiley, 1966); T. Hodgkin, "The African Middle Class," in Wallerstein, *op. cit.;* Martin Kilson, "The Masses, the Elite, and Post-Colonial Politics in Africa," in Jason Finkle and Richard Gable, *Political Development and Social Change* (New York: John Wiley, 1966); and Guy Hunter, *The New Societies of Tropical Africa* (New York: Praeger, 1964).

[5] Urbanization

THE spread of cities and the concomitant spread of the problems that develop in the cities are facts of everyday experience in America today. The newspapers write daily about the problems caused by the immense concentrations of people in our metropolitan areas: housing congestion, traffic congestion, water shortages, air pollution, strains on public services of all kinds, intergroup tensions exploding in overcrowded spaces, and many more. At the same time, it is a fact of everyday experience that the cities and their way of life are reaching out to embrace more people and to cover ever larger portions of what remains of the countryside. Large stretches of the Atlantic and the Pacific coastlines threaten to become urban sprawls, as spreading metropolitan areas link up with each other—Boston with New York, New York with Philadelphia, and so on. Nor is the problem a peculiarly American one. Considerable sections of industrial countries elsewhere (for instance, central Holland or northern Switzerland) already have the appearance of gigantic cities, with towns and their surroundings linking together into vast areas of compact urban settlement. And, outside the industrial nations, in the underdeveloped world, cities are also growing at a rapid rate, with vastly graver problems than even the worst ones in America or Western Europe. Urbanization is worldwide today. Before we turn to an examination of its contemporary patterns, however, we will first attempt a sociological definition of the concept of "city," surveying the historical development of cities in Western civilization, as this forms the background of our present situation.

TABLE 5-1

Estimated Percent Distribution of World Population, and Percentages of Population in Places of 20,000 or More Inhabitants for the Regions of the World, 1950-1960

AREA	ESTIMATED PERCENTAGE DISTRIBUTION OF WORLD POPULATION		PERCENTAGE OF POPULATION IN PLACES OF 20,000 OR MORE					
			ESTIMATED AVERAGES FOR ALL COUNTRIES			AVERAGES FOR COUNTRIES HAVING 1950 AND 1960 DATA		
	1950	1960	1950	1960	PERCENTAGE INCREASE IN PROPORTION URBAN[a]	1950	1960	PERCENTAGE INCREASE IN PROPORTION URBAN[a]
World Total	100	100	21	24-25[b]	12-17[b]	27	30	12
Less Developed Regions	70	72	14	17-18[b]	17-28[b]	18	22	19
Africa	9	9	10	13	37	14	18	27
North Africa	—	—	21	26	23	25	31	23
Sub-Sahara Africa	—	—	6	9	50	8	11	35
Asia	55	56	14	16-18[b]	11-26[b]	19	21	14
Excluding China (mainland)	33	34	17	19	15	19	21	14
China (mainland)	22	22	10	10-15[b]	0-50[b]	—	—	—
Latin America	6	7	25	32	28	28	36	29
Argentina, Chile, Uruguay	—	—	47	56	19	48	57	20
Remainder of Latin America	—	—	21	28	33	21	29	40
More Developed Regions	30	28	37	41	10	38	41	10
Northern America	7	7	43	46	6	43	46	6
Europe (excluding U.S.S.R.)	16	14	37	40	8	37	40	8
Northwestern	—	—	52	54	3	52	54	3
Central	—	—	37	40	9	37	40	9
Southern	—	—	23	27	16	23	27	16
U.S.S.R.	7	7	31	36	17	31	36	17
Oceanic	c	c	46	53	15	56	64	13
Australia and New Zealand	—	—	58	65	12	58	65	12
Remainder of Oceania	—	—	—	3	—	—	15	—

[a] From unrounded data. [b] Range of estimated values corresponding to alternative estimates for China (mainland). [c] Less than 1 percent.

Source: Gerald Breese, *Urbanization in Newly Developing Countries* (Englewood Cliffs, N. J.: Prentice-Hall, 1966), p. 33. Copyright 1966. Reprinted by permission of Prentice-Hall, Inc., Englewood Cliffs, N.J.

Concept of the City

In our daily life, of course, we have some sort of unarticulated notion of what constitutes a city, but as soon as we try to make a sharp conceptualization of it, we discover how difficult it is. For instance, our ordinary notion certainly presupposes that a city is a settlement of a certain size; but precisely how large must it be to be termed "city"? Rather than describe and evaluate various definitions of the concept (which would quickly become tangential to our present purpose), we will simply work from Max Weber's definition, which is relatively straightforward.[1]

Weber's conceptualization of the city has three principal facets. First, a city is a form of human settlement in which people live together in close *proximity* within a compact, continuous area. Second, a city is a *large* settlement of people. For Weber, the element of size, however, is historically and geographically relative: what is reckoned as a large city in one age or country need not be so considered in another. Third, a city is a place where people do not generally know each other personally and where, therefore, social relations are organized in complex, more or less *impersonal* forms; these forms Weber called "associational," as against the "communal" forms of preurban or nonurban settlements. This definition certainly leaves room for many questions, but it serves pragmatically to point to what it is that we are talking about.

Closely related to Weber's conceptualization of the city is his typology or characterization of it.[2] Again, this is not exhaustive, but it will serve to suggest the great diversity embraced by the single concept. Cities, by definition, are always centers for some sort of human activity; what the activity is varies greatly. First, and possibly the most ancient type, is the city as a religious center. These normally develop around a shrine or sanctuary, with religious performance as their original and central activity, although other functions may later accumulate there as well, such as juridical, economic, and so forth. Many ancient cities began in this way, for example, Memphis, Babylon, Jerusalem, or Delphi, and such modern cities as Mecca and, at least originally, Salt Lake City.

Second, some cities develop as administrative or military centers, that is, centers of governmental activity, such as the District of Columbia and New Delhi. Third, some cities are trade centers, and naturally are located most frequently at strategic points in terms of transportation, as Hong Kong today or Venice in an earlier time. Fourth, there are cities that are industrial centers, not only in the modern, post-industrial-revolution sense, but in terms also of ancient financial and productive institutions. Within this category there are various subtypes: cities are centered on the exploitation of raw materials for production, such as Johannesburg, a mining city; cities are centered on actual manufacturing, like Pittsburgh or Manchester; cities are centered on the distribution and administration of manufactured commodities, such as New York.

These various types, if we take account of the many modifications they are subject to, may all be found in every period of history. In different periods one or the other type comes into prominence. Thus, during periods of empire-building, cities of the governmental type are most prominent, while today most urbanization is of the fourth type. As we will see, every type and every epoch entails a very different structural and institutional nature: for example, the stratification system of a military city is, obviously, not like that of a city centered on trade.

Historical Development of the City

Cities are a late development in human history.[3] When they finally made their historical appearance, they ushered in a transformation of human life so radical that some historians and cultural anthropologists have identified the "urban revolution" as the root of what we call civilization. Because the existence of cities coincides, more or less, with development of writing and the consequent keeping of records of man's doings, it may be said justifiably that the coming of the city inaugurated the historical memory of man; whatever preceded this time is veiled, probably forever, in the mist of mythology and legend.

Although cities and their problems are not as old as man himself, it should be obvious that they are not peculiarly modern phenomena. The available archaeological evidence indicates that cities existed at least as early as 3,000 B.C. in Egypt, in Mesopotamia, in the Indus Valley, and in the river basins of China. Civilizations flourished in all these areas at the same time that they became urbanized. Even then, one may distinguish cities with different purposes at their inception. It is safe to say that the earliest cities were religious and/or governmental centers, with trade cities developing only later.

There are a number of general sociological characteristics of cities, holding cross-culturally with great consistency.[4] A prerequisite for the existence of the city as a form of human settlement is a surplus of agricultural production. A subsistence economy, in which all available labor must be dedicated to the sheer task of survival, will not be able to afford city life. Only the existence of such a surplus can free a sizable proportion of the population from what cultural anthropologists call the "commissariat," that is, the institutionalized activity of supplying food. And, only then can there be the division of labor that creates occupations, ranging from astrology to fine metal artisanship, that are typical of people dwelling in cities. Therefore, cities are closely tied to technological innovation: originally this involves innovations in agriculture, making for increased per capita food production, but eventually it becomes innovation in other areas as well and finally creates what may be called the autonomous spirit of innovation. This means, from another perspective, that cities are places where tradition counts for less. This fact is of immense significance, and has been so ever since the first appearance of the city in history.

The social structure of cities is based on the division of labor that makes them possible; it may vary with the city type, but in every case involves a structure of considerable complexity and, compared with preurban patterns, "artificiality." It is artificial because people of diverse backgrounds commingle, and therefore are forced to devise social structures other than those of family, clan, or tribe. The city deemphasizes consanguinity and all its attendant social forms. Once again, this is a trait that makes for change, innovation, and depreciation of tradition. Also, because the occupational diversity and specialization in cities produce new types of people and new ways of life (for example, intellectuals and artisans, each with highly distinct conduct, outlook, and even personality), cities require forms of social association that are functional and limited to specific tasks, and that are, in comparison with the forms of consanguinity, abstract and impersonal. Not surprisingly then, cities are important centers for the development of informal regimentation and of codified law.

In antiquity a "natural" limit to the size of cities was set by the

How the City Was Formed

Fustel de Coulanges has made the classic, comprehensive study of religious and civic institutions in ancient Greece and Rome. In these excerpts we desire to isolate Coulanges' notion of the rise of the ancient city.

There seem to us to be two truths equally manifest: the one is, that the city was a confederation of groups that had been established before it; and the other is, that society developed only so fast as religion enlarged its sphere. We cannot, indeed, say that religious progress brought social progress; but what is certain is that they were both produced at the same time, and in remarkable accord.

We should not lose sight of the excessive difficulty which, in primitive times, opposed the foundation of regular societies. The social tie was not easy to establish between those human beings who were so diverse, so free, so inconstant. To bring them under the rules of a community, to institute commandments and ensure obedience, to cause passion to give way to reason, and individual right to public right, there certainly was something necessary, stronger than material force, more respectable than interest, surer than a philosophical theory, more unchangeable than a convention; something that should dwell equally in all hearts, and should be all-powerful there. This power was a belief.

Now, an ancient belief commanded a man to honor his ancestor; the worship of the ancestor grouped a family around an altar. Thus arose the first religion, the first prayers, the first ideas of duty, and of morals. Thus, too, was the right of property established, and the order of succession fixed. Thus, *in fine,* arose all private law, and all the rules of domestic organization. Later the belief grew, and human society grew at the same time. When men begin to perceive that there are common divinities for them, they unite in larger groups. The same rules, invented and established for the family, are applied successively to the phratry, the tribe, and the city.

Let us take in at a glance the road over which man has passed. In the beginning the family lived isolated, and man knew only the domestic gods. Above the family was formed the phratry with its god. Then came the tribe, and the god of the tribe. Finally came the city, and men conceived a god whose providence embraced this entire city; a hierarchy of creeds, and a hierarchy of association. The religious idea was, among the ancients, the inspiring breath and organizer of society.

During the Republic the basic rights of a citizen were two: the right of appeal (*provocatio*) to the Assembly of the Roman people; and the vote (*suffragium*) in that Assembly. Both rights were ascribed to a very early date; both were regarded as mainstays of freedom, and illustrated as such on the Republican coinage. The right of appeal remained the basic privilege of a citizen.

Source: Fustel de Coulanges, *The Ancient City* (New York: Doubleday, n. d.), p. 26.

limited capacities of technology. Thus ancient technology (except, possibly, that of the Romans) simply could not handle the problems of food and water supply, of sewerage and of transportation facilities, on the scale required by the large modern conglomerations of people. Also, the location of cities, with the occasional exception of those developed for purely religious reasons, was heavily dependent on geographical factors, such as the availability of water and the proximity to food supplies. (Logically, riverways were of great importance for this.)

Obviously, we cannot here provide a history of the city, not even of the city in Western civilization, but a survey of its various historical manifestations may be helpful. The Greek city, of course, is of paramount importance to the creation of Western civilization.[5] According to Aristotle, Greece had 154 different city constitutions, which indicates great diversity; both Sparta and Athens fall within the category of *polis,* but what a difference in character! Indeed, the long conflict between Sparta and Athens, which led to the collapse of Greece as an autonomous historical force, may be conceptualized as a conflict between two contradictory ideas of the city and of civilization. Sparta was a completely integrated, closed community in which the warrior held the key position, whereas Athens was a community of relatively peaceful and enlightened people where the scribes of various kinds marked the character of city life. It may be argued, however, that despite Athens' failure to impose its pattern on the rest of Greece during its days of political autonomy, it was the Athenian rather than the Spartan conception on which most later Western developments were patterned.

The history of the Greek *polis* makes it clear that the emergence of urban social forms from a structure of consanguinity inaugurates a profound revolution wherever it appears. The early social structure of the *polis* was founded on the old forms of con-

Ancient Rome—A City of the People

Thomas Africa's informative *Rome of the Caesars* provides a vivid picture of life in that ancient city. He claims that, in many respects, imperial Rome was New York on the Tiber River.

A center of international finance, the city attracted enterprising businessmen and speculators. For artists and writers, Rome provided many opportunities to display their talents and snare wealthy patrons. Since the city was also the seat of government, ambitious politicians from the provinces visited Rome to win or buy favors from influential members of the imperial court. To countless people throughout the empire, the capital was a symbol of worldly success and conspicuous consumption, a distant scene of glamor, wealth, and power. The residents of Rome relished the excitement of life in the city and enjoyed a sense of proximity to the rulers of the world.

Under the emperors, Rome was a vast melting pot of many ethnic groups, but the common use of Latin prevented the city from becoming a polyglot babel. In the crowded streets of the capital, Berbers and Negroes jostled Greeks and Sicilians, and Spaniards, Germans, and Celts might idly watch a snake-charmer from Egypt or a fire-eater from Syria. In the markets, which resembled oriental bazaars, Italian farmers haggled with Jewish merchants, and African grain importers often bargained with bakers of Balkan origin. The cosmopolitan complexion of the city reflected the international society which the Roman empire was becoming. Though conservatives complained that the minorities had become the majority, the city was enriched by its variegated population. With the sincere bias of a small-town Italian, the emperor Augustus tried to slow the alien tide and limited the freeing of slaves, but his efforts were in vain and even emperors would soon be drawn from the provinces.

Michael Grant describes precisely what Roman citizenship entailed.

In origin, Roman citizenship had been a privilege for the free inhabitants of Rome, and long after the establishment of the Roman confederation in Italy large areas of the peninsula had still been excluded from its benefits. In order to break the great revolt (90–99 B.C.), Rome had been obliged to concede citizenship to all Italians south of the river Po (89 B.C.), together with a halfway step toward the franchise for Transpadane Gaul (Italy north of the Po) which reached full Roman citizenship in 49 B.C. So what was, in origin, a municipal Roman franchise had now developed into a quasi-national citizenship of Italy.

Source: Thomas W. Africa, *Rome of the Caesars* (New York: John Wiley, 1965), p. 23; Michael Grant, *The World of Rome* (New York: World, 1960), p. 77.

sanguinity and kinship—families, groupings of families and clans; but over this foundation there was created something entirely new, an association of free urban citizens, tied to one another by political obligations, unrelated to any common kinship. This, quite rightly, the Greeks saw as the birth of liberty, and it is expressed wonderfully in the conclusion of the great dramatic trilogy, the *Oresteia* by Aeschylus (525–456 B.C.). Orestes, who had killed his mother to avenge his father whom his mother and her lover had murdered, pursued by the avenging goddesses of the blood— that is, of kinship and consanguinity—sought refuge in Athens, where he was tried and, indeed, absolved by a jury of Athenian citizens. As the rational political order of the *polis* is superimposed on the old order of consanguinity, not only a new law but a new outlook on life altogether is established. In the *Oresteia* the avenging goddesses, the Erinyes, whose names as of this moment were changed to the Eumenides (connoting their change to benevolence), were bound and imprisoned beneath the Acropolis, the shining symbol of lucidity and reason of the new order.

The Greek *polis* succeeded in laying the foundation for the new, nonconsanguinous way of life in the Western world. It failed, however, to expand its order into imperial dimensions, although Alexander did try to achieve world domination in order to integrate masses of people within its order. It was Rome that achieved what Greece could not: the Roman city, the *urbs*, became a world, or *orbs*, imposing its order on an entire imperial civilization.[6]

Also, Rome succeeded in including within its order the masses of "plebeians" that, originally, had not been citizens and thus not participants in the "polity." At the height of Rome's imperial power, finally, Roman citizenship was a status available in principle to anyone, even to "barbarians" with no "natural" connection whatever with the city on the banks of the Tiber. It was Roman law, above all, which created for the future a concept of corporate personality distinct from all "natural" bonds of kinship, language or region—a crucial element for the later history of Western

The Rise of an Urban Middle Class
in the Medieval City

The various writings of Henri Pirenne on the medieval city are well known. Pirenne traces the emergence of a new class of merchants who found themselves at odds with the countryside and its institutions, and whom he sees as the real founders of the European medieval city.

In the need of security which the merchants felt there lies, therefore, the explanation of the fundamental characteristic of the towns of the Middle Ages. They were strongholds. It is impossible to imagine a town existing at that era without walls. It was an attribute by which towns were distinguished from villages. It was a right, or, to use the expression of that time, it was a *privilege* which none of them lacked. Here again heraldry conforms very exactly to reality, in surmounting the crests of cities by a walled crown.

But the rampart was the symbol not only of the city; it was from it also that came the name which served and which still serves to designate the population. Because of the very fact that it was a fortified place, the town became a burg. The mercantile center, as has been shown, was designated by the name of "new burg" to distinguish it from the original "old burg." And hence its inhabitants, at the beginning of the eleventh century at the latest, received the name of "burghers" (*burgenses*). The first known mention of this word occurs in France in 1007. . . . It was therefore the inhabitants of the "new burg," that is to say, of the merchant burg, who received, or more probably who created it to describe themselves, the appellation of "burghers." It is curious to see that it was never applied to those of the "old burg." These latter were known as *castellani* or *castrenses*. And this is further, and particularly significant, proof that the origins of city populations should be sought not in the older population of the early fortresses but in the immigrant population which trade brought to them and which, in the eleventh century, began to absorb them.

It is somewhat difficult to define this original middle class of the commercial centers. Evidently it was not composed exclusively of widely traveled merchants. It must have comprised, besides them, a more or less important number of men engaged in the unloading and the transporting of merchandise, in the rigging and the equipping of the boats, in the manufacture of carts, casks, chests or, in a word, of all the necessary accessories for carrying on business. As a result, men from the whole neighboring territory were drawn to the nascent city in search of a profession. A definite and positive attraction by the urban population for the rural population is clearly manifest by the beginning of the eleventh century. The greater the concentration of population, the greater the effect it had roundabout. It needed, for its daily existence, not only a quantity but also an increasing variety of skilled workmen. The few artisans who heretofore had sufficed for the limited needs of the towns and the burgs evidently could not satisfy the multiplied exigencies of the newcomers. Members of the most indispensable professions therefore had to come from outside—bakers, brewers, butchers, smiths, and so on. But trade itself stimulated industry. In every region where industry was carried on in the country, trade made a successful effort first to lure it to the city and then to concentrate it there.

Source: Henri Pirenne, *Medieval Cities* (New York: Doubleday, 1956), pp. 107, 108.

cities and of Western civilization at large. Only with Rome does the city become a center of *masses,* and thus the locale of the peculiar revolutionary forces endemic to masses.[7]

Medieval cities were of three principal types: defensive conglomerations of people around powerful feudal centers, military castles, or burghs from which they derived names like Strasbourg and Salzburg; episcopal centers, such as Cologne and Canterbury; and trading centers, such as Venice and the littoral cities of Northern Germany. During the Middle Ages, the third type gained importance, eventually giving birth to interurban alliances —the league of Hanseatic cities and, later, imperial Venice—that developed economic and then political power in opposition to that of the feudal system. As described in Chapter 4, these cities were producing a new social stratum, the nonfeudal townspeople or bourgeoisie, that was to help create modern Europe. By the time of the Renaissance, there was a distinctly urban way of life, characterized by political independence from the feudal aristocracy, commercialism, and a propensity for intellectual ferment. The spirit of the city-states of northern Italy,[8] of the German-speaking areas, and of the Low Countries was expressed in a patriotic poem written in Basel, which proudly proclaims that the burghers of that city were beholden to no one, and even had their own coinage and gallows.

These interurban economic alliances achieved a new dimension when political power became concentrated on a national scale in the hands of kings. The royal courts, and their cities, like Paris and London, established themselves as national centers for a novel cultural form. Once more, cities were centers of enlightenment—intellectually, artistically, in matters of mores and morality, and eventually in terms of political innovation. So there developed the notion of a fundamental dichotomy between the "backward" countryside and the "progressive" city, which by now has been deeply impressed on the consciousness of both rural and urban people alike.

This notion of the progressive city was founded on the part it played in making technological innovations, which became increasingly important with the coming of the Industrial Revolution.[9] The Industrial Revolution has been an urban phenomenon *par excellence*. Since then, urbanism, industrialism, and "modernity," have been correlated phenomena. After the Industrial Revolution, due to the technology engendered by it and because of the population expansion related to it, cities have grown to vast proportions, unthinkable in any previous period of history. More than that, modern urbanism is more than just gigantic cities and metropolitan regions, as it also means that entire national cultures are formed from and supported by the urban centers. Urbanism is the dominant mode of life in industrial societies, affecting the countryside almost as much as the cities themselves. Agrarian enclaves, sheltered from the impact of urban life, are rapidly disappearing everywhere. Moreover, even outside the sphere of industrial societies, urbanism is an ideal and a goal. The "good things" associated with modernity are, above all, things belonging to the urban life style. Of course, there continue to be important differences among various types of cities, regardless of size (consider, for instance, San Francisco, Detroit, and Washington, D.C., in America). But, urbanism has had a generally leveling effect wherever it has reached, creating global similarities both physically (traffic jams are the same in Chicago, Frankfurt, and Tokyo) and culturally. Urbanization is a revolutionizing process that is worldwide today.

Population and Ecology

Of the three central facets of the "city" as Weber defined it, two concern the gross fact of its immense and highly concentrated population, while the third describes the uniquely impersonal organization of human relationships that this size makes necessary. We will briefly describe and conceptualize several aspects of the city's population, turning then to a more elaborate analysis of the nature of city life.[10]

The process of urbanization in the West has been accompanied by a steady decline in the birth rate and a consequent decrease in average family size. Commonly, the explanation of this has been in economic terms: many children are an asset to an agrarian family, but a liability to an urban family. However, the exceptional rationality of this explanation calls it into question, especially since it is not certain that urbanization brings a population decrease in non-Western societies. In any case, even in the urbanized West, there are considerable differences in the fertility, as in the mortality, rates of different classes and ethnic groups, and this seems clearly relevant to each group's relationship to the industrial process, as we noted earlier.

Urbanization involves not only an increase in the absolute number of people, but also a change in the constitution of the population, and especially in regard to age and sex. In the early days of industrial urbanization the city contained a heavy concentration of working-age people, whereas today it seems the home of the elderly and, to a lesser degree, the very young. This is not difficult to understand, for the rapid industrial revolution involved an influx of workers into the new manufacturing centers; the very old and young remained in their rural homes, as the city had nothing to offer them. In developing countries today there is a similar pattern, and for the same reasons. Urban age ratio is a rather accurate indicator of the stage of industrial urbanization in a particular society, although it need not, of course, apply to nonindustrial urbanization.

There is a similar pattern in the sex ratio. Historically, there was at first a great concentration of males in Western cities. As these cities grew, the proportion of females in the population enlarged to create a balance. So, sex ratio, too, may serve as an indicator of the stage of industrial urbanization. Again, the explanation of the phenomena is obvious: in the early stages of industrialization, men from the countryside tend to come into the cities alone, leaving their families behind, which is even today the pattern in Asian and African cities; the eventual increase in the number of females is indicative of the presence of permanently settled families, as urbanism becomes an established way of life.

Sex Ratio in Urban Areas of Underdeveloped Countries: The Cases of Madras and Bombay

In underdeveloped countries there is a larger proportion of males than females in a city. The larger the city, the wider will be the gap. In India, for instance, in 1964, the city of Bombay had a population of 11,450,000, and the city of Madras a population of 1,825,000. In this table we represent the sex and age distribution of 10,000 residents in these two cities, based on Brij Raj Chauhan's calculations.

	MALES		FEMALES	
AGE GROUPS	MADRAS	BOMBAY	MADRAS	BOMBAY
Less than 1 year	126	117	116	119
1 to 4	348	393	324	387
5 to 14	1164	924	1057	847
15 to 34	2142	3094	1752	1552
35 to 54	1106	1443	1023	663
55 and over	383	260	452	201

Source: T. K. N. Unnithan, Deva and Singh, eds., *Toward a Sociology of Culture in India* (Englewood Cliffs, N. J.: Prentice-Hall, 1965), p. 396.

Also, advancing industrialization brings a greater participation of women in the labor force, especially in what we have called the "tertiary" phase. In cities where there are strong concentrations of administrative offices and white-collar jobs, there even tends to be a disproportionate number of females, whether the administrations are public (for instance, governmental offices in Washington, D.C.) or private (as with the central offices of insurance companies in Hartford, Connecticut). There are here, too, of course, differences between classes and ethnic groups that often complicate the picture, but the basic point is clear: urbanization entails a demographic revolution, not only in the size but also in the composition of the population.

We have been defining the city in terms of certain physical relations between human beings and their space, or to say it another way, between people and the use of land. These relations are commonly referred to as "ecological," a concept originated by biologists to denote the relation between organisms and their environment, and later adopted by sociologists, especially in the study of cities.[11] Every city has a certain ecology. However, since this does not remain constant, every city has its ecological history. The use of the land changes as does the distribution of the population over the territory.

In studies of cities in America, particularly those made in the 1920s, sociologists have distinguished a number of basic ecological processes or phases in the history of cities.[12] Throughout most of the world, these phases have been unplanned. Only recently, as a result of the development of planning in different countries has there been the notion that urban development could be carefully controlled from the beginning; so far, such planning experiments are few and are generally limited to smaller communities, such as the "New Towns" in England or the "Maerkische Viertel" in Berlin. This means that most cities studied by the sociologist are the result of unplanned, uncontrolled growth.

The first phase of urbanization is characterized by *concentration*. Both people and activities become concentrated within a space that is small when compared to their preurban dispersion. Initially, people and their activities tend to cluster most heavily around the geographical center of the city, the "inner city" or the "downtown area." Naturally, this eventuates in a tremendous overcrowding at the center, which, in turn, produces an outward movement, a redispersion or decentralization of both people and activities. Industry moves from the city to the periphery; commerce becomes diffused; and, of utmost significance, the residential areas move outward from the center, pushing the geographical limits of the city further and further into the surrounding countryside, creating the phenomenon of suburbs.

Closely related to decentralization is the process of *segregation*, that is, of ecological differentiation. Simply, different activities take place in different areas of the city, physically segregated from each other. The business district becomes distinct from the civic center. Industrial areas are segregated from nonindustrial ones. There may be special districts dominated by a university or a military installation. And the residential areas may be segregated within themselves by class or ethnic groups; this is the general rule in America, although it is not common everywhere in the world: there are "better addresses" and slums, ghettos and ethnic neighborhoods. For better or worse (depending on one's values), the city becomes "profiled," as a result of this. There are great

*Patterns of Urbanization in an
East African Town*

In 1952, the town of Kampala, the commercial center of Uganda, had
a population of approximately 70,000 living under urban conditions.
This was estimated to be composed of 4,250 Europeans, 17,000
Asians, 16,800 Africans in the municipality of Kampala itself, and at
least another 30,000 Africans living in a narrow belt around the municipality. A. W. Southall uses this town to illustrate the main factors
that determine the ecological structure of African urban population.

The mass of urban Africans start off in town as members of their
respective tribes, relying on such kinsmen as are also in town, or
failing these, extending something of the attitudes of kin toward
any of the same language and culture as themselves. Since there is
an ever flowing stream of new migrants to town, the kinship system
of each tribe, its type of marriage and family life, its expectations as
to the political ordering of society and the sources of cohesion, are
all of continuing importance. Thus, on a horizontal plane, there is
dependence on a series of tribal social structures of different types,
each offering varying possibilities of adaptation to urban needs. The
urban community is based on highly dispersed kinship and descent
groupings of an *ad hoc,* ephemeral kind. Residence is usually based
initially on the use of tribal and kinship ties as a jumping-off
ground, followed by the hunt for jobs and the adjustment of residence to the location of work in conjunction with the enjoyment of
such amenities as are offered. One must suppose that, as his familiarity with urban existence increases, and his economic status im-
proves, the individual becomes less dependent on his tribal background for his sense of security, and more and more relationships
develop with neighbors, with workmates, and with those whose interests are similar to his own.

The general pattern of residence seems to depend on economic
distinctions, though these still follow tribal differences fairly closely.
Of the 30,000 unskilled labourers employed within the municipality
in firms with five or more employees, little more than a tenth live
within the municipality. Three-fifths of them live in the belt immediately surrounding the municipality, which for convenience is referred to as Greater Kampala. This belt lies within two-and-a-half
miles of the center of the municipality. The rest of the unskilled
group live beyond this limit, but very few beyond four miles from
the center. Two-thirds of this whole unskilled group belong to tribes

other than the Ganda (the dominant local tribe). The main body of African residents within the municipality consists of domestic servants, and those in the quarters provided by the East African Railways, the Uganda Police, and the African Hospital. Thus, broadly speaking, the Africans who live within the municipal boundary are those for whom quarters are provided by their employers. The rest live beyond this boundary, but as near to it as possible, because they cannot afford bicycles or any other form of transport to and from work.

The better-paid workers, of whom the clerks make up the largest group, live mainly further out than the two-and-a-half-mile zone, remarkably large numbers coming in on bicycles, and the best paid on motorcycles, from as far as ten or even twelve miles away. The majority of this group are Ganda. They try to combine urban employment with rural residence. This solves the problem of food supply, money expenditure on food being begrudged where it can possibly be avoided. The great objective of this group is to acquire *mailo* (land) and so to enter at least the bottom of the class of landed gentry. With the appreciation of land values near the town they are driven further out to get hold of land at a reasonable price. Those who cannot afford *mailo* try to obtain plots under customary tenancy, but this too is difficult near the town, and high premiums have to be paid.

The better paid workers of tribes other than the Ganda form a special group. There is nothing to prevent them . . . from acquiring land or customary holdings from the Ganda. But very few have done so as yet. . . . These people therefore, like the unskilled labourers, try to rent accommodation as near the town as possible. It is with them that accommodation provided by the Government or by employers is particularly popular.

It is only the wealthiest section of the Ganda who can afford to live near the town and in their own land and housing. Most of them belong to the principal Ganda families, who received land in the original distribution of *mailo* and took care to secure part of their allotment in plots near to the town and to their own capital of Mengo.

Source: A. W. Southall, "Determinants of the Social Structure of African Urban Populations, with Special Reference to Kampala (Uganda)," in Immanuel Wallerstein, *Social Change* (New York: John Wiley, 1966) pp. 332–333.

variations, of course, in the particular pattern of segregation, but one fairly general rule is true wherever urbanization of the industrial type has reached a certain stage of development—people do not live where they work. One consequence of this is that transportation is becoming an increasingly crucial urban problem.

As times passes, these patterns also shift, as the condition of a growing city is that values and locations change on all levels. These dynamic processes, when they alter the established patterns of segregation in a city, are called *invasion* and *succession*. An area may be invaded by new activities or a new population, as when an industrial area extends itself into what was hitherto a residential area, or lower classes move into what was once a "good part" of the city. When such an invasion has been accomplished, one can speak of succession: the character of the area has been changed, temporarily at least, as one activity or group has more or less completely replaced its predecessor.

These concepts are very general and formal, and we do not mean to deny the great variability that exists in all empirical reality; nevertheless, we believe they are useful in alerting the student to the often manifest patterns in the development of the city. In every case, it is also important to recognize the fundamental difference between urbanization under industrial and urbanization under preindustrial conditions. For example, the tremendous growth of cities in India has not been accompanied by an equivalent growth of industry, and this is the reason for their unmanageable problems. Although the relationship generally holds true in contemporary Western societies, we must be aware that, in principle, urbanization is *not* the same as industrialization.

Urban Institutions

It will already be clear that the great shifts and reorganizations of populations that occurred in the cities entailed as well a variety of institutional changes. This is most clear, perhaps, in regard to the political institutions. A number of observers regard the development of municipal government as a key factor in defining the nature of urban life.[13]

The political institutions of the city have so great an effect on the lives of urban people because they are superimposed on previous political structures. In other words, urban political institutions everywhere erode and eventually replace earlier forms of political traditionalism. So they have, actually or potentially, an intrinsic character of dynamism and innovation; because the old traditions are incapable of dealing with explosive urban growth, there is an unavoidable demand for rational organization—of activities, resources, and people. The larger the city, the more pressing the need for rational regulation of a larger segment of its life. Food and water, sewage, transportation and traffic, public security —all these must be handled rationally, if the city is to avoid disaster and anarchy. Inevitably, compared to the preurban or nonurban situation, a great expansion of governmental functions is necessary to examine the quality of food sold in the city, inspect buildings for cleanliness and safety, issue licenses for the exercise of many occupations, control the movements of vehicles, and so on. Since these activities naturally cost a great deal of money, municipal government always requires a greater amount and complexity of taxation and other levies, whether imposed directly by the government itself or a larger political unit.

Because of the complex functionings of the city, there must be a municipal government that can serve as arbiter and administrator. Rational management and therefore rational personnel and processes are required: in other words, urbanization demands bureaucratization. The water supply, say, must be continuously maintained, and the water must be kept free of pollution. The knowledge of how to accomplish these particular functions is not likely to be in the possession of officials who owe their positions to political favor, whether achieved through their skill as democratic politicians or through political or economic bribery. Therefore, there will have to be bureaucrats with the necessary competencies. Yet, because the nature of city life makes the city the focus, also, of our most intensive *political* interests and our most important *political* decisions, there will often and understandably be tensions between the rational functions and administrators of the bureaucracy, and the various irrational methods of selecting the officials of this government. In this sense, democracy may be just as irrational as corruption.

In the West, there has been a close link between urbanization and the development of representative political institutions. Weber analyzed this in his work on the sociology of the city: he explained that the city, as a *political community,* was a peculiarly Western phenomenon and the source of our conception of "citizenship," which itself is the source of modern democracy.[14] Later writers, such as Harold Laski and S. M. Lipset, have corroborated this linkage of urbanization and democracy in Western history,[15] but it has not necessarily held true in other parts of the world. Western influence (colonial or other) has introduced the representative form of municipal government into different parts of the world, as a replacement for earlier traditional forms, but the process of democratization, however, has frequently been unsuccessful, because it lacked the cultural foundation for representative government found in Western cities. Sometimes, as in many African cities, there is found a strange coexistence of the modern-democratic and the traditional-tribal political forms, the former "artificially" introduced from outside, the latter constituting a strange survival of preurban patterns in the urban situation. Whatever may be the historical relationship between urbanization and democracy in the West is not automatically transmitted to all other societies in which urbanization takes place.

Although urbanization in underdeveloped non-Western societies does not necessarily produce democratization, it does have the general effect of weakening the traditionalism, that is, eroding traditional political institutions.[16] In addition to the process of political rationalization that usually occurs in the urban situation, the disintegration of traditionalism is rooted also in the very conditions under which new arrivals live in such cities. People are suddenly deprived of the all-embracing and sheltering institutions in which political authority is vested, say, an African tribe. Naturally, these institutions can be transferred to the city only in broken or changed form, as "residual" patterns in a drastically changed context. The new urban population comes typically from many different tribal backgrounds; but tribal institutions, almost by definition, are not suitable to a pluralistic situation. Therefore, the new arrivals are uprooted and disoriented, not only politically, but in other aspects of their life as well. Consequently, the new urban situation is highly volatile politically as well as culturally. It is a situation that is congenial not to democracy but rather to political demagoguery, to radical political movements, and to the eruption of mob violence. The politics of this situation is most likely to be authoritarian, since the uprooted masses, the new urbanites, crave some kind of certainty and stability to replace the lost structure of tradition—and it is authoritarian political figures who most easily satisfy this craving, at least psychologically. Authoritarianism is especially potent because it has at its disposal the propaganda means of modern mass communications: the radio, loudspeakers, and the like. Urban politics in underdeveloped societies typically consists of using modern propaganda technology on masses of semitribal, illiterate or barely literate, and profoundly uprooted people; this is obviously a combination full of potential for violence.

Both in politics and in other areas of social life, the city is the "natural" habitat of *associations*—that is, of groups, in principle voluntary, which express specific interests of their members.[17] The structural roots of urban associationism are in the fact that the city no longer constitutes a unified community in which all interests are somehow represented; rather, it has become a highly complex collectivity within which special interests must be individually attended to. This is true of economic interests which in the West were organized in the guilds that developed into the labor unions, as well as of cultural interests of other kinds, from religious sects to bird-watching groups. What all these groups have in common is their associational character: each is voluntary, and expresses only a part of a person's total social participation. In contrast, the individual has no choice about belonging to the tribe or, later, to the political community of the city; but, whereas the former expresses, in principle, one's entire social existence, the city and its associations regulate, functionally and specifically, only a limited part of this existence. The political community of today's city does not represent the religious interests of its inhabitants, as did the tribe, which was both a political and a religious institution. The contemporary urbanite, even in underdeveloped societies, to express his religious interests, must join one of the several available religious groups.

The psychological product of this pluralistic social structure is that the new urbanite has a sense of rootlessness and disorientation (which sociologists since Émile Durkheim (1858–1917) have called "anomie") that particularly afflicts newly arrived people in the city. Urbanites are "joiners." Quite apart from the specific interests (political, economic, or religious) represented, such associations provide a feeling of roots, or orientation in the world, of belonging, which replicates or helps to recapture the psychological security offered by traditional structures. Interestingly, even traditional beliefs are forced, in the urban situation, to organize themselves in associational forms. For example, there are tribal *associations* in African cities and caste *associations* in Indian cities. These, of course, can be described as traditional in aims. But,

Voluntary Associations: A Peculiar Urban Feature

Kenneth Little, in his excellent study *West African Urbanization: A Study of Voluntary Associations in Social Change,* aims to discover the new patterns of interaction that are coming to the fore among people involved in the process of urbanization. He attends, therefore, to the new institutions that are created under the influence of a developing urban industrial economy: the voluntary associations. He found that there is a variety of types of associations in West African towns: tribal associations, syncretistic cults, mutual aid associations, recreation associations, as well as a host of what he calls "modern associations," that is, cultural associations as well as those which are branches of a Christian church, all introduced originally by European administrators and missionaries. In the following we quote two passages on mutual aid associations.

Migrants who have left behind their rural villages and families are confronted by a more impersonal system of relationships than exists at home. It operates through the economic laws of supply and demand but offers as yet few of the safeguards of a modern welfare state. There is no scheme of social insurance to cover sickness or disability and no pension scheme for widows, orphans and old people, nor is there any national assistance to provide for the destitute or the unemployed. Ethnic associations alleviate these drawbacks to some extent, but their provision of mutual aid only covers a limited number of contingencies. Nor does a tribally based system meet the needs of people earning their living under industrial conditions. True, there is a tendency, for historical reasons, for certain occupations to be mainly the province of particular tribes, and a few tribes have a virtual monopoly of some minor types of trade. But the general situation is that the principal activities of the town—commerce, administration, transport, mining—are organized irrespective of tribe. In the main, economic considerations alone—the demand for special skills and forms of training—determine who the workers are.

These facts account for the wide incidence of associations concerned with mutual benefit or with the furtherance of occupational aims. They also explain why in these organizations the economic interest of their members is the primary purpose of association. In Accra, for example, benevolent thrift societies claim to be open to all without regard to tribe or religion. Some of these organizations had been in existence for more than thirty years when they were studied in 1954, and they had a total membership between them of 26,193. All of them gave assistance to members in sickness and bereavement and donated sums of money to the kinsfolk of a deceased member.

Source: Kenneth Little, *West African Urbanization: A Study of Voluntary Associations in Social Change* (New York: Cambridge University Press, 1965).

the new, self-conscious form has a nontraditional effect, even on the traditional content. It is one thing to belong from birth to a tribe that effectively organizes all important aspects of its members' lives; it is quite another thing to belong to a tribal association that meets in a clubhouse on Tuesday evenings. The associational form itself weakens tradition, even if such tradition is the avowed aim of an association. Many other urban associations, of course, are explicitly and intentionally antitraditional. Among these should be specially mentioned trade or labor unions, which in some countries (for example, in Latin America) are important antitraditional forces.

One of the hallmarks of urban life, then, is *voluntary participation,* expressed in regard both to associations, and, in some parts of the world, to a political life that tends toward representative forms. This is one reason that cities tend to be centers of education. Educational institutions become particularly important in situations where the political participation of all citizens is a matter of policy—ideally by means of education the individual gets to the point where he can conceive of himself as a participant in larger social and political processes. This point has been made very well by Daniel Lerner, in his study of social change in the Middle East.[18] Lerner even feels this sense of participation is a crucial psychological component of modernity, as it enables an individual to think of himself as a participant in the fate of the Turkish nation, rather than as just a participant by virtue of birth in the life of his family or village. This is of critical importance in societies just emerging from tribal culture, as in the new countries of Africa, which must create a unifying, yet rational sense of national identity.

The rapid rate of urbanization in the underdeveloped world today is historically unprecedented.[19] Western urbanization was a much slower process. One consequence of this was that, although

TABLE 5-2

Population in Large Cities (100,000 and Over) by Major Continental Regions: 1800-1960

AREA	1800 IN MILLIONS	1800 AS PERCENTAGE OF TOTAL POPULATION IN REGION	1850 IN MILLIONS	1850 AS PERCENTAGE OF TOTAL POPULATION IN REGION	1900 IN MILLIONS	1900 AS PERCENTAGE OF TOTAL POPULATION IN REGION	1950 IN MILLIONS	1950 AS PERCENTAGE OF TOTAL POPULATION IN REGION	1960 IN MILLIONS	1960 AS PERCENTAGE OF TOTAL POPULATION IN REGION
World	15.6	1.7	27.5	2.3	88.6	5.5	313.7	13.1	590.0	19.9
Asia	9.8	1.6	12.2	1.7	19.4	2.1	105.6	7.5	203.6	12.3
Europe[a]	5.4	2.9	13.2	4.9	48.0	11.9	118.2	19.9	189.0	29.6
Africa	0.30	0.3	0.25	0.2	1.4	1.1	10.2	5.2	20.4	8.1
America	0.13	0.4	1.8	3.0	18.6	12.8	74.6	22.6	169.9	42.0
Oceania	—	—	—	—	1.3	21.7	5.1	39.2	7.0	43.3

[a]Including the U.S.S.R.

Source: Gerald Breese, Urbanization in Newly Developing Countries, (Englewood Cliffs, N.J.: Prentice-Hall, 1966), p. 22. © 1966. Reprinted by permission of Prentice-Hall, Inc., Englewood Cliffs, N.J. From Kingsley Davis and Hilda Hertz, "Patterns of World Urbanization." Table reproduced in United Nations, *Report on the World Social Situation*, including studies of urbanization in underdeveloped areas, prepared by the Bureau of Social Affairs, United Nations Secretariat, in cooperation with the International Labor Office, Food and Agriculture Organization, World Health Organization, and the United Nations Educational, Scientific, and Cultural Organization (New York: United Nations, 1957), p. 114, Table 3. The 1960 data are based on Homer Hoyt, *World Urbanization: Expanding Population in a Shrinking World* (Washington, D. C.: Urban Land Institute, 1962), p. 31, Table 2. Data are approximately comparable with those for 1800-1950.

The Role of Caste Associations in India

As discussed, the rise of voluntary organizations is a typical feature of the urbanization process. In the following, we are quoting a short passage from George Rosen, *Democracy and Economic Change in India,* on the role of caste associations.

> Of even greater importance than traditional caste factors, on the state or national electoral level, is the emergence of caste associations into a political role. . . . These caste associations were started in many cases as voluntary organizations of people of the same general caste for setting and enforcing caste rules, frequently as part of a sanskritization process. In the process they set normative rules of behavior that were of greater ritual purity than the existing practice, and they frequently operated schools and welfare societies for their members, or lobbied for their members in relations with the government. They are generally statewide and have a permanent bureaucracy that consists normally of an educated and aspiring leader supported by a small staff. These associations are an obvious target for political parties wooing mass support, and they themselves see politics as a method of improving the position of their members in the caste hierarchy, especially since one of their major aims is to improve that position in relation to the government. The Rudolphs have described the role of caste associations in India, but with emphasis upon Madras, and they pointed out that the caste association provides a traditional framework that makes the new democratic processes in India comprehensible to the politically unsophisticated masses. But these caste associations vary in strength from state to state. In Orissa and Rajasthan, among the less developed states, they are weak; in such states as Madras and Kerala, they are strong. Madras is developing rapidly, and both have a high rate of literacy; jockeying for position among the castes is a characteristic of their social life. The caste associations are very influential in economic, social, and political areas in those two states.

Source: George Rosen, *Democracy and Economic Change in India* (Berkeley: University of California Press, 1966), p. 76. Reprinted by permission of The Regents of the University of California.

Western urbanization produced great misery for large numbers of people, the social strains it caused were less cataclysmic than they are in many countries today. The pressure created by the rapidity of contemporary urbanization is multiplied by a demographic factor discussed in Chapter 4: their unprecedented, virtually astronomic population explosion. The effects of this can be seen in the impact of urbanization on the economy of underdeveloped societies. As large masses of people move from the countryside into the cities, the latter are swamped with an oversupply of unskilled labor. Clifford Geertz, an American anthropologist who has worked in Indonesia, has used the terms "shared poverty" and "involution" to describe the resulting situation.[20] Shared poverty means that the oversupply of labor leads to the limited income derivable from available jobs being spread among an inordinate number of people: for example, an entire extended family of some twenty individuals may subsist on the wages of one or two of its members who have found employment. In Indonesia, apparently, these pressures also are felt by employers, who will deliberately hire as many people as possible on a part-time basis, so as to spread the available income as much as possible. Obviously, this situation is not conducive to a rationalization of the labor force. The term "involution" refers to the overall paralysis of the economy, the inhibition of economic evolution, that is the final consequence of these processes, and that ultimately frustrates development plans, especially capital formation.

Urban areas in contemporary underdeveloped societies tend to be centers of unprecedented misery. This fact, furthermore, has direct consequences on the economic fate of these societies as a whole. What happens in the cities has direct consequences in the countryside as well. This particularly applies to what Geertz has called "involution." Some observers have felt that urbanization should be controlled and slowed down in many of these societies, and that attention should be given to the development of the countryside as it has been to that of the cities. It has also been maintained that most underdeveloped societies should be careful not to stimulate a total commitment of too many people to urban employment, but instead should seek to preserve the rural ties of industrial workers coming into the cities.[21]

An important role in urbanization has always been played by minority groups.[22] The city, because of its relative freedom from traditional structures of exclusiveness, has always been hospitable to alien groups. A number of racial, ethnic, and religious groups have shown particular affinities to the urban situation, and have even become "carriers" of urbanization. The Jews have played this role in several European countries and, to a considerable extent, in America; other minority groups playing this role today are the Greeks and Armenians in the Middle East, the Chinese in Southeast Asia, the Indians in East Africa, and the Arabs (mostly Lebanese and Syrians) in a number of African countries. In various excolonial countries Europeans may now be regarded as a minority group in this sense. Such groups occupy a peculiar and often a strategic, profitable place in the urban stratification system. Commonly they occupy strategic positions, on the top or in the middle, in the occupational system, sometimes completely monopolizing certain occupations. Because these are the very positions and occupations that are aspired to by the upwardly mobile new urbanites of indigenous origin, there often erupts a "class struggle" with racial or ethnic antagonism as a prime motivating force. The savagery this can unleash was shown in recent years by the massacres of Arabs in Zanzibar and of Chinese in Indonesia.

We will discuss the family as an institution in Chapter 6, but let us only note here that the general consequence of urbanization is the weakening of kinship as an all-embracing institution, a loosening of family ties and thus a tendency toward dependence on the Western-type "nuclear family," a unit consisting only of parents and children.[23] This tendency, it may be added, is a factor with antitraditionalistic consequences.

Urbanism as a Way of Life

A classical description of the effects of the city on social life may be found in two essays by the German sociologist Georg Simmel, "The Metropolis and Mental Life" and "The Stranger." [24] In these essays, Simmel anticipated, albeit in a very formal and general manner, many of the subsequent findings of urban sociologists.

Simmel saw the large city, the metropolis, as, above all, an enormous assault on the nervous system of the individual. It confronts the consciousness of the individual with an infinitely larger number of stimuli and impressions than are available under preurban or nonurban conditions. Psychologically, and presumably even physiologically, it is impossible to remain attentive to all of these; consequently, the individual in the urban environment must shield himself by selecting which few of his many experiences he will allow to "get to" him. This psychological and physiological necessity is the source of the sophistication and the intellectualism of the urbanite. Only through heightening his intellectual awareness can the individual find his way through the heterogeneous multitude of his daily experiences. Thus the urbanite is "quick," because he must be. And urban life, of necessity, is characterized by a heightened rationality in all spheres of life.

This psychological rationality is closely connected with the rationality of a money economy, which is also typical of the city. A money economy and the presence of large masses of people within a limited space together produce an orientation toward life that is calculating, deindividuating, and typifying. Things are measured by their abstract exchange value, rather than their unique, nonexchangeable individuality. Similarly, people are dealt with as types, for there is no other manageable way of dealing with them, with the exception of the small number of them that form the individual's immediate circle. Outside of it, the city is the realm of abstraction and anonymity, qualities that affect all aspects of its culture in one way or another. This, however, has paradoxically resulted in making the city the realm of freedom, of individual differentiation, even of individualism. The paradox resolves itself when one understands that the individual, precisely because he must organize most of his life in abstract and anonymous forms, can carve out for himself an area of personal autonomy—something that is impossible or at least very difficult in the closely-knit rural community, where all of life takes place under the continuous scrutiny of everyone.

Urban culture, therefore, has produced a highly distinctive type of human being, which despite variations, has a high cross-cultural predictability. Although Simmel did not write "The Stranger" explicitly as a portrait of urban man, the appropriateness of his description is undeniable. The city is, by definition, a conglomeration of strangers, and urban life, like the typical situation of the stranger, is a peculiar combination of closeness and distance. People share space, at times even very intimately and crowdedly, but they are nevertheless distant from each other in their personal lives. They relate to each other in peculiar ways—with "objectivity" (that is, with detached attitudes rather than with total mutual commitment), abstractly (that is, as types rather than as individuals), and often with mutual suspicion.

The alienation amidst neighbors, which Simmel describes on the level of the individual, exists also on the sociological level of urbanism as a way of life.[25] The city is, above all, a dynamic phenomenon: it contains a large variety of contending groups and forces, and it is a situation of continuous change. The rate of this change is directly proportional to the degree of urbanization. We have already emphasized the dynamics of social change in connection with specific institutions; it is equally true of urban culture as a whole. The city is the realm of cultural vitality, and of innovation and rapid transformations of all kinds. It is also the realm of fashion, that is, of the quick succession of cultural styles. Urban culture puts a high premium on being and remaining "with it," of knowing what is "in" and what "out." We should recognize that cities have always had this property, even in antiquity. In the New Testament, the Apostle Paul, on his missionary travels, saw that "all the Athenians and the foreigners who lived there spent their time in nothing except telling or hearing something new." [26] This absorption in fashion and change, however, has deepened in the modern city, principally as a consequence of modern mass communication.

The modern media of mass communication ensure that "something new" is rapidly and almost universally transmitted through all or most strata of the urban population, as well as from one city to another and from the city to the countryside. This has the effect of accelerating, diffusing, and standardizing the cycles of "fashion": innovating ideas and patterns of conduct, as well as new commodities and services, are available to everyone. And since most people are exposed to the *same* media of communication, all diffusable items—and this includes ideas and behavior as well as material goods—tend toward a high degree of sameness. When access to the communication media was limited by literacy, the impact of any change was still comparatively limited—limited, of course, to those who could read. The advent of nonliterary means of mass communication has lifted this limitation. In underdeveloped societies today, where the large majority of the population is illiterate, radio and film have become crucially important vehicles of cultural integration (and, at the same time, of the diffusion of urban culture). In developed societies, the importance of television as against literary communication has also had both accelerating and standardizing effects on cultural processes. There may be some important difference in what is communicated when

The Town Enterprisers in Jordan

Daniel Lerner confirms our position that the mass media have an essential influence on the formation of the modern, urban personality. In the following we present some of his findings pertaining to a sample of fifty-five enterprisers in Jordan, thirty-seven of whom lived in towns, the rest in rural areas.

The shopkeepers and government clerks who compose this group represent the growing class of newly articulate people in Jordan. They have left traditionalism far behind and are now situated just above or below the fine line of Modernity. Most have had elementary or high school education; their opinions indicate a good, though unsophisticated, knowledge of world affairs; they are well acquainted with press, film, and radio. Almost half are Palestinians in moderate circumstances, with good education, and claim to speak some English. To compare those living in larger towns with those in more rural settings, the fifty-five enterprisers were divided into two groups.

RURAL AND URBAN ENTERPRISERS COMPARED IN PERCENTAGES

Education	Rural	Urban
Almost none	28	19
Elementary	28	35
High School	44	46
College	—	—
TOTAL	100	100
Socioeconomic Status		
Destitute	5	5
Poor	34	19
Modest	56	54
Well Off	5	22
Rich	—	—
TOTAL	100	100
Communication Habits		
Listen to Radio	84	79
Read Newspapers	55	67
Attend Motion Pictures	50	62

The relatively small differences indicate that occupational mobility is the key attribute—an individual tends to modernize if he makes his living in a typically urban occupation, even though he actually resides in the countryside. The urban enterpriser is somewhat more educated and media-participant than his rural counterpart—but this may reflect only greater availability of papers and movies.

Source: Daniel Lerner, *The Passing of Traditional Society* (New York: Free Press, 1958).

masses of Indian villagers go to the movies and masses of American teenagers sit before the television set. What both instances have in common is that the "screen" of individual discrimination has been removed, as it never has been in literary communication.[27]

Modern mass communication has produced the new phenomenon of "mass culture" or "popular culture." [28] To understand this, we must distinguish between what is peculiarly modern and what has always been true of human societies. There have been "masses" before and they have had a "culture"; what is historically new is the extreme homogenization of this culture of the masses, and also its dominant position in the general culture. Contemporary mass culture is not, because it is linked with the media of mass communication, thereby viewed as the despicable product of the downtrodden strata by the elitists of the "high culture." On the contrary, the culture "carried" by the mass media is of the highest influence and (not incidentally) highest cash value in the society as a whole. Even the upper strata are significantly affected by it. Those who wish to uphold a non-mass-communicated high culture, be they upper-class individuals or more or less independent intellectuals, are forced to maintain protective enclaves so as to insulate themselves, as far as feasible, from the omnipresent "vulgarity" they despise. Whether this is good or bad cannot concern the sociologist; his job, though, is simply to point out the distinctive features of the situation.

This situation, as we have described it, is not, of course, limited to the cities proper, for the whole of modern culture is urban both in origin and in character. It perhaps goes without saying that the urban situation has lasting effects on personal conduct. We will discuss in Part II of this book some of the psychological consequences of urbanism, but here we can summarize some of its key cultural traits. Urban culture is characterized by a number of dichotomies, as earlier explained. It is, on the one hand, characterized as a mass culture and a mass social structure that forces the

individual into an anonymous, or highly impersonal, mode of interaction; on the other hand, it leaves leeway for individual and
group differentiation, even idiosyncracy. The double character of
the city as the realm of anonymity and the realm of freedom is
only seemingly a paradox, as we have seen. Also, urban culture is
on the one hand characterized by a high degree of tolerance toward individual and group deviances, on the other hand by strong
pressures toward conformity. This dichotomy is experienced on
the level of individual existence as a segregation between contiguous aspects of our life: the individual is pressured to conform in
certain matters, such as his economic life, his "on the job" behavior, but individual and group deviances, the freedom to choose
any alternative is inalienable in other areas of his life, as for instance, in his choice of friends or in his religious activities. What
we have called the associational character of urban life is of great
importance in this. Within the heterogeneous population of the
city, the individual is likely to find others with similar values or
interests to his own, no matter how deviant these may seem. He is
able here to band together with these others in voluntary associations, which have the sole purpose of fostering the values or interests in question. In other words, in this realm, as in others, the
city may be seen in terms of the decline of overall community and
the rise of associations that structure specific, limited aspects of
social life. Some of the problems of the young generation in Western countries may stem from precisely this loss of community feeling.

The urban situation also is marked sociologically by high mobility and a fluid class structure. Many urbanites have roles and
status that are of recent vintage. Consequently, they feel insecure.
To counteract this insecurity, they are led to adopt various means
of symbolizing status, to themselves quite as much as to others.[29]
For example, in a traditional society, in which most of the people
have their place and hold it throughout their lifetimes, it is not of
great significance in what part of the city an individual lives—
everybody knows who he is anyway. By contrast, in the modern
city "a good address" is of critical importance in locating an individual in the status system, because, without this physical sign,
people are likely to make mistakes in placing him. Status symbolism assumes innumerable, and pervasive, forms. It includes site
and quality of residence, membership in different associations

(clubs, churches, and so on), use of cultural and educational facilities (such as sending one's children to the "right schools"). A strategic factor in the mechanism of status symbolization, though, is one's material consumption: since material goods have prices that are generally known or can be guessed, and since the means to acquire them directly indicates status in a rational, materialistic class society, consumption ("conspicuous consumption," as Thorstein Veblen called it) is a favored indicator of status.[30] Once more, that is not an altogether novel social phenomenon, but what is peculiarly modern is its scope. Thus, when Veblen coined this term, he was writing about the American upper class; this was in 1899. Today the term is appropriate throughout the whole range of classes, with the possible exception of the very top and the very bottom, where "conspicuous consumption" is respectively unnecessary and unattainable, changing at the bottom into "compensatory consumption."

Urban culture, consumer culture, has something it peculiarly calls the problem of leisure.[31] Again, Veblen provides an instructive comparison: his work of 1899, *The Theory of the Leisure Class,* developed the concept of "conspicuous consumption," which dealt with the American upper class. Leisure, and even more startling, the "problem of leisure," is a universal phenomenon today in all classes in America as well as in other developed and developing societies. Of course, even in ancient Rome the masses craved "bread and circuses," and even in the impoverished urban sprawls of contemporary *under*developed societies there are similar demands, often met by the extravaganzas of political mass movements and propaganda. What is peculiar about the urban culture of developed societies is that the structuring of leisure-time activities has become the permanent concern of vast organizations, both commercial and governmental. In America, characteristically, one speaks of an "entertainment industry," which accounts for an astonishing amount of economic activity: in addition to the vast organizations directly linked to mass communications (from Hollywood to Madison Avenue), there is the commercial organization of spectator as well as participant sports, the tourist industry (extending into the large economic complexes of mass transportation and the hotel business), the multiplicity of institutions concerned with adult education, the rapidly expanding publishing industry (for instance, in the so-called paperback explosion), and the manufacture of games, gadgets, and the like for adults (for instance, the "hobby industry" in all its forms). Government agencies also have entered the leisure field, constructing and operating parks, recreational facilities, public libraries. Often these activities are organized associationally in "Great Books" clubs, discussion groups, sports clubs, groups gathered around hobbies, and so on. Frequently these voluntary associations are linked symbiotically to commercial enterprise, as the "do-it-yourself" movement was supported by the firms who supplied materials necessary "to do it yourself"; some of them are subsidized by the government, as in Germany public funding is available to sports associations. A general characteristic of all these leisure-time activities has been their shift of locus from the family to various artificial groups. Furthermore, the processes of fashion, standardization, and status symbolism—as we have described them—undergird many of these activities. An interesting feature of urban leisure, which we can only mention here, is the incidence of *illegal* activity: the anonymity and freedom of modern urban culture affords protection to various leisure-time activities outside the law, some of them also organized commercially, as narcotics, or in voluntary associations, as in the clubs devoted to illicit sexual experimentation.

Urban culture is characterized by, and, indeed, is completely dependent upon, the ubiquity of modern technology. This further augments the rational character of modern city life. The contemporary urbanite lives every day in a highly complex environment shaped and maintained by modern science and technology. Very probably this has had an important influence on his general outlook (as, for example, in the area of religion). On this, however, there is as yet a paucity of data.

Finally, let us reemphasize that urban culture is *the* culture of modernity. What happens in modern cities is what defines the fate of modern and modernizing societies. Urbanization equals modernization. And since modernization means, in a fundamental way, the diffusion and adaptation of Western patterns of society and culture, urbanization equals Westernization. Urbanization has thus become a global force driving divergent societies toward a common pattern: this process is of fundamental importance for the possibility of a genuinely *comparative* sociology.

NOTES

1. For his definition of the city, see Max Weber, *The City,* trans. and ed. Don Martindale and Gertrud Neuwirth (Glencoe: Free Press, 1958). The reader may also wish to consult Max Weber, *General Economic History* (Glencoe: Free Press, 1950), Chapter 28.

2. Weber, *The City.*

3. For general reference on the history of the city, see the various publications of Lewis Mumford, such as *The Culture of Cities* (New York: Harcourt, Brace, 1938), and *City Development* (New York: Harcourt, Brace, 1945).

4. Louis Wirth, "Urbanism as a Way of Life," *American Journal of Sociology* 49 XLIX (July 1938): 1–25; Kingsley Davis and Hilde Hertz, *The Pattern of World Urbanization* (New York: 1954); Rose Hum Lee, *The City* (Philadelphia: Lippincott, 1955); and P. K. Hatt and A. J. Reiss, eds., *Reader in Urban Sociology* (Glencoe: Free Press, 1951).

5. A. H. M. Jones, *The Greek City from Alexander to Justinian* (New York: Oxford University Press, 1940); Michael Rostovtseff, *The Social and Economic History of the Hellenistic World,* 3 vols. (New York: Oxford University Press, 1942); N. D. Fustel de Coulanges, *The Ancient City* (New York: Doubleday, n. d.).

6. Jerome Carcopino, *Daily Life in Ancient Rome* (New Haven: Yale University Press, 1940); Michael Rostovtseff, *The Social and Economic History of the Roman Empire,* 2nd ed. (New York: Oxford University Press, 1957); and de Coulanges, *op. cit.*

7. Henri Pirenne, *Medieval Cities: Their Origins and the Revival of Trade* (Princeton: Princeton University Press, 1925), and *A History of Europe from the Invasion to the Sixteenth Century* (New York: W. W. Norton, 1948).

8. Jacob Burckhardt, *Die Geschichte der Renaissance,* 10th ed. (Leipzig: Kroener, 1908).

9. Patrick Geddes, *Cities in Evolution* (New York: Oxford University Press, 1950); Lewis Mumford, *The Culture of Cities* (New York, Harcourt, Brace, 1938) and Lee, *op. cit.*

10. See Davis and Hertz, *op. cit.;* J. A. Quinn, *Human Ecology* (New York: Harper & Bros., 1950); and Hatt and Reiss, *op. cit.*

11. See R. E. Park, E. W. Burgess, and R. D. McKenzie, eds., *The City* (Chicago: University of Chicago Press, 1925); R. E. Park, *Human Communities* (Glencoe: Free Press, 1952); and A. H. Hawley, *Human Ecology* (New York: The Ronald Press Co., 1950).

12. See Charles Abrams, *Man's Struggle for Shelter in an Urbanizing World* (Cambridge: M. I. T. Press, 1964); R. D. McKenzie, "The Scope of Human Ecology," in E. W. Burgess, ed., *The Urban Community* (Chicago: University of Chicago Press, 1926); and Quinn, *op. cit.*

13. D. G. Bishop and E. E. Starret, *The Structure of Local Government* (Washington: National Council for the Social Studies, 1945); and Victor Jones, *Metropolitan Government* (Chicago: University of Chicago Press, 1942).

14. Max Weber, *General Economic History,* pp. 315–338.

15. Harold J. Laski, "Democracy," in *Encyclopedia of the Social Sciences* (New York: Macmillan, 1937); and S. M. Lipset, *Political Man* (New York: Doubleday, 1963), p. 34.

16. See William McCord, *The Springtime of Freedom* (New York: Oxford University Press, 1965); and Kenneth Little, *West African Urbanization* (New York: Cambridge University Press, 1965).

17. See Little, *op. cit.*

18. Daniel Lerner, *The Passing of Traditional Society* (New York: Free Press, 1958).

19. Gerald Breese, *Urbanization in Newly Developing Countries,* Modernization of Traditional Societies Series (Englewood Cliffs, N. J.: Prentice-Hall, 1966).

20. Clifford Geertz, *Agricultural Involution: The Processes of Ecological Change in Indonesia* (Berkeley: University of California Press, 1963).

21. See the chapter, "Urban Characteristics in Indonesia" in W. F. Wertheim, *East-West Parallels* (Chicago: Quadrangle Books, 1965).

22. Wertheim, *op. cit.,* Chapter 3, "Trading Minorities in Southeast Asia."

23. See C. C. Zimmerman, *Family and Civilization* (New York: Harper & Bros., 1947); and Sidney M. Greenfield, "Industrialization and the Family in Sociological Theory," in Bernard Farber, ed., *Kinship and Family Organization* (New York: John Wiley, 1966).

24. Kurt Wolff, ed., *The Sociology of Georg Simmel* (Glencoe: Free Press, 1950), pp. 409 ff. and 402 ff.

25. See Wirth, *op. cit.,* and Weber, *General Economic History.*

26. Acts 17:21 (RSV).

27. See Marshall McLuhan, *The Gutenberg Galaxy* (Toronto: University of Toronto Press, 1962).

28. See Bernard Rosenberg and David M. White, *Mass Culture* (New York: Free Press, 1964).

29. See David Riesman, *The Lonely Crowd* (New York: Doubleday, 1953); J. R. Seeley, R. A. Sim, and E. W. Lossley, *Crestwood Heights* (New York: Basic Books, 1956).

30. Thorstein Veblen, *Theory of the Leisure* (New York: Doubleday Mentor, 1953).

31. Martin H. and Esther S. Neumeyer, *Leisure and Recreation* (Cranbury, N. J.: A. S. Barnes and Co., Inc., 1949); and Bernard Rosenberg and David Manning White, *Mass Culture* (New York: Free Press, 1964).

[6] Family and Youth

VARIOUS factors have been suggested as explanations of why the family occupies a central position in the institutional fabric of society—because of its foundation in man's biological nature, because of the potentially overwhelming strength of the sexual drive that it is supposed to regulate, because of its crucial function in socializing the young. From a sociological viewpoint it is this last that appears most meaningful. Whatever else the family as an institution may be or do, since the earliest times its most important task in society has been the support, care, and training of the young. And, as we will see, the deepening crisis faced by the family as an institution in modern industrial society is precisely that the family is being forced to surrender this task to other institutions.

Cultural anthropologists have sought to determine whether the family is a universal human institution.[1] The consensus today is that it is. Commenting upon situations where, at first glance, it seems there is no defined institution of the family at all, Claude Lévi-Strauss has said that the institution reveals itself as soon as one turns to study the manner in which children are supported.[2] Anthropologists also agree that the family can and does occur in an immense variety of patterns in different cultures. This variety at first seems nearly infinite; indeed a large part of the accomplishment of cultural anthropology has been to order these diverse patterns into distinctive types. Despite the cross-cultural variousness of the institution, there are several basic structural areas it almost always has. Among these the most important are: some means of regulating sexual relations among the members of the society, the incest taboo being the most archaic and fundamental way; some form of household, with provision for the economic support of children; and some method of reckoning the descent and legal status of individuals.

We are not interested here in the cross-cultural aspects of the family, but only in the fate of the institution under modern conditions. It is well to keep in mind, however, that the family is the most ancient social phenomenon, which makes all the more significant its recent transformations.

Western Historical Developments

The historical background of the modern Western family is important for us to examine, not simply out of an abstract interest in origins, but because it provides a perspective for other contemporary trends as well. As we shall try to show, these trends generally are related to the family patterns first developed in the West; however, the differences also must not be overlooked.

The modern Western family has two central sources, one in ancient Rome—particularly in Roman law—the other in the Judaeo-Christian religious tradition. Compared with other cultures, the Western family, in general, has several distinguishing features, most of which can be traced to one or the other, or a combination, of these roots. It is monogamous, a trait with both Roman and Judaeo-Christian background.[3] The father has the dominant role, both in law and in fact. In the Roman family this power of the father (*potestas patri*), awesome and almost absolute, had both a religious and a political dimension. The father was the bearer and officiant of the household cult, which was originally, and largely remained, the fundamental religious unit of ancient Rome. At the same time, the father carried on a political function in the government of the city. Both of these dimensions still persist in our language: the religious one in the title of "holy father" (of course, this also derives from the complex, Judaeo-Christian religious concept of "fatherhood"), the political one in our notion of "town fathers." Correspondingly, the Western family has until very recently assigned an inferior status to women. This is not of Roman origin, for there, despite paternal authority, the woman played an important role in the family.[4] The degradation of women is a product of Greek tradition and its influence on Christianity.

Also, the Western family has taken as another Roman inheritance its crucial role as the source of education. In contrast with Greece, education took place entirely within the family, with a strict sexual division of labor in this activity—fathers educated the sons, mothers, the daughters. This changed somewhat in later Roman times, under the strong influence of Greece: the Greek institution of the gymnasium was taken over, as well as that of the pedagogue, who was often a Greek, or at least Greek-speaking, slave. Yet the Greek ideal of education never really took hold in the Roman mind, and the older Roman pattern reasserted itself in the Middle Ages. Schools and other pedagogic institutions disappeared with the exception of the Church schools, where, significantly, the population was one of celibates, that is, of individuals detached from the family. For the most part, education was reattached to the family: both apprentices and aspirant knights took their training in a family, although, to be sure, it was not their own. Furthermore, the Roman notion of morality as the be-all and end-all of education reasserted itself in a Christian garb, as against the Greek ideal of education as enlightenment. The Roman and, after it, the medieval family was completely what contemporary educationists would call "adult-centered."

Like every social institution, the Western family has undergone a continuing process of change in which a number of critical transformations, like that in educational methods, may be stressed: the first is from the Roman to the medieval feudal family. In some respects this was more a petrification than a metamorphosis, as certain Roman patterns became rigidified and legitimated in a new way by Christianity. This was made possible by the disappearance of direct Greek influence, which came to be regarded as pagan by the new Christian ideologues, while, strangely enough, the equally pagan traditions of Roman law were rather smoothly "baptized" into the new religion. To be sure, some features of the "classical" family were of both Greek and Roman origin: thus the religio-political basis of the family, particularly as vested in its presiding father, pertained to the Greek polis as much as to the Roman republic. It is safe to say, however, that the solidarity and self-sufficiency of the family was considerably stronger in Rome, and this quality was adopted by feudal, Christian society.

Family and Education in Ancient Rome

The family in ancient Rome was central to political, economic, and religious life. It is therefore not surprising that the individual was always viewed essentially as an extension of his family and the bearer of a family tradition. The following describes family education in ancient Rome.

The basis and backbone of education was the family. Legal historians love to emphasize the Roman family's strong constitution—the sovereign authority that was invested in the *pater familias,* the respect that was accorded to the mother—and nowhere is this more evident than in the matter of education. In the eyes of the Romans the obvious place in which children should grow up and be educated was the family. Even under the Empire, when it had been the custom for a long time to educate children together in schools, they still went on, as we can see in Quintilian, discussing the advantages and disadvantages of the two systems; and it was not always the old one of keeping the child at home—*domi atque intra privatos parietes*—that was given up.

The mother's influence lasted a lifetime—hence the symbolic value of the famous tale that was handed down about Coriolanus. Coriolanus had revolted against Rome and was advancing upon the great city at the head of the Volsci. Ambassadors come out from the Roman people and pleaded with him, and they were followed by the city's priests, but despite their entreaties Coriolanus remained inflexible. Finally his mother appeared and upbraided him; and he yielded. The story may have been a myth, but it expressed a genuine feeling. We know the part played in their sons' lives in historical times, in the second and first centuries B.C., by Cornelia the mother of the Gracchi, Aurelia the mother of Caesar, and Atia the mother of Augustus, all of whom brought up their sons to become leaders of men.

When the mother was unable to do her job properly, a governess was chosen to look after the children, and she was always a relative, a woman of experience whom all the family respected, and a person who knew how to maintain an atmosphere of severity and a high moral tone—even when the children were playing games.

From the age of seven onwards the child ceased, as in Greece, to be entirely in the hands of the women, but in Rome he came under his father. This is absolutely typical of the Roman system of teaching. The father was looked upon as the child's real teacher, and even later on, when there were proper teachers, they were still supposed to behave more or less like fathers.

While the girls tended to remain at home with their mothers, industriously spinning wool and doing the housework—this was still the custom when the austere Livia was bringing up Augustus's granddaughters—the boys went off with their father, right into the "curia," even when the senate was sitting in secret, and so they saw all sides of the life ahead of them, learning from his precepts and still more from his example.

It was with a strong sense of duty that the Roman pater familias applied himself to his job as an educator: he was a very different figure from the careless and incompetent Greek fathers who appear in the pages of Plato's *Laches*. There is an excellent chapter in Plutarch describing the care Cato the Censor took over his son's education: Plutarch shows what an eagle eye he kept on his progress, how he taught him all his subjects, and he emphasizes the gravity and the respect for the child that he showed throughout. "Maxima debetur puero reverentia" ("Above all, show respect to a child"), Juvenal was to write later. This was one of the fundamental features of the Roman tradition.

Source: H. I. Marrou, *A History of Education in Antiquity* (New York: Sheed & Ward, 1964), pp. 313 ff.

As Christianity sanctified certain key figures of the Roman family, it also modified them. For example, it intensified the Roman conception of the family as sacred by attributing to marriage the status of a sacrament. At the same time, by also declaring marriage to be indissoluble, Christianity diminished the power of the husband; the Roman husband could easily get rid of his wife by divorce, the medieval husband could not. Again, the feudal family continued to play a key political role, though within an overall structure that was vastly different from that of the Roman world. And, as we have already seen, the Middle Ages returned to the family the Roman role of nearly sole agency of education and greatly increased the Greek subordination of women. Compared with Roman antiquity, particularly the later imperial period, under feudalism the family became the *total* social context for the individual's life, with only the Church providing a potential alternative. Unless an individual took orders and escaped into the Church, almost everything that was likely to happen to him in the course of his life (particularly his economic and political relations as defined in the feudal system), occurred within the context of his family. One very significant aspect of this, which we will later elaborate on, is the absence of any real conception of "childhood" as a separate, distinct stage in life.[5] Essentially, children were conceived of and treated as young adults, a view that is revealed by the manner in which they were dressed. Consistent with this, the individual started to work, marry, and became legally responsible at a very early age in comparison with our own notions.

A second important transformation in the Western family took place between 1500 and 1800 A.D.[6] The beginnings of this transformation are related to the Renaissance and the Reformation. The humanist ideals of the Renaissance led to the re-emergence of classical Greek influences. The Reformation deprived the family (or, strictly speaking, marriage) of sacramental status—a fact that possibly was not of decisive significance *per se,* but which opened the door to other secular influences. The net effect of these fundamental changes was to make available new ways of conceiving of the family, ways more appropriate to the nonfeudal society then developing in Europe.

The global social events underlying this transformation of the family have already been discussed: the disintegration of feudalism as a functioning social system; the rise of cities; political centralization; economic diversification; and the profound shifts in the stratification system brought about by all of these processes. Out of these shifts the bourgeoisie emerged as the dominant class of the new era, and it developed its own specific bourgeois pattern of family life, which gradually became the model throughout the whole society, radiating, as it were, both upward and downward from the central strata of the bourgeoisie. Since then the history of the Western family has been largely that of this bourgeois pattern, in its various manifestations, first in Western civilization and now increasingly everywhere in the world.

The emerging bourgeois family was open to the humanist ideal of education, partly because learning and the formation of character in the humanist sense were greatly emphasized, and partly because these were seen (correctly) as vehicles of social success and mobility. There continued, however, a stress on the family as a Christian moral institution. The bourgeoisie was, in the name of self-betterment, becoming most earnestly concerned with the education of its children, at a time when the aristocracy still scoffed at such ideas. The child was moving into the forefront of attention, as the social hopes of the family came to be vested in him. And, new methods of hygiene, which steadily reduced infant and child mortality, gave the evolving "child-centeredness" a realistic foundation it would previously have lacked. This focus on the child has increased steadily over the generations, first in the bourgeoisie, then in other strata. At the same time, a change in the status was beginning. As mobility was becoming ever more possible, "marrying up" was becoming secondary only to working up as a way of rising in the world. Therefore, there was an increased interest in the education of girls as well as boys, and again it occurred first in the bourgeoisie. A new type, "the cultured woman," began to emerge, a person not only educated in the formal sense, but also given to the cultivation of individuality, including the highly individuated emotion of romantic love. In this woman the bourgeoisie was producing a new kind of personal sensibility, which was to become of tremendous historical significance.

The interest of the bourgeoisie in education led to the development of schools independent of the existing system of the church schools, and education developed as an independent social institution of steadily increasing importance. In this new system there was for the first time in Christendom a conception of age specialization in education, with different schools handling material appropriate to different age groups. Ideologically, this was related to the evolution of the specifically modern conception of childhood as a very special age of life—again sharply illustrated by new, distinctive ways of dressing children.[7]

One major effect of these various transformations was the beginning of a shrinkage in the social functions of the family.[8] Other institutions, particularly the newly institutionalized system of education, were preempting many of the family's functions. At the end of the eighteenth century, the family was diminishing its hold on some areas of life: this can be seen as the triumph of the bourgeois family. With the eminent success of bourgeois capitalism, its family patterns were increasingly emulated by others, including the aristocracy, which also began to take an interest in the education of its children.

The third major transformation of the Western family occurred with the Industrial Revolution.[9] As we have seen, industrial revolution is not an inexorable process with identical results everywhere, as always the basic pattern is modified by the idiosyncra-

The Changing Role of the Child in the Family
from Medieval to Modern Times

The following is taken from Philippe Ariès excellent study, *Centuries of Childhood;* these paragraphs summarize key aspects of the change of the medieval into the modern family.

In the Middle Ages, at the beginning of modern times, and for a long time after that in the lower classes, children were mixed with adults as soon as they were considered capable of doing without their mothers or nannies, not long after a tardy weaning (in other words, at about the age of seven). They immediately went straight into the great community of men, sharing in the work and play of their companions, old and young alike. The movement of collective life carried along in single torrent all ages and classes, leaving nobody any time for solitude and privacy. In these crowded, collective existences there was no room for a private sector. The family fulfilled a function; it ensured the transmission of life, property, and names; but it did not penetrate very far into human sensibility. Myths such as courtly and precious love denigrated marriage, while realities such as the apprenticeship of children loosened the emotional bond between parents and children. Medieval civilization had forgotten the *paideia* of the ancients and knew nothing as yet of modern education.

Between the end of the Middle Ages and the seventeenth century, the child . . . won a place beside his parents to which he could not lay claim at a time when it was customary to entrust him to strangers. This return of the children to the home was a great event: it gave the seventeenth-century family its principal characteristic, which distinguished it from the medieval family. The child became an indispensable element of everyday life, and his parents worried about his education, his career, his future. He was not yet the pivot of the whole system, but he had become a much more important character. Yet this seventeenth-century family was not the modern family: it was distinguished from the latter by the enormous mass of sociability which it retained. Where the family existed, that is to say in the big houses, it was a center of social relations, the capital of a little, complex, and graduated society under the command of the paterfamilias. The modern family, on the contrary, cuts itself off from the world and opposes to society the isolated group of parents and children. All the energy of the group is expended on helping the children to rise in the world, individually and without any collective ambition: the children rather than the family.

This evolution from the medieval family to the seventeenth-century family and then to the modern family was limited for a long time to the nobles, the middle class, the richer artisans, and the richer laborers. In the early nineteenth century, a large part of the population, the biggest and poorest section, was still living like the medieval families, with the children separated from their parents. The idea of the house or the home did not exist for them. The concept of the home is another aspect of the concept of the family. Between the eighteenth century and the present day, the concept of the family changed hardly at all. It remained as we saw it in the town and country middle classes of the eighteenth century. On the other hand, it extended more and more to other social strata. . . . Finally family life embraced nearly the whole of society, to such an extent that people have forgotten its aristocratic and middle-class origins.

Source: Philippe Ariès, *Centuries of Childhood, A Social History of Family Life* (New York: Knopf, 1962), pp. 403, 411.

cies of each national society. Yet, its fundamental effect on the family can be observed almost everywhere.

Industrial labor removed the husband from the household during his working hours. This did not always happen immediately, as in early industrialism there were "cottage industries," in which work was "farmed out" to the household. (The merchant supplied the raw materials, and then he brought the work of the household by the piece, subsequently marketing it at some considerable distance.) This type of industry naturally declined with the increasing complexity of modern machinery. Also, the distance of the worker's separation from his household increased as industries began to gather in large agglomerations which were necessarily separated from residential areas. Institutionally, the family progressively ceased to function as a unit of production, and became instead primarily a unit of consumption, which had far-reaching consequences. This change from production to consumption has particularly affected the stability of the family, making it less stable as a unit. It is not difficult to understand the reason. It is, simply, that one is far more inclined to separate from a wife who helps one to eat than from a wife who helps one to produce food for eating. It is for the same reason that children have ceased to be an economic asset and have instead become an economic liability—with the

The Conjugal Family in Industrial Society

William J. Goode, a sociologist at Columbia University, in his many studies on industrialization, argues that the family and industrialization interact through independent variables. Nonetheless, his findings support the general notion that family systems, under the influence of the industrial mode of life, are moving toward a conjugal pattern, despite the fact that the change of specific family traits may vary from one industrial society to another. Some of his major findings are listed in a summary fashion below.

1. Freedom of marital choice, with the following concomitant changes:
   a. Marital bargaining is taken from the hands of elders;
   b. The young couple must be economically independent;
   c. The age of females at marriage is likely to drop in Japan, but to rise slightly in China and substantially in Arab countries and India; the age of males depends on several additional variables; at a minimum, there develops the notion of a "proper maturity at marriage" for both;
   d. The pattern of class homogamy does not change greatly;
   e. In cultures where there was nearly universal marriage (India, Japan, China), there may be a slight diminution in the percentage married; and
   f. Age-discrepant marriages, that is, between spouses of very different ages, diminish.
2. Marriages between close kin (for example, between cousins) decrease.
3. The dowry or bride price begins to disappear.
4. Illegitimacy rates increase in systems where most marriages have been consummated between children (for example, India —but not China and Japan). Since most civilizations seem to have various forms of marital unions which are not fully legitimate, the movement toward a conjugal system may (as in Japan) actually reduce the illegitimacy rate.
5. Concubinage and polygamy decline.
6. Theory cannot predict whether fertility in a conjugal system will be high or low—but fertility will be controlled in the interests of the couple, and not of the kin group. Under industrialization, of course, the rate usually falls. And any movement toward a conjugal system reduces the size of the household—even in Africa, where possibly the marital fertility ratio may be increasing.

7. Infanticide decreases—though we have no firm numerical data with which to measure its past rate in those countries where it allegedly once existed (India, Japan, China, and the Arab world).

8. Matriliny weakens—although here our Western bias may exaggerate changes in lower-caste Indian or Central African systems; that is, because the system seems strange, we are more alert to changes in it.

9. The divorce rate will be high, but the trend in any given culture will depend on its prior level. It may drop if the rate was already high and the new system yields some new elements of stability (for example, the removal of the Japanese parents-in-law's right to send the bride to her parents).

10. Remarriage after divorce or the death of one's spouse becomes common in areas where it was rare. Here, stereotypes confuse somewhat, since divorce was certainly more commonly supposed, as was remarriage of the widow or widower (as in China and Japan).

Source: W. J. Goode, "Industrialization and Family Patterns," in B. F. Hoselitz and W. E. Moore, eds., *Industrialization and Society* (Mouton: UNESCO, 1963). By permission of UNESCO.

consequence that there has been a tendency to have fewer children. The overall effect of industrialization in most cases has led to a decline in the birth rate.

The self-sufficiency of the family has decreased, both materially and culturally. Not only does the family no longer produce the material goods it needs, but it can no longer take care of most of its cultural needs either: both education and entertainment, which is more critical than might be assumed, become the domain of specialized agencies outside of the family. The members of the family therefore tend to disperse not only during working hours but in their leisure time as well. This dispersion of family energy and orientation is related also to women entering the labor force in large numbers. Their status and self-image changed as economic independence became a real possibility for them and undermined their ancient subordination to the male. The new independence and status of women is an aspect of our ideology of "individualism," in accordance with which marriage has become understood as a locale for individual satisfactions and fulfillment; the related idea that women as well as men have sexual needs and

sexual rights has been an important factor in the steady liberaliza-
tion of sexual morality and mores. This change in social status has,
of course, produced legal consequences (for example, in herit-
ance law) as well as political consequences (for example, suffrage). But the crucial point for us is this: marriage has become
basically a civil contract, opening the door ever more widely to
family instability, as marked by the steady increase in divorce in
Western societies.

The industrial revolution furthered the process we have already
described, removing education from the family and making it an
autonomous and specialized institution. It also spread education
throughout the population in two directions: the norm became
compulsory education for all strata, over a lengthened span of the
child's life. As a longer period of life was "taken over" by education, the family began to lose control over its own children (a phenomenon which has had special virulence in America). This created a new social reality, the age of "youth," as the period between
childhood and adulthood steadily grew and is still growing. (We
will examine this curious matter later.) As the child and the youth
began to be seen as special classes of people, rather than as "small
adults," mounting tensions between the family and the state
erupted over particular questions concerning them, for instance,
over laws prohibiting children's work. The general notion today is
that society (that is, the state) must protect childhood, and a great
array of laws and special agencies has sprung up with this function. An unintended consequence of this protection, however, has
been a separation of the child from meaningful social participation. The child's life, as well as the youth's, have become, in essence, periods of *anticipation* and *waiting,* a state of affairs that
produces obvious psychological strains.

Generally, the industrial revolution has led to a fluidity and an
instability of all family patterns. Criteria for marriage, for sexual
practice, for child rearing, for dealing with older people—all have
become subject to constant change and, consequently, to fashion
and uncertainty. To deal with this situation, there have developed a
large number of specialized agencies for family advice and assistance. In America this can be studied in the complex system of
psychotherapeutic, social work, and guidance agencies, many of
which are operated directly by the state, some of them buttressed
by legal sanctions. The family, shrunk both in size and in func-
tionality, has become the "nuclear family," a place, above all, for

the fulfillment of its younger members. The problem this causes older people, and the grandparent in particular, further intensified by the lengthening life expectancy in modern societies, cannot be discussed here. Nor can we examine the national and class differences in some of these patterns. We are merely drawing a general picture of a whole constellation of features and problems that increasingly affect industrial and industrializing countries.

The Spread of Western Patterns

So far, only the family has been discussed. But the comparative sociologist is aware that the Western patterns now constitute a worldwide trend.[10] As we have seen, industrialization and urbanization everywhere tend to disrupt traditional forms of social life. However, in most preindustrial societies, the family (and kinship, in the broad anthropological sense) is the "keystone" of the traditional social order. Thus a good case can be made for measuring modernization in terms of the decline of traditional family patterns. The family patterns of modernizing/industrializing societies and advanced industrial societies are converging toward the Western patterns, despite differences in the historical backgrounds. Two examples may help to show this.

One of the most interesting studies of African family patterns was made by Remy Cliquet in the Ivory Coast, a former French colony.[11] Cliquet studied two tribes, the Aboure and the Bete. Traditionally, their family patterns were very different. Both were polygynous, but the Aboure were matriarchal, the Bete patriarchal. In both groups there were close ties between brothers and sisters, although for different duration and for different reasons. Among the Aboure, the ties were permanent because the position of the sister was never independent of her brother; among the Bete, the ties were temporary, ending when the early marriage of the sister provided the bridal price needed by her brother to purchase his own bride. The relation of the wife to her husband's family differed greatly, however. Among the Bete, relations were close: the wife had to ensure her children's position within the husband's family; and, because the wife worked the land and produced wealth, bridal prices were quite high, and many wives were a sign of great prosperity. Among co-wives, strong frictions developed. On the other hand, among the Aboure, the wife's connection with her husband's family was very loose, because the position of the children in the wife's family, not the husband's, was what mattered. Bridal prices existed, but they were low. There was polygyny, but rather rarely, and where it existed, there was little friction between the co-wives, since the position of each wife and of her children was established in her own family, making rivalry pointless.

Both tribes had members who migrated to the city, although geography had led the Aboure to start migration earlier and to develop a higher migration rate. Hence, there were more Aboure than Bete women in the city, proportionally. Also, because the Aboure had been exposed more strongly to French influence, they had more French-speaking males; consequently, they found more and better jobs. Yet, despite the differences both in traditional patterns and in migration history, the city caused similar problems for both groups.

In both groups a loosening of ties between the urban family and the rural home family occurred and in both cases it was the women who maintained stronger ties, as they do in America also. Both groups showed a trend toward the "nuclear family," as a result of the economic conditions of urban life. Both groups tended away from early marriage, and thus the extended family grew less influential and marriage became a more individualized affair. The figures on this are interesting: in the rural situation, 82 per cent of Aboure women married immediately after their first menstruation, and 56 per cent of Bete women; in the city, it was only 57 per cent of Aboure and 33 per cent of Bete women. Also, there were more intertribal marriages in the city, including marriages between Aboure and Bete. In the rural situation, 2 per cent of Aboure and 1 per cent of Bete women married outside their respective tribes; in the city, 25 per cent of Aboure and 8 per cent of Bete women did so. A similar trend was found with regard to choosing partners from another village. But, while the extended family, in its traditional patterns, became less important in the city, kinship and tribal links continued to be important, though now in forms not traditionally provided for. For example, the role of the brother might be taken over by a distant relative or just by anyone from the home village (a pattern reminiscent of American ethnic groups, as that of the *paisano* among Italian immigrants).

In both groups women gained a new independence, in regard

to crucial underlying matters, such as independence in buying clothes, and polygyny made it easier for some women to take jobs. An interesting finding was that friction between co-wives in the city *increased* among Aboure women but *decreased* among Bete, in contradiction to the traditional differences. In this as in other matters, the two groups came to resemble each other more, as both moved toward the universal modern-urban pattern. Generally, the authority of women increased with their capacity to be economic contributors in their own right. This also resulted in what may be called psychological independence. At one point in the study women were asked whom they would save first in a situation of disaster—their husband, their mother, or nobody. These were the results:

TABLE 6-1

	Aboure		Bete	
	RURAL	URBAN	RURAL	URBAN
	(in percentage)		(in percentage)	
Husband first:	84	47	79.5	54
Mother first:	13	31	18	40
Nobody:	1.8	13.5	0.4	3.8

Overall, the inclination to save the mother increased at the expense of the inclination to save the husband. To see the meaning of this, one must recognize that the mother rarely is present in the urban situation: she serves, rather, as a kind of remote security symbol, not present as a source of friction in the actual experience of these women. Most important, the figures just cited indicate a loosening of marital ties, as the women grow more secure that they could take care of themselves.

We have already suggested that Japan is sociologically a fascinating case; despite its history of rapid, highly successful industrialization, it has nevertheless retained some non-Western traditional patterns. This may also be seen with regard to the Japanese family. It has moved toward Westernized patterns in some aspects, but remained strongly traditional in others.[12] One possible explanation of this may be the continuing role of the "cottage industry" in Japan, which mitigates the disruptive effects of industry on traditional family patterns.

In the traditional Japanese family the *ie,* or "stem family," held the key place: this direct line usually ran through the oldest son, while the younger sons formed "branch families." All property passed to the stem family; however, total primogeniture could be modified by adding a second son to the *ie* whenever the father deemed the eldest to be unsuitable. The *ie* thus retained its concentrated economic strength, as well as its political position, especially in the village councils. Ancestor ritual was vested in the *ie*. It also decided the education of all family members, on the basis of the individual's function in relation to the needs of the family as a whole. The *ie* dominated and was responsible for the welfare of all members of the extended family. Both Shinto and Confucianism reinforced these patterns. Under this dispensation marriages were always arranged, usually with the aid of professional go-betweens. The selection of a wife depended on "objective" criteria, both material and in terms of character—such as size of dowry and evidence of amiability. The wife was completely subservient to her husband and her mother-in-law, and her ties of affection were generally much stronger with her own parents than with her husband: within the household there was little or no privacy, not even between the spouses.

With the coming of industrialization, despite the prevalence of "cottage industry," many men began to be taken out of their households by their jobs. Even farmers began to accept additional jobs in industry that took them away from home either seasonally or part time. The same happened with small shopkeepers, who left their wives to run the shops. Thus, here as elsewhere industrialization turned the family unit from production to consumption, and thereby diminished the importance of the heir, who was delegated to continue the *ie* economy. Furthermore, since the *ie* economy was typically rural, the branch families often grew more prosperous than the *ie,* and their subservience disappeared.

With the decline in the economic functions of the family there emerged a new emphasis on individual emotional relationships. In the earlier stages of industrialization many women worked in industry. Younger women still do, before marriage, but the norm has become that married women stay at home and do not work (except in those cases where work can be taken home). Thus there has been a continuation of the traditional division of labor between the spouses. Social disapproval of working wives exists in both middle-class and working-class strata. Nevertheless, if only because of the frequent absence of the husband, the wife's authority within the family has increased. Her most important task is to raise the children, and the strong emphasis on education is supported by the family as a whole. The total influence of the family on the children is more intense and more enduring than it is in Western countries.

In other words, the family remains the social keystone, and often in traditional terms, although its form shifted from the *ie* to the nuclear family. Despite urbanization, there has been a decline in the divorce rate. Although marriages are now increasingly based on affection, the parents' consent is still widely sought. At one time it was dowry; today the most important criterion for selecting both husband and wife is education, as it relates to the mobility chances of the new family unit. The family has retained its strong sense of responsibility for the welfare of all its members, which is related to Japan's relative lack of social legislation. Interestingly, the growing concern for individual emotional fulfillment has led to a new desire for privacy, which causes tensions, particularly between wives and their mothers-in-law.

How long this odd combination of traditional and modern patterns will last is difficult to answer. Will the need for private emotional satisfaction destroy the sense of family responsibility? The combination of mushrooming industrialization and stabilizing population is likely to create change, if only because more women will be required in the labor force. Thus far, however, the Japanese family offers one of the best examples of a traditional system that has adapted itself to Western patterns no more than was minimally necessary under the new economic conditions.

The Family and Other Institutions

We cannot investigate here the many and complex relations between the family and other institutions in modern Western society. However, we shall briefly consider three of these—relations with the state, with the economy, and with the class system.

THE FAMILY AND THE STATE

The relations between the modern state and the family are marked by a paradox.[13] On the one hand, the state recognizes the importance of the family to society and takes various measures to protect it. On the other hand, some of these very measures actually serve to weaken the family as an institution. The supportive measures of the state inevitably occur within a bureaucratic structure, while the family is probably the *least* bureaucratized of the large institutions of modern society. The state programs on behalf of the family thus have an odd, sometimes even a comical, character, by virtue of this imposition of bureaucracy upon a profoundly nonbureaucratic even antibureaucratic social phenomenon.

The favorable attitude of the state toward the family has its root in the widespread notion (partly Roman, partly Judaeo-Christian in origin) that a stable family guarantees a stable social order and therefore a stable state. We cannot be concerned here with the sociological validity or invalidity of this notion, but only with the practical consequences of believing it. For some two hundred years the state has played a double role in this area. On the one hand, it has acted as the protector of the individual within the family, by allowing, for example, rights of divorce; on the other hand, however, it has acted as the protector of the family as an institution, even against the rights or desires of the individual, by placing, for example, limits on the rights of divorce, even in cases where there are no children (and thus no "third party" individuals to be protected). This ambivalence is reflected in the curious legal status of marriage, which is defined as a civil contract between individuals, but which is a contract that changes the legal status of the individuals involved and, therefore, cannot be freely dissolved as other contracts.

The state has recently been encroaching upon the autonomy of the family with various new controls that, unlike the limits on individual as against family freedom (mentioned above) are not grounded in older traditions. Examples of such controls are the compulsory education laws (I cannot choose to educate my children at home), or the various laws relating to medical care (I cannot refuse to have my children inoculated). The state has also set up a large number of bureaucratic agencies concerned with the family. Some of these are voluntary agencies, such as counseling services or (recently) birth control clinics. Others, though, have legal powers of compulsion, such as those connected with family ("domestic relations") and juvenile courts.

There are differences among national societies in the degree of state support of (or, if one prefers, encroachment upon) the fam-

State Influence upon the Family in Japan

The following excerpt demonstrates the influence the modern Japanese government tries to exert upon family life.

A government-approved textbook, published in 1952 for use in the Social Studies course in secondary schools (ages 12–15), deals with the family. In the author's evolutionary historical presentation, monogamy is represented as the product of "modern civilization" and as such is given all the authority of inevitability and all the associations surrounding the word "progress." The following extract will give an idea of the reformist tone of the book.

"It can not be said today that mistresses have entirely disappeared. Nor can it be honestly said that marriages no longer take place in which the wishes of the individuals concerned are ignored . . . It is our task to build a real, and not simply a formal, system of monogamous marriage . . . That men and women should be truly equal, that marriage should be guaranteed economic security, that marriage should be free—these are the foundations of a healthy and undistorted system of monogamous marriage. Only on such foundations can the union of two people who truly love one another be assured." [a]

[a] Tamaki Hajime, *Kazoku*, (Tokyo, Shakaika Zensho Series, 1952), pp. 32–37.
Source: R. P. Dore, *City Life in Japan* (Berkeley: University of California Press, 1959), p. 164. Reprinted by permission of The Regents of the University of California and Routledge & Kegan Paul.

ily. The Soviet Union, Sweden, and the United States may be taken as representative of three different types of state/family relations.[14]

The Soviet case is particularly interesting, because it went through a complete circle in a relatively short period. Immediately after the Russian Revolution the Soviet state had what could be called a negative policy toward the family, which it regarded as an obsolete bourgeois institution. It did not actively seek to destroy the family, as it tried to destroy other institutions of the old order, but all its actions with regard to the family were geared to protect the individual rather than the family unit. There were no limits on divorce. Official policy encouraged sexual liberality, as an emancipation from the "exploitation" of bourgeois morality. Contraception and even abortion were freely available. But this changed dramatically during the Stalinist period and the family code of 1936 formalized a new policy aimed at protecting the family as a unit important to the stability of society as a whole. The measures taken to do this were quite similar to those instituted during the same period by dictatorial regimes of the right, as in Italy and Germany. Divorce was made quite difficult; abortion became illegal and contraception was frowned upon as bourgeois decadence; heavy tax burdens were imposed on bachelors and childless couples, while subsidies were given to families with large numbers of children, and particularly fertile mothers were even given state decorations. Daycare centers and creches were made available for children of working mothers. And a new concept of "socialist morality" introduced a strongly puritanical flavor into Soviet life. According to one Soviet source during this period, "The aim of Soviet legislation is to promote the stability of the family. . . . In strengthening the family the state strengthens itself, strengthens its power and might." [15] This essentially conservative or neoconservative attitude has remained characteristic of Soviet policy, though there have been some relaxations in the post-Stalinist period.

Sweden has a well-organized family and population policy, conceived in terms of both the stabilization of the family and its democratization. The state disclaims any interest in increasing the population, but attempts to assist families to have as many children as they desire without thereby suffering in their standard of living. This policy is expressed in tax benefits for couples with children, state loans to the newly married, and state clinics for prenatal and infant care, as well as for birth control. Yet, despite these intensive welfare programs, there is great concern for the individual's rights and desires, especially in regard to sexuality. The state provides "education for family life" in school programs that cover both sexual instruction and training in cooking, child care, and the like. These programs are funded jointly by the state and by various private agencies. Other Western countries with strong socialist influences, such as Britain, have developed family policies very similar to the Swedish one.

In the United States, until very recently, the state per se has been reluctant to take direct initiative in family policy. It relied on the formal laws, leaving direct social action in this area to private programs. Thus, marriage counseling, birth control, and, indeed, social work in general have all in the past largely depended on private enterprise. Change has come only recently, as the United States has moved toward the welfare state. Increasingly, welfare and medical agencies concerned with the family have been established by the state, remaining under state control and often functioning under the sanction of compulsory state laws. The development of family courts has been particularly significant. Most recently the state has even entered the once forbidden area of birth control. And the controversy over the so-called Moynihan Report on the Negro family has raised the possibility of an even more active governmental role, on both the Federal and state levels, in family policy.[16] Generally, there has been a move from a moral to a supposedly "scientific" attitude for this. Thomas Szasz has coined the apt term "therapeutic state," suggesting that the legal and political order form an all-embracing therapeutic establishment.[17]

Generally, despite differences between national societies, all modern states have had the problem of finding some sort of balance between the protection of the family and the protection of the individual's rights within the family, both being declared aims of the state. Not surprisingly, there has been a general convergence in governmental policies in this area.

THE FAMILY AND ECONOMY

Enough has been said about the way economic developments have affected the family to allow us to be brief here.[18] As we have seen, the basic change has been the transformation of the family from a production to a consumption unit. In this process, the key factor has been the participation of women in the labor force, a role opened to them by the technology that developed labor-saving devices for the household. These devices, however, have themselves become consumption goals. There is thus an inexorable process in which high consumption expectations lead to increased labor by members of the family, which itself in turn creates new consumption needs. As a consumption unit, then, the family is of great importance to the economy. This is most easily seen in the family orientation of consumer advertising, which has, incidentally, had an effect on the place of women as great as did their entry into the labor force, giving them the role of family decision-maker about consumption. It is quite possible (though precise evidence is lacking) that there is today *more* economic pressure on

*Fertility Rates and Social Strata in the
United States and in Sweden*

FERTILITY RATE, BY MOTHER'S
EDUCATIONAL LEVEL, U.S.A.

MOTHER'S EDUCATION	YEARS	NUMBER OF CHILDREN PER 1,000 WOMEN
Elementary school	<8	3,118
Elementary school	8	2,465
Secondary school	1–3	2,347
Secondary school	4	1,940
College	1–3	1,812
College	4	1,592
Average	4	2,188

The censuses of 1935 and 1945 in Sweden produced a more complicated picture of fertility in towns. In both years, the average number of children was lowest in the middle groups, in 1935 the upper-income group had as high a figure as the lower-income group, but in 1945 it had a figure that was considerably higher than any of the others. The lowest-income group seems to have more children than they can afford, presumably because many of these people can not or do not want to plan the family's children. But in the upper-income groups in the towns, income and number of children tended to move together.

Source: Gunnar Boalt, *Family and Marriage* (New York: McKay, 1965), pp. 91–93.

the family than there was when it was still geared to production.

These economic factors have had a paradoxical effect. The family has given up most of its traditional societal functions, leaving it only the private relationships among its own members, but it has little time or impetus to find new activities in which these relationships can be cultivated. Children are increasingly left to themselves or to extrafamilial influences. The common life of the family is strongly dominated by material interests, which conflicts with nonmaterialistic ideology toward contemporary marriage. In behavioral terms, one no longer marries for economic gain, yet, once married, economic concerns dominate the activities, and, most likely, the conversation of the spouses.

THE FAMILY AND THE CLASS SYSTEM

In all countries for which data are available, there are variations in the family patterns from class to class.[19] There is now a larger body of data for America than for other countries, but there are sufficient cross-national data to make some generalizations.

The various classes have different fertility rates. Generally, the lower classes have the highest rates, a fact discovered as early as 1906 in a comparative study made in Paris, Berlin, Vienna, and London.[20] This is related, of course, to the fact that contraceptives are used more frequently as one goes up the class scale. There has been much research into the effect of class on sexual behavior; in America, the most important data come from the Kinsey studies, and similar studies have been made in other countries.[21] It is thus possible to pinpoint a cross-national pattern, as, for instance, that premarital intercourse takes place at an earlier age and that marital intercourse is more frequent in the lower classes, that extramarital intercourse is more frequent among older men in the upper strata and least frequent among older men in the lower strata, and so on. One's age at marriage also rises with one's class position (except in the old European upper class, where there is still control over mate selection by the family), as does family stability (that is, the durability of individual marriages). Child-rearing practices are more rigid, or authoritarian, in the lower classes, more permissive in the middle classes where there is the "child-centered family," and again more rigid in the upper classes.[22]

Some class differences are evident in practices dating to infancy, such as weaning, swaddling, and toilet training. This has two significant implications: one, that outside influences determine even this innermost area left to the individual, private family; two, that, if one grants the validity of modern psychology's basic assumption, that personality is formed early, one must expect there to be class differences in personality as well. The available data would seem to support the second implication: there does seem to be a distribution of certain psychological traits by class.[23] For example, lower-class children tend to be less ready to wait for the fulfillment of their wishes (that is, tend to lack a capacity for what psychologists call "delayed gratification"). Studies of the Negro American particularly have revealed that these psychologi-

*Class Differences in Child Disciplinary Methods
in England*

J. and E. Newson found that there was a class factor in the use of
smacking to control one-year-old children.

	1 and 2	3 WHITE COLLAR	3 MANUAL	4	5
No smacking	56	38	32	42	35
Smacking for danger only	5	9	8	4	7
Smacking for other offences also	39	53	60	54	58

Source: John and Elizabeth Newson, *Infant Care in the Urban Community* (London: George Allen &
Unwin, 1963), p. 284. © George Allen & Unwin Ltd. 1963.

cal traits often serve to inhibit social mobility, quite apart from
the restrictions imposed by the stratification system as such. There
are also class differences in family authority and sociability: male
authority decreases as one goes up in the class scale, except in
particular ethnic or racial groups; for instance, the Negro in
America. Also, there is more common sociability of spouses in
the middle than in the lower class.

Particularly interesting is the Soviet Union, where such class
differences seem to exist despite the official denial of the reality of
class. This has been illuminated by Kent Geiger's study of the Soviet family.[24] Geiger differentiates among three family types, each
type directly related to class position. First, there is the type that
continues traditional Russian patterns: strong male dominance,
high fertility (and, incidentally, high abortion) rates, and relatively
little family attention directed toward children. This type is found
in the lower strata, especially in the rural areas. Second, there is
the child-centered type, with some egalitarianism between the
spouses, planned and therefore lower fertility rates, and exceptionally great attention directed toward the children, who frequently
are described as spoiled; there is even a tendency for the mothers
in this group to stop working and devote themselves full-time to
the household. This type is found predominantly in the urban,
middle strata of clerks, technicians, and skilled workers. Third,

there is the type that Geiger, perhaps rightly, considers the pattern of the future. Both parents work; servants are often used to help with the household and children; and the attitude toward the children is "instrumental," involving affection, but not allowing them to become the focus of family attention. These children are less spoiled than those of the second type, and they are trained to be independent and aspiring. This third type is characteristic of the elite stratum of professionals and upper-echelon bureaucrats.

In non-Western societies, insofar as there are data, it is possible to say that class differences in family patterns are even more exaggerated.[25] The reasons for this are obvious. The higher classes are the carriers of the revolutionary, new, industrial values, whereas traditional patterns are still adhered to in the lower classes of these societies.

Youth

"Youth" is not a universal social reality, but a concept created in Western history by specific, and largely economic, developments. In the world of today, it has emerged as a distinct subculture, with amazing cross-national diffusion, composed of young people in the interstitial years between childhood and adulthood who have banded together. This phenomenon, commonly called "youth culture," has been most intensively studied in America, but much material is also available about its manifestations in other countries.[26]

A number of factors have created this phenomenon. Most important, probably, is the length of the educative process in modern industrial societies. During the whole span of the individual's involvement (which is largely involuntary), he is economically and politically dependent. In other words, in this period of life society allows the individual no responsible role. At the same time, however, this individual is both biologically and psychologically an adult: indeed, the age of biological maturation, puberty, has been *decreasing* over the last half century.[27] Puberty, in both sexes, now takes place two to three years earlier, on the average, then fifty or sixty years ago. It can readily be seen that such an unfortunate juxtaposition of social and biological facts will engender great

TABLE 6-2

Age Composition of Population in Twenty-five Countries

YEAR	COUNTRY	TOTAL POPULA-TION (in thousands)	30 YEARS AND OVER	15-29 YEARS	UNDER 15
1963	Belgium	9,290	5,279	1,700	2,212
1963	Sweden	7,604	4,386	1,605	1,613
1965	England and Wales	47,763	26,956	9,902	10,905
1964	France	48,411	26,378	10,026	12,008
1962	Italy	50,946	26,720	11,730	12,496
1965	U.S.A.	194,583	92,631	42,043	59,909
1964	Japan	97,186	43,635	27,961	25,590
1960	U.A.R. (Egypt)	25,984	9,011	5,864	11,110
1960	Syria	4,565	1,413	1,041	2,111
1961	India	438,775	149,006	109,750	180,019
1960	Turkey	27,755	9,390	6,938	11,427
1961	Pakistan	90,283	28,726	21,378	40,179
1960	Senegal	3,110	1,020	769	1,789
1961	Indonesia	96,319	31,603	24,172	40,544
1963	Ceylon	10,625	3,515	2,790	4,320
1965	Venezuela	8,722	2,615	2,147	3,960
1961	Peru	9,907	3,053	2,563	4,290
1960	Ghana	6,727	2,013	1,717	2,997
1960	Brazil	70,119	21,676	18,512	29,931
1960	Mexico	34,923	10,484	8,987	15,452
1960	Dominican Republic	3,047	850	756	1,441
1962	Kenya	8,636	2,449	2,212	3,976
1963	Morocco	12,665	3,605	3,254	5,806
1957	Tanzania	8,663	2,585	2,399	3,679
1965	Philippines	32,345	8,780	8,453	15,112

Source: United Nations, *Demographic Yearbook*, 17 (1965), Section 6.

pressures on the individual. The age of youth is, above all, an age of psychological turmoil.

Also, young people have become a distinct economic market, despite their overall economic dependency. In an affluent society, even the economically dependent children of the affluent have money to spend. Business is aware of this fact: increasingly, advertising and the mass media generally have taken an interest in young people, that is, in the "youth market." [28] Adult consumer patterns are encouraged in the very young, while at the same time the distinctiveness of youth is emphasized. Idiosyncratic styles of dress, cosmetics, automobiles, drinks, and other commodities are advertised as appropriate for youth, as are styles of entertainment entailing the consumption of goods or services. Thus the whole phenomenon of youth culture, especially in America and recently in Western Europe also, has a synthetic character, invented "of airy nothing" by the mass media for commercial reasons. In other words, many of the traits of youth culture have been exaggerated, if not totally created, by an adult society to which youth is interesting precisely to the degree that it can be integrated into adult socioeconomic patterns.

But, regardless of the degree to which youth is a spontaneous or artificial grouping, most of the social interaction of young people today takes place in age-segregated groups. The peer group, the community of those of the same age, is the focus of the individual from an early age,[29] and the family, as we have seen, is ill-equipped to provide a counterfocus. The social and economic bases of this are reinforced by psychological and ideological factors, like the uncertainty of parents as to their proper parental roles and their consequent subjection to shifting fashions in educational philosophy. Also, the parents' own orientation toward mobility serves to estrange them from their children. The intention may be to educate children to get further ahead, but necessarily this directs the children *not* to identify with the patterns of their parents, and not to aspire to their occupation and position, so that many quarrels between parents and children are caused by essentially economic issues, like, in America, the possession or the use of an automobile. The push to perform successfully and to be upwardly mobile, which the parents teach, often produces unanticipated tensions. The parents often fail to understand that the very behavior that shocks them in their children is an indication that mobility-training has been successful, and that the children are engaging in behavior characteristic of a social stratum beyond that of the parents. For example, lower-class parents are anxious that their children should attain middle-class positions, but are shocked when they practice sexual behavior appropriate in the upper middle class but still disapproved in the lower-class milieu. In America this process of social "outgrowing" is further accentuated by the ethnic factor, as often the children must learn to outgrow not only their parents' class but their ethnic subculture as well. Of course, all these tensions are escalated by increasing mobility. Since the family in these classes cannot adequately supply the children with the necessary norms to function in the anticipated new class role, the peer group becomes then, among other things, a kind of training ground for mobility aspirations, where new roles that already anticipate future positions in society can be "tried out." Robert Merton has coined the happy term "anticipatory socialization" for this phenomenon.[30]

A considerable difference between the rebellions of working-class and middle-class youth against their families is frequently noted by sociologists. Working-class youth (especially in America, where ethnic factors, as well as other subcultural factors, may be involved) commonly rebels against relatively intact traditional patterns, embodied in and practiced by the parental generation. Middle-class youth, on the other hand, is typically confronted with an absence of defined patterns of any kind, or rather with constantly shifting and highly tenuous patterns. The difference may be put graphically as that between a rebellion against "something" and a rebellion against "nothing." Indeed, middle-class culture is commonly perceived as a "nothing" by the youthful rebels within it. It seems likely that this kind of rebellion is psychologically more difficult to bear than rebellion against a clearly defined, cleanly profiled antagonist. It would also seem that this kind of rebellion has a built-in tendency to escalate, since the wish to shock the culture is rendered impotent by the culture's lack of defined values, patterns, mores, or convictions. So, youth culture is as highly stratified as adult culture, because its solidarity can only embrace those with similar objects of rebellion. In youth culture, in other words, tolerance and group feeling does not extend to cutting across class lines any more than it does in the parents' world. One crucial focus of these tensions is, of course, the educational system.[31] The pressure to achieve academically has been pushed back earlier and earlier partly because of the organization of the educational process, partly because of parental ambition; childhood has shrunk in duration to make way for youth, as we can see in patterns of dress and comportment. Within the educational system proper, there is the need to make far-reaching decisions at a time when the individual is not ready to do so, because the goals and life to which these decisions refer (typically, of course, an occupational career) are still quite unreal in terms of the youngster's age-segregated life. That is, the young individual is forced by the educational system to *orient himself* in terms of adult realities from which the societal definition of youth has systematically excluded him. Thus an early fixation on one or another occupation is made, in ignorance, and frequently regretted later on. One reaction to these pressures, on all levels of the educational system, is "dropping out," but this too is a choice, and may be much regretted and difficult to remedy later on. The pressure on all individuals is increased by the educational system's giving preference, not just to a certain level of intelligence, but also to a certain personality type, variously described as introvert, compulsive, or achievement-oriented. The system places in this way additional barriers in the way of those, however intelligent, who do not fit into this mold. In this, of course, the educational system is representative of the society in general, so every student is aware that in school he is defining the pattern of his whole life. The cross-national rise of suicide rates among young people is eloquent testimony to the psychological ravages produced by this situation.[32]

Another focus of tension is sexuality.[33] Success with the opposite sex, ranging from general popularity to sexual score-keeping, is of utmost moment within the youth culture, and probably even more so for girls than for boys. Based on the biological fact that adolescence is the "springtime" of sexuality, sexual or erotic activity is one of the few domains where success actually may be sought by young people, because in other areas they are relegated to impotency and irresponsibility by society. Therefore, young people must get much of their success in sexuality. Inasmuch as it involves the consumption of commodities ranging from cars to lipstick, it is actively, albeit subtly, supported by the mass media. Closely related to this drive for success is the concern with athletics, particularly among boys (an emphasis that also has a biological appropriateness at this age). Unhappily, the constellation of sex, consumption, and athletics is dysfunctional for success, thus engendering additional tensions in the youth culture toward the educational system. American data show that the academic achiever tends to be unpopular within the peer group.[34]

Generally, the sexual patterns of modern youth comprise earlier, more intensive, and more variegated behavior than was experienced by youth in an earlier period. It also tends toward greater sophistication, as in the use of contraceptives. Nevertheless, data reveal a steady rise in illegitimacy, abortions, and venereal disease among young people in all Western countries.

Some of this tension is not internalized, but is directed toward the society at large, which parents and the educational system are usually taken to represent. This is evidenced by the great increase in juvenile criminology, which is a cross-national phenomenon.[35]

The Emergence of Youth Groups in Changing Societies

A very important example of ideological and social transformation may be seen in some processes of social change in modern China, and in the transformation of the traditional Chinese society. . . . With the transformation of the traditional Chinese society under the impact of Western ideological, economic, and military processes, which have necessarily given rise to more individualistic and universalistic ideas and criteria of social action, we witness increasing stress on absolute age, and on the growing common identification of the *ch'ing-nien* (the young adults). This common identification has served as the basis for many active social groupings, which formed parts of the incipient Chinese youth movement and of various social and political movements.

A similar development can be traced in the disintegration of the traditional Jewish community—one of the most familistic societies known—under the impact of emancipation and modern commercial and industrial development. Even in the traditional familistic society, various youth groups of *bakhurei yeshiva* (youngsters of the college) would be formed in those centers of learning which drew students from many localities and in this way took them out of the familistic setting. With more modern developments within the traditional society, these groups developed even more distinct youth ideology and activities. Later these groups also formed the nucleus of numerous Jewish Socialist and Zionist group activities. Similar developments can be found in most non-European countries which felt the impact of Western institutions. Most of the nationalistic movements in the Middle East, in India, Indonesia, etc., consisted of young people, quite often students, or young officers who rebelled against their elders, against the traditional familistic setting in which there existed a very strong emphasis on the authority of elders. They tried to develop new social values and groups, and within most of these movements there was a very strong emphasis on a specific youth consciousness and youth ideology. In fact, the need to "rejuvenate" the country was strongly emphasized by these nationalistic movements.

Source: S. Eisenstadt, *From Generation to Generation* (New York: Free Press, 1956), pp. 173, 174. Reprinted with permission of The Macmillan Company. © by The Free Press of Glencoe, 1956.

On another level is the growth of various, more or less organized forms of sociopolitical rebellion, such as the "Berkeley syndrome" among middle-class college youth or the motorcycle cult among lower-class youth.[36] In some places this rebellion has led to explosions with far-reaching effects in the society at large, as in the recent politics of practically all Western industrialized countries.

One important factor today is the rapid international diffusion of youth patterns.[37] This is true of material things like fashions, the various incarnations of the "young look"; for example, the English "mod" style is worn worldwide. But, it is true also of nonmaterial patterns: musical tastes, forms of political protest, and so on. One condition for this is simply technological, the diffusing power of modern mass communications. But of greater sociological significance is that the crisis of youth is quite similar in all industrial countries: the student rebellion at Berkeley was quickly emulated in Berlin, Paris and Rome, and the motorcyle has been a protest symbol from California to Yugoslavia. Jazz is an international symbol of youth culture's protest against the alleged stuffiness of their elders. Even the communist countries, which tried to resist this symbol of "bourgeois decadence," have had to capitulate before it: today there are discotheques in the Soviet Union, operated by the Komsomol, the youth organization there. And, there is an instantly recognizable "internationale" among American hipsters, Dutch "provos," and Soviet "hooligans," despite their national differences in such matters as the extent to which there is a *political* dimension in their youth protest. Youth culture, in every case, signifies a withdrawal, more or less rebellious, from the values and goals of adult society.

The situation of youth in the developing countries is quite different.[38] There, youth typically forms the political and social leadership of the future. Far from being excluded from responsibility, youth is adulated and called upon to play an elite role, particularly in political matters: this was true in the Cuban and Indonesian revolutions (no matter that the first was leftist, the second rightist), and we may recall the astounding phenomenon of the Red Guard in China. These revolutionary movements often appeal to Western young people as well, not so much because of their politics (one may assume) but because of the responsible roles performed in them by young people, precisely such roles as are unattainable in industrial societies, Western and non-Western alike.

NOTES

1. See Claude Lévi-Strauss, "The Family," in H. L. Shapiro, ed., *Man, Culture, and Society* (New York: Oxford University Press, 1956). For general reference on anthropological literature on the family, see John Beattie, *Other Cultures* (New York: Free Press, 1966), chapters on "Kinship" and "Marriage and Affinity." An excellent bibliography on cross-cultural studies of the family can be found in M. F. Nimkoff, *Comparative Family Systems* (Boston: Houghton Mifflin Company, 1965).

2. Lévi-Strauss, *op. cit.,* indicates that the anthropologist working in the field has no trouble identifying married couples, because they cooperate economically and in the rearing of their children. He suggests that there is a comprehensive and universal basis for the family in this: in tribal societies, and in more developed ones, labor is divided between the sexes, which makes them mutually dependent on social and economic as well as cultural and sexual grounds.

3. See E. O. James, *Marriage and Society* (New York: John DeGraff, 1955), gives a short, summary history of Christian marriage; and Bernhard J. Stern, *The Family, Past and Present* (New York: Appleton-Century-Crofts, 1938). Classics on the history of the family which still deserve attention are: Lewis Henry Morgan, *Ancient Society, or Researches in the Lines of Human Progress from Savagery Through Barbarism to Civilization* (New York: Holt, 1877); Edward Westermarck, *History of Human Marriage* (London: Macmillan, 1891); Bertrand Russell, *Marriage and Morals* (New York: Horace Liveright, 1929); W. E. H. Lecky, *History of European Morals,* 2 vols. (London: Cambridge University Press, 1934).

4. See M. Cary and T. G. Haarhoff, *Life and Thought in the Greek and Roman World* (London: Methuen, 1946); J. Carcopino, *Daily Life in Ancient Rome* (New Haven: Yale University Press, 1940); H. I. Marrou, *A History of Education in Antiquity* (New York: Mentor, 1963), is excellent on the role of the family in education in Greek and Roman society; Janine Assa, *The Great Roman Ladies* (New York: Evergreen Profile Book, 1960). There are excellent fictional reconstructions of family life in antiquity in the writings of Mary Renault and Marguerite Yourcenar.

5. Philippe Ariès, *Centuries of Childhood, A Social History of Family Life* (New York: Knopf, 1962); a most perceptive analysis of changing family life in European society, especially French, between 1400 and 1700.

6. F. Musgrove, in *Youth and the Social Order* (Bloomington: Indiana University Press, 1965), makes an excellent sociological analysis of the changing role of the child in the European family, specifically English, in the late eighteenth and nineteenth centuries; see particularly chapters 3 and 4. Also see Arthur W. Calhoun, *A Social History of the American Family,* 3 vols. (Cleveland: Arthur H. Clark, 1917–1919); Ruth N. Anshen, ed., *The Family: Its Function and Destiny* (New York: Harper, 1959); and Willystine Goodsell, *A History of the Family as a Social and Educational Institution* (New York: Macmillan, 1915).

7. Ariès, *op. cit.,* Part 3, "The Family."

8. See Talcott Parsons and Robert F. Bales, *Family, Socialization and Interaction Process* (Glencoe: Free Press, 1955).

9. William J. Goode, *World Revolution and Family Patterns* (New York: Free Press, 1963); and W. F. Ogburn and M. F. Nimkoff, *Technology and the Changing Family* (Boston: Houghton Mifflin, 1955). Also see Stern, *op. cit.;* see 3 above.

10. See M. F. Nimroff, *op. cit.;* Bernard Farber, ed., *Kinship and Family Organization* (New York: John Wiley, 1966); Norman W. Bell and Ezra F. Vogel, *A Modern Introduction to the Family* (Glencoe: Free Press, 1960); Dorothy Blitsten, *The World of the Family: A Comparative Study of Family Organizations in Their Social and Cultural Settings* (New York: Random House, 1963); David and Vera Mace, *Marriage: East and West* (New York: Doubleday, 1960); Stuart Queen, Robert W. Habenstein, and John B. Adams, *The Family in Various Cultures* (Philadelphia: J. B. Lippincott, 1961); and William N. Stephens, *The Family in Cross-cultural Perspective* (New York: Holt, Rinehart, and Winston, 1963).

11. Remy Cliquet, in *Comparative Studies in Society and History,* VIII, 4.

12. Ezra F. Vogel, "The Japanese Family," in Nimkoff, *op. cit.;* R. P. Dore, *City Life in Japan* (Los Angeles: University of California Press, 1958); and Richard K. Beardsley, "Cultural Anthropology: Prehistoric and Contemporary Aspects," in John W. Hall and Richard K. Beardsley, *Twelve Doors to Japan* (New York: McGraw-Hill, 1965).

13. Compare recent studies of the family in highly industrialized and urbanized countries such as the United States of America, England, Sweden, Germany, and France.

14. Kent Geiger, "The Soviet Family," in Nimkoff, *op. cit.;* Alva Myrdal, *Nation and Family: The Swedish Experiment in Democratic Family and Population Policy* (New York: Harper, 1941); U. S. Department of Health, Education and Welfare, Office of the Secretary, Washington, D. C. *Release* T 67, May 8, 1962; see also implications of *The Moynihan Report* and *The Politics of Controversy* by Lee Rainwater and William Yancey including the text of Daniel Patrick Moynihan, *The Negro Family: The Case for National Action* (Boston: The Massachusetts Institute of Technology Press, 1967).

15. Helmut Schelsky, *Wandel der deutschen Familie in der Gegenwart* (Dortmund: K. Specht, 1951).

16. Moynihan, *op. cit.*

17. Thomas Szasz, *Law, Liberty, and Psychiatry* (New York: Macmillan, 1963).

18. Compare Arnold Rose, ed., *The Institutions of Advanced Societies* (Minneapolis: University of Minnesota Press, 1958).

19. Various American community studies are concerned with the class perspective in family life. See, for instance, A. B. Hollingshead, *Elmtown's Youth* (New York: John Wiley, 1961); J. R. Seeley, R. A. Sim, and E. W. Loosley, *Crestwood Heights* (New York: Basic Books, 1956); Herbert J. Gans, *The Urban Villagers* (New York: Free Press, 1965). Comparable data for England are summarized in Josephine Klein, *Samples from English Cultures* (London: Routledge and Kegan Paul, 1965).

20. Dennis Wrong, "Trends in Class Fertility in Western Nations," in R. Bendix and S. M. Lipset, *Class, Status, and Power* (New York: Free Press, 1966), pp. 353–354.

21. A. C. Kinsey *et al., Sexual Behavior in the Human Male* (Philadelphia: Saunders, 1948); A. C. Kinsey *et al., Sexual Behavior in the Human Female* (Philadelphia: Saunders, 1953); Harold T. Christensen, "Cultural Relativism and Premarital Sex Norms," *American Sociological Review,* 24

(1960), 31–39; Gunnar Boalt, *Family and Marriage* (New York: David McKay, 1965); Hans Heinrich Muchow, "Sexualreife und Sozialstruktur der Jugend," *Erde*, 94 (Hamburg, 1959); Eustace Chesser, *The Sexual, Marital, and Family Relationships of the English Woman* (New York: Roy Publishers, 1957); and Lester David, "The Controversy over Swedish Morals," *Coronet*, 41 (December 1956), 126–132.

22. Martha White, "Social Class, Child Rearing Practices, and Child Behavior," *American Sociological Review*, 22 (December 1957), pp. 704–712; Hollingshead, *op. cit.*; Helmut Schelsky, *Wandel der deutschen Familie in der Gegenwart* (Dortmund: 1953) and Klein, *op. cit.*

23. Hollingshead, *op. cit.*; Gans, *op. cit.*; Seeley, *op. cit.*; and Martin Deutsch *et. al.*, *The Disadvantaged Child* (New York: Basic Books, 1967).

24. Geiger, "The Soviet Family," in Nimkoff, *op. cit.*

25. See P. Mercier, "Problems of Social Stratification in West Africa (1954)," in I. Wallerstein, *Social Change: The Colonial Situation* (New York: John Wiley, 1966); T. Hodgkin, "The African Middle Class," in Wallerstein, *op. cit.*; George Rosen, *Democracy and Economic Change in India* (Berkeley: University of California Press, 1966); Hans-Dieter Evers, *Kulturwandel in Ceylon* (Baden-Baden: Verlag August Lutzeyer, 1964). The peculiar situation of ethnic minorities and their place in the socialization processes is implied in the studies of W. F. Wertheim.

26. A comprehensive description and discussion of this modern phenomenon is in James S. Coleman's *The Adolescent Society* (New York: Free Press, 1961), p. 3 ff.

27. See the studies of Kinsey *et al.*, *op. cit.*

28. See articles on the "youth market" by Dwight MacDonald, "A Caste, A Culture, A Market," in *The New Yorker Magazine*, November 22, November 29, 1958.

29. See David Riesman, *The Lonely Crowd* (New Haven: Yale University Press, 1950); and Coleman, *op. cit.*

30. Robert K. Merton, *Sociological Theory and Social Structure* (Glencoe: Free Press, 1957).

31. See Seeley, *op. cit.*; and James B. Conant, *Slums and Suburbs* (New York: McGraw-Hill, 1961); John Hersey, *The Child Buyer* (New York: Knopf, 1960); and Hillel Black, *The Truth about College Entrance Exams and Other Standardized Tests* (New York: Hart, 1963).

32. The census data of such diverse countries as Germany, Japan, France, and the United States over the last fifteen years show a clear pattern of a rising suicide rate among young people.

33. Compare, for instance, Ernest Smith, *American Youth Culture* (New York: Free Press, 1962); Ira L. Reiss, *Premarital Sexual Standards in America* (New York: Free Press, 1960); Gerald Brenan, "Courtship in Granada," *Atlantic* (August 1957), pp. 33–38; U. Undeutsch, "Das Verhaeltnis von koerperlicher und seelischer Entwicklung," in L. Friedeburg, ed., *Jugend in der modernen Gesellschaft* (Koeln, Kiepenheuer, and Witsch, 1965); E. H. Erikson, *Childhood and Society* (New York: Norton, 1951); and E. H. Erikson, ed., *The Challenge of Youth* (New York: Doubleday, 1963).

34. Coleman, *op. cit.*; see 26 above.

35. A good general analysis of the rising delinquency rates in eighteenth century European and Asian countries, as well as the United States and Israel, can be found in Joachim Helmmer, *Jugendkriminalitaet in unserer Zeit* (Frankfurt: Fischer, 1966).

36. J. L. Simmons and Barry Winograd, *It's Happening: A Portrait of*

the Youth Scene Today (Santa Barbara: Marc-Laird Publication, 1966); and the articles on the Provo in *Delta, A Review of Arts, Life, and Thought in the Netherlands,* 10, 3 (Autumn 1967).

37. See *Delta, op. cit.* Compare special article on student movements in Germany in *Der Spiegel,* 21 (24 Oktober 1967). See also reports on "Hooliganism in the U. S. S. R." in daily newspapers.

38. See Darcy Ribeiro, "Universities and Social Development," and Aldo Solari, "Secondary Education and the Development of Elites," in S. M. Lipset and A. Solari, *Elites in Latin America* (New York: Oxford University Press, 1967); United Nations Children's Fund, *Children and Youth in National Development in Latin America,* Report of Conference held in Santiago, Chile, 28 November–11 December 1965. Also see Helen Kitchen, ed., *The Educated African* (New York: Praeger, 1962).

PART II

Social Change—
Ideas and Personality

[7] Ideas and Personality— Theoretical Considerations

In the preceding chapters we have discussed various institutional structures in relation to social change in different contemporary societies. This is clearly the natural way for the sociologist to proceed; by the very nature of his intellectual focus, social structures and social institutions will be his favorite "diet," indeed will be that slice of the science pudding that can most readily and unambiguously be called "sociological." In the following chapters, however, we will focus our attention on the role of ideas and the forms of personality in the process of social change in different societies. This we will do despite the artificial lines dividing scientific disciplines. Our concerns will take us particularly into areas of investigation commonly assigned to the sociology of knowledge and to social psychology. It will be important, though, to keep in mind the structural and institutional background in all these considerations.

Why is this shift of attention necessary in terms of the overall purpose of this book? It is because people not only live in institutional structures, they also perceive these structures, reflect about them, evaluate them, and try to understand their own location in them. Their definitions of the situation become a social reality that has, in turn, its own effects on the institutions concerned. More-over, people not only have thoughts and ideas; they also have per-sonalities. They fear, admire, recoil, hope, and even dream in ways that are profoundly related to their social context. For these reasons social change not only occurs on the structural level, but it also takes its toll on people's thoughts, norms, aspirations, and emotions. The sociological observer must confront change on all these levels, as a totality that extends even to the innermost core of human personality.

While the relation between institutions and human ideas and personality may sound, as we have presented it, only theoretical, it is part of the concrete experience of people involved in situations of rapid social change, as are American businessmen and govern-ment officials who work in underdeveloped countries. An Ameri-can manager in, say, Saudi Arabia will quickly discover the signif-icance of our approach when he tries to cope with an indigenous labor force.[1] His problem will be not only that his Arab work-ers are unskilled in the performance of their jobs, nor even that they are at first unfamiliar with such nonvocational skills of West-ern civilization as opening a faucet or turning a doorknob but even more fundamentally that these people are organized inside themselves in a way that is not at all conducive to efficient modern industry. Their sense of time and space is different. They do not live by the precise time units of the clock, and thus are not punc-tual in their work habits. They also resist the precise organization of space necessary for modern industrial work, and so will wander on and off the areas assigned to them. Their imaginations are not geared to the requirements of productivity, neither are their aspi-rations and anxieties. For very practical reasons, therefore, Amer-ican management in countries such as Saudi Arabia will have to be interested in the inducement of change not only on economic and technological levels but also on the levels of thought and per-sonality. The sociologist will pursue this interest in a more sys-tematic and less manipulative study.

There are alternative approaches to understanding the relation-ship between social change and human ideas. At one extreme we find theories that conceive of ideas as being nothing but the ex-pression of structural processes, that is, fundamentally as products or "dependent variables" of the hard, material aspects of social life. This is the viewpoint of what is called "vulgar Marxism," [2] which is a simplified, dogmatic adaptation of Marx's ideas to the requirements of Soviet ideology. From this viewpoint, Marx's notions of the "substructure" and "superstructure" are diminished to the level of socioeconomic determinism. The substructure is the economic level of society and the institutions directly connected with it (such as the class system, as Marx saw it); the superstructure is the level of culture and ideas: vulgar Marxism states that the former directly produces the latter, in a simple cause-effect relation. This is what is meant by "Der Mensch ist was er isst," or "Man is what he eats." In other words, all that humans feel, think, and aspire to is directly produced by their economic circumstances. From this viewpoint ideas are mere epiphenomena, with no change-inducing power or even autonomy of their own: merely passive reflectors of the real (that is, structural) processes that underlie them. The same perspective obtains in what we might call "vulgar functionalism" in contemporary American sociology.[3] Here the sophisticated ideas of theoretical functionalism, made by such sociologists as Talcott Parsons and Robert Merton, are trivialized by dogmatic sociologists who are trying to make specific research applications. They, too, act as though ideas simply mirror structures; it is their work, incidentally, that has created the image of sociologists as intellectual simplifiers.

At the other extreme are those theories that conceive of change as the product of the movement of ideas. The theoretical work of Arnold Toynbee and Pitirim Sorokin tend in this direction.[4] Again, however, their sophisticated viewpoint is often given less articulate forms, though less by social scientists than, understandably, by those engaged in the humanities. To such thinkers, societies are seen as essentially the realization of certain ideas, which operate as the motor forces of history. As ideas develop and change, so do the social structures that are founded on them.

We would contend that neither the materialism of the former viewpoint nor the idealism of the latter does justice to sociohistorical reality. The sociological observer is better advised to recognize that the structural and the ideational levels of society stand in a reciprocal relationship (or, if one prefers, a dialectical relationship) with each other. Social structure and social change do not relate to ideas and culture in an undirectional way. At any particular instant in the ongoing stream of sociohistorical change, one or the other level may be considered of causal primacy.

Max Weber conceptualized this balanced position in his notion of "elective affinity," which affirms the principle of the autonomy of both the social-structure and ideational processes, yet says that, under certain social conditions, social groups and ideas "seek each other out," as it were.[5] Then social groups become carriers of ideas and ways of thinking. For example, Weber's sociology of religion stresses that it is the lower-middle stratum of society that is most apt to become the carrier of radical doctrines of salvation and that, generally, leans toward religious innovation. This is true because their social position predisposes them to look for this type of religious solution. It does *not* mean that the religious ideas in question are simply the outgrowths of this social position; indeed, they may have originated in quite different social circumstances. It also does *not* mean that the religious ideas created the social position, with its special interests and problems. Rather, there is a coincidence, a correlation, between idea and interest, between religious constellation and social group. Similar analyses abound throughout Weber's work, as in the work of Vilfredo Pareto, who discusses, for instance, the particular value orientations that are found in various types of political elites.[6]

We shall have occasion for this kind of analysis throughout the chapters to come, but one example will suffice for the moment. In recent years, groups of alienated youth in America have shown a predilection for Asian religious ideas. During the "best" period, the alienated subcultures took to Zen Buddhism; later, with the advent of the hippies, attention turned to Hindu rather than Buddhist themes. It would be patently foolish to understand these Asian religious ideas as products of the American situation; as a matter of historical fact, they have been propagated in America by various missionaries for at least a half-century, that is, long before they attracted young refugees from respectable middle-class secularism. On the other hand, it would be equally erroneous to understand American youth culture, and its lurid Haight-Ashbury avatars, as the product of Oriental evangelism. The American youth subculture antedates this dalliance with Asian religions. Its origins are, as we have seen in Chapter 6, in specific features of the contemporary social structure. What we have, then, is a clear case of elective affinity, of a set of ideas and a particular social group "seeking each other out" in a given situation. This linkage having once been established, however, it may well be that the group will now become a carrier in the Weberian sense, diffusing these ideas over much broader sectors of American society and thus itself becoming an agency for social change.

As there were various ways of grasping the relationship between social structures and ideas, so in the matter of social change and personality there are a variety of approaches. Again we may distinguish two extremes and a more satisfactory middle position. At one extreme there are theories that conceive of "human nature" as a constant, more or less unchanging *datum,* which persists intact through all sociohistorical changes. This view assumes there are a certain number of human "needs," which different societies satisfy or frustrate in varying degrees. One can then nicely develop something like a psychopathology of societies, distinguishing healthy societies that satisfy human nature from sick (or pathogenic) societies that frustrate it and us, and thus one has a purportedly scientific method of grading the mental health of historical phenomena. This type of theory is particularly liked by (or, if one prefers, has an elective affinity with) conservative temperaments. For, if human nature remains constant, and *plus ça change, plus ça reste la même chose,* then proposals for radical change are, by definition, futile.

Such a notion existed as long ago as Thucydides. Freud clearly tends toward this viewpoint, and the neo-Freudian attempts to modify his theories in the light of historical social factors have not overcome this tendency.[7] Bronislaw Malinowski, however, successfully adapted this viewpoint to the social sciences, positing an inventory of human needs to which different societies relate in more or less satisfactory ways.[8] British social anthropology was influenced by Malinowski and his followers, and in turn passed his position along to the functionalist theorists of American sociology. The principal spokesman for this viewpoint in sociological theory is Pareto.[9] For him, all of society, and *ipso facto* all of history, are founded on a limited set of psychological patterns or predispositions, called "residues." Social change consists of varying combinations of these underlying forms, while they themselves remain unchanged. Logically, then, social change moves in great cycles— sooner or later everything repeats itself. A similar viewpoint is often, and always with a conservative animus, expressed in the language of politics and in the wisdom of the man-in-the-street. The use of the idea of "human nature" is a rather good sign of such, for example, when a businessman tells us that it is "against human nature" to limit the acquisitive urge, or when a labor leader says that corruption is a "natural" fact of life.

At the other extreme are the theories asserting that personality

Identity and the Social Structure

As we pointed out, the relationship between ideas, personality, and the social structure has been the domain of the sociology of knowledge and social psychology. The following, from Peter Berger's "Identity as a Problem in the Sociology of Knowledge," may provide a basis for a theoretical discussion of the relationship among these phenomena.

> Every society contains a repertoire of identities that is part of the "objective knowledge" of its members. It is "known" as a matter "of course" that there are men and women, that they have such-and-such psychological traits and that they will have such-and-such psychological reactions in typical circumstances. As the individual is socialized, these identities are "internalized." They are then not only taken for granted as constituents of an objective reality "out there" but as inevitable structures of the individual's own consciousness. The objective reality, as defined by society, is subjectively appropriated. In other words, socialization brings about symmetry between objective and subjective reality, objective and subjective identity.
>
> This dialectic between social structure and psychological reality may be called the fundamental proposition of any social psychology in the Meadian tradition. Society not only defines but creates psychological reality. The individual *realizes* himself in society—that is, he recognizes his identity in socially defined terms and these definitions *become reality* as he lives in society.
>
> The sociology of knowledge is concerned with a related but broader dialectic—that between social structure and the "worlds" in which individuals live, that is, the comprehensive organizations of reality within which individual experience can be meaningfully interpreted. Every society is a world-building enterprise. Out of the near-infinite variety of individual symbolizations of experience, society constructs a universe of discourse that comprehends and objectivates them. Individual experience can then be understood as taking place in an intelligible world that is inhabited also by others and about which it is possible to communicate with others. Individual meanings are objectivated so that they are accessible to everyone who coinhabits the world in question. Indeed, this world is apprehended as "objective reality," that is, as reality that is shared with others and that exists irrespective of the individual's own preferences in the matter. The socially available definitions of such a world are thus taken to be "knowledge" about it and are continu-

ously verified for the individual by social situations in which this "knowledge" is taken for granted. The socially constructed world becomes the world *tout court*—the only real world, typically the only world that one can seriously conceive of. The individual is thus freed of the necessity of reflecting anew about the meaning of each step in his unfolding experience. He can simply refer to "common sense" for such interpretation, at least for the bulk of his biographical experience.

It is important to stress that the social construction of reality takes place on both the pretheoretical and the theoretical levels of consciousness, and that, therefore, the sociology of knowledge must concern itself with both. Probably because of the German intellectual situation in which the sociology of knowledge was first developed, it has hitherto interested itself predominantly in the theoretical side of the phenomenon—the problem of the relationship of society and "ideas." This is certainly an important problem. But only a very few people are worried over "ideas," while everyone lives in some sort of world. There is thus a sociological dimension to the human activity of world-building in its totality, not only in that segment of it in which intellectuals manufacture theories, systems of thought and *Weltanschauungen*.

The relationship between a society and its world is a dialectic one, because, once more, it can not be adequately understood in terms of a one-sided causation. The world, though socially constructed, is not a mere passive reflection of the social structures within which it arose. In becoming "objective reality" for its inhabitants it attains not only a certain autonomy with respect to the "underlying" society but even the power to act back upon the latter. Men invent a language and then find that its logic imposes itself upon them. And men concoct theories, even theories that may start out as nothing but blatant explications of social interests, and then discover that these theories themselves become agencies of social change. It may be seen, then, that there is a theoretically significant similarity between the dialectics of social psychology and of the sociology of knowledge, the dialectic through which society generates psychological reality and the dialectic through which it engages in world-building. Both dialectics concern the relationship between objective and subjective realities, or more precisely, between socially objectivated reality and its subjective appropriation. In both instances, the individual internalizes facticities that appear to him as given outside himself and, having internalized them to become given contents of his own consciousness, externalizes them again as he continues to live and act in society.

These considerations, especially in the compressed form in which they have had to be presented here, may at first seem to be excessively abstract. Yet, if one asks about the combined significance of these root perspectives of social psychology and the sociology of knowledge for the sociological understanding of identity, one may answer in a rather simple statement: Identity, with its appropriate attachments of psychological reality, is always identity within a specific, socially constructed world. Or, as seen from the viewpoint of the individual: One identifies oneself, as one is identified by others, by being located in a common world.

Source: Peter Berger, "Identity as a Problem in the Sociology of Knowledge," Reprinted by permission from the *European Journal of Sociology*, 7 (1966), pp. 105–115.

is a social product, pure and simple. Social structures are understood to produce men on some sort of psychological assembly line, constructing personalities to meet society's requirements. This viewpoint is characteristic of both vulgar Marxism and vulgar functionalism, expressing what Dennis Wrong, the sociologist, has aptly called an "oversocialized view of man." [10] A grotesque example of this was in the Stalinist era that produced Lysenko, the geneticist. His absurd distortions of the facts of genetics were motivated by his social and ideological interest in proving that new social forms would produce a new type of man; Lysenko "proved" that socially induced changes could run so deep as to be transmitted genetically. [11] This type of theory is probably less common in America, but it lurks in the background of some sociological teaching and research, especially that which is geared to the requirements of personnel management that seeks to produce people who can do "this and that."

Once more we shall contend that neither extreme is theoretically or empirically satisfactory, but that a middle, dialectic position adequately will meet our need for sociological understanding. Such a perspective is intrinsic to the tradition in American social psychology that derives from George Herbert Mead, and which has proved useful in a wide range of applications. [12] From this perspective society and personality are seen as complementary, interacting entities. On the one hand, society socializes or defines personality: personality types thus vary with social structures and change as these structures change. On the other hand, psychobiological factors impose limits on socialization's influence. Also, the characteristics of a personality type, both of a group and an individual, are capable of reacting against and modifying social structures. It should be noted that recent work in human biology, particularly that associated with the so-called ethological school of Konrad Lorenz, suggests that congenital, instinctual determinants of human conduct may limit society's impact more than had heretofore been assumed by social scientists.[13]

Needless to say, this theoretical outline has been sketchy, but it will serve to place a broadened context of interpretation around the following description of several facets of modernization. Our focus is rationalization, and the type of rationalized ideation and sense of selfhood that exists today, in our rationalized Western society.

The modernization of ideas involves certain peculiarly Western developments that Weber has analyzed exhaustively, especially in his work on the sociology of religion.[14] The crucial concept in Weber's analysis is "disenchantment of the world." Although Weber was concerned primarily with the paradoxical role of Protestantism in this process, as it expressed forces whose origin was in the most ancient residue of Old Testament religion, and although other scholars argue that Weber mistakenly traced the historical chain of causes to the Reformation rather than to, say, the consequences of the Renaissance, nevertheless "disenchantment of the world" is a wonderfully apt way of describing the spirit of modernity. This modern spirit has, speaking negatively, moved away from the luminous backdrop of most previous human history: to a great degree the gods have fled the modern world, which is what we mean by secularization.

Secularization, speaking positively, is the spirit of modernity: this-worldly, historistic, and activistic. As attention is turned away from the "other worlds" of the sacred and the supernatural, it is turned toward the realities of the empirical universe. Modern science and technology are, of course, the most impressive manifestations of this-worldliness (though it is not altogether clear to what extent they are the *causes* or the *effects* of this attitude). History has become the frame of reference for all human conduct. To an unparalleled degree, categories such as evolution, development, and progress have become guideposts for both collective and individual endeavors. Our view of the world has become thoroughly dynamic: the spirit of modernity extols the virtues of activity and achievement, and the world is seen as an immense agglomeration of tasks. History and biography are the records of tasks being accomplished or at least attacked. As Weber saw clearly, this rapid expansion of rationality has brought about what is probably the era of the most revolutionary changes in human history.

The modernization of personality entails similarly far-reaching transformations, which are similarly rooted in structural changes. On the most general level, this change is from the *Gemeinschaft* to the *Gesellschaft* structure.[15] The former refers to groupings that are totally unified and are held together by one central agency of social control; within them the individual has a clear sense of belonging. In *Gesellschaft* groupings, on the other hand, social relations are limited to specific and usually utilitarian goals; different agencies control the numerous sectors of social life; and the individual does not feel he belongs, or owes loyalty to, his groups. A comparison of a peasant community and a modern city will demarcate the difference. In modern societies both types of social groupings coexist: thus the modern business enterprise is of the *Gesellschaft* type, but the modern family continues to be a *Gemeinschaft* grouping. What distinguishes modern society is not a complete disappearance of *Gemeinschaft* groups, though it is true that no *Gemeinschaft* exists on the level of the total social context within which the individual lives, as it once did. What is peculiarly modern is that life is divided between *Gesellschaft* and *Gemeinschaft* relations, and that the overall society can therefore only be organized along *Gesellschaft* lines.

This is of far-reaching psychological consequence. Modern man lives in widely discrepant social milieus, and only in a few of these does he have human relationships that are of great importance to him, that are with the kind of people George Herbert Mead called "significant others"; most of his relationships are limited, pragmatic, and of low emotional intensity. In a peasant community, on the other hand, the individual is highly interested in almost everyone he contacts in the community: this does not at all mean that he *likes* everyone, which he rarely does, but everyone is "significant" to his own life. People, in other words, live with and experience each other as totalities. In a modern city, however, the individual relates only to a few people in this way. Most of the people he has to deal with (at work, while traveling, in his neighborhood, even in his leisure-time activities), he is interested in to only a very limited degree. Of course, in view of the large number of people an individual must, willy-nilly, cope with every day, anything else would be psychologically intolerable. In sociological

Some Essential Features of a Modern Industrial Society

F. X. Sutton describes some of the general sociological features of modern industrial society.

As essential sociological features of a modern industrial society I suggest the following:

1. Predominance of universalistic, specific, and achievement norms.
2. High degree of social mobility (in a general, not necessarily "vertical," sense).
3. Well-developed occupational system, insulated from other social structures.
4. "Egalitarian" class system based on generalized patterns of occupational achievement.
5. Prevalence of "associations," that is, functionally specific, nonascriptive structures.

I trust that a few comments will serve to illuminate this list and make the necessary explanations of technical terms. The prevalence of universalistic and achievement norms implies a marked restriction of the significance of kinship systems. These norms also act as a kind of solvent to barriers among local, ethnic, and other groups. Spatial mobility is facilitated and stimulated by legitimate access to different possible statuses. A highly differentiated occupational system is governed by universalistic and achievement norms. Holding some sort of occupational role becomes a normal expectation for adult men and for those women for whom kinship duties do not take precedence. This is one sense in which the occupational system becomes generalized in the society. Another is that occupational roles have the common features of 1) demanding relatively continuous application; 2) being the principal "instrumental role" activity of the incumbent; 3) money remuneration, which in the typical case is the principal source of income of the jobholder. These common features and the criteria that make any qualified person the potential incumbent of any occupational role serve to produce an effective generalization.

Source: F. X. Sutton, "Analyzing Social Systems," in *Comparative Studies in Society and History*, 2, no. 1 (New York: Cambridge University Press, 1959).

terms, this means that social life entails a high degree of role differentiation. The individual must play highly divergent roles in
various social situations; and this inevitably introduces differentiation into his personality. He "is" as well as "acts" a different
"person" from moment to moment. Personality is a thing variegated, flexible, and (of utmost importance) prone to change.

The differentiating process begins quite early in life, certainly
no later than the child's first entrance into the educational system.
Indeed, it occurs even on the nursery school level, which is a time
when even the basic personality is still in the process of formation. Many individuals, from diverse social groups, join in the
business of socializing the child, whereas once a single set of parents did it all. Sometimes, to be sure, this pluralistic socialization
presents the child with problems and conflicts, but it teaches the
child from an early age that he can and perhaps must be a different person as his situation, his environment changes. And, of
course, unless he learns this, his chance of getting ahead in modern society suffers greatly.

Modern society has been described as "atomizing" in its psychological effect, in that the individual no longer feels totally
embedded in his social group. In other words, in modern society
"individualism" is not only a value but a psychological fact. Personality, the self, becomes "open" in a new way—open to different people and situations, and open to change. Personality is less
"profiled" than it was in previous periods of history. For better or
for worse, a peasant *was* a peasant, an aristocrat *was* an aristocrat,
and so on. Very few people today *are,* in quite the same way, the
roles that they play: they are, indeed, this or that in society, but
they could become something else in the future, and even in the
present their particular roles rarely exhaust what they consider
themselves to be. To be a knight, totally and permanently, was a
matter of ultimate honor. To be a college professor with such an
ultimate commitment would only be ridiculous.

Furthermore, modern personality is highly reflective. A contemporary sociologist, Helmut Schelsky, has originated the term "permanent reflectiveness" for this phenomenon: modern men are
compelled to reflect continuously about their social interaction because it takes place in a context of extreme role differentiation.[16]
In concrete terms, one must constantly be on the alert to make
sure that one is always acting in harmony with the social signals
that are forever changing. Thus a very high level of deliberate

awareness, of being always "with it," is required by modern social life. And this means that a high degree of empathy with other people is necessary, for they *are* the environmental signals one must respond to.[17] In other words, one must be able to put oneself imaginatively in the place of many different people from diverse social milieus. Inevitably, this entails a decrease in stability, both in terms of values and beliefs, and in terms of personality. It is this new sensitivity to others and to the changing demands of social situations that David Riesman has aptly called "other-direction." [18] Riesman contrasts the contemporary, other-directed character with an older type he calls the "inner-directed character." The latter had, built into his personality, something like an inner compass that told him what to do; contemporary man has something like a radar system that is sensitively geared to read the social expectations others hold of him and to direct him accordingly.

A consequence of such a psyche is a permanent crisis.[19] Premodern man, for better or for worse, *was* what he was supposed to be and he knew it. Everyone in the *Gemeinschaft* around him confirmed his identity, which therefore was relatively unambiguous and stable. Such identity-confirmation no longer exists to anything like the same degree. Since different identities are recognized in their appropriate contexts, the individual's image of himself becomes ambiguous, tenuous, shifting. He simply can no longer be sure just who he really is. Regardless whether we think this to be good or bad, desirable or undesirable, it must be understood if we are to understand the psychological dynamics of modern society.

Modernization, then, is comprised not only of fundamental structural and ideational transformations, but also of a psychological revolution.[20] While fine nuances and applications of this revolution are not generally understood by those who have experienced it, nevertheless it is manifested in their radical awareness of the importance of socialization. The socialization of the individual into a modern psychological type (in addition, of course, to his acquiring modern skills and modern ideas) is understood as a task of primary importance. A crucial feature of this is to acquire the capacity to change, to be able to anticipate becoming someone other than one is at the moment, which Robert Merton has called "anticipatory socialization." [21] Appropriate socialization is a prerequisite not only of social mobility, but of modern social life itself.

These remarks should suffice to orient us for the chapters that

Sources of Identity Problems

Orrin E. Klapp observes that in the last fifty years there has been a curious shift of concern from "making one's way" to "finding oneself," that is, finding one's identity. His *Collective Search for Identity* is based on the idea "that there is a disturbance of symbolic balance—a loss of nondiscursive symbolism—behind the identity problem of modern times," and takes its theoretical orientation from George Mead. In the following paragraphs, some of the underlying sources of identity formation of modern man are described.

The furious pursuit of status and ego symbols, past a certain point, becomes a vicious circle. It is now true, in our land of ambiguous identity, that anyone may adopt almost any status symbol which he can afford. He may have his Cadillac, the new look of fashion, the fashionable address, the fancy letterhead. He announces and maintains any identity that he can get away with. But to consider the ultimate effect of free adoption of symbols on identity itself, we might imagine a play in which the actors were free to costume themselves as they pleased. Would it not soon become impossible to tell who was really who? Would not the action become, instead of a meaningful play, a confusing masquerade? The changeability of symbols makes life like a masquerade.

Another detrimental [effect] . . . of identity mobility in a pluralistic setting is inconsistency and unreliability of signals. From the conflict of subcultures, confusion of styles, rapidity of changes, diversity of viewpoints, shifting of positions, and difficulty of sorting out poses, a person has a hard time feeling he is right—whether he follows or rejects a certain position. He has trouble, first, in deciding which persons, styles, and authorities are right and true among the poses, pretexts, and rationalizations of those playing "games." Secondly, when he takes a position, he doesn't know whether the expressions of opinion and concern of others are sincere, so he doesn't know whether he will be really supported or whether he is "going out on a limb." An undetermined number of people with whom he deals in a mobile society are "phonies" (inauthentic role-players)—he cannot be sure which [people]—and their responses do not help him become authentic by sincere revelation or, ordinarily, by challenging encounter.

Source: Orrin E. Klapp, *Collective Search for Identity* (New York: Holt, Rinehart, and Winston, 1969), pp. 31–32.

follow. We should add that there is much more authoritative data on comparative institutions than on comparative ideation and personality (with the exception of anthropological data on primitive societies, which is of minimal interest to us here). This means that, even less than in Part I, we can make no claim to anything like "full coverage." We can, however, in the following chapters, deal with a number of key areas in which the changes outlined above are apparent.

NOTES

1. James Sidney Slotkin, *From Field to Factory: New Industrial Employees* (New York: Free Press, 1960).
2. The so-called vulgar Marxistic perspective can be found in the works of Lenin, Trotsky, Svetlov, and many others.
3. We do not mean to describe any particular author in this way. Rather, we refer to the manner in which "functionalism" is loosely used in American society generally, especially in college courses.
4. Arnold Toynbee, *A Study of History,* 6 vols. (London: Oxford University Press, 1934–1939); and Pitirim A. Sorokin, *Social and Cultural Dynamics,* 4 vols. (New York: Bedminister Press, 1962).
5. The term "elective affinity" is taken from Max Weber, *Gesammelte Aufsaetze zur Religionssoziologie,* Tuebingen, 1, (1920), p. 83, pp. 257 seq.; see also Max Scheler, *Die Wissensformen und die Gesellschaft* (Halle, 1926), p. 127. The classical exposition of the concept is on pp. 30 seq.
6. Pareto's "fox" elite is composed of individuals who resort to their wits, are quick in recognizing new situations, cunning in exploiting their advantage, open to new insights. The contrasting type of elite, the "lions," is composed of individuals who excel in personal courage, traditional values, religiosity in the widest sense. They are averse to innovation and are more likely to use force than cunning to remain in power. Cf. Vilfredo Pareto, *Mind and Society,* 4 vols. (New York: Harcourt, Brace, 1935). The fourth volume is concerned mainly with the interaction between these two types of elites, who are sharply distinguished from each other by their values.
7. See especially the various publications of Erich Fromm and Karen Horney, especially Fromm, *Escape from Freedom* (New York: Farrar and Rinehart, 1941), Fromm, *Man for Himself* (New York: Farrar and Rinehart, 1947), and Horney, *The Neurotic Personality of Our Time* (New York: Norton, 1938).
8. Bronislaw Malinowski, *A Scientific Theory of Culture* (Chapel Hill: University of North Carolina Press, 1944).
9. Pareto, *op. cit.*
10. Dennis Wrong, "The Oversocialized Conception of Man in Modern Sociology," *American Sociological Review,* 26 (April 1961), pp. 187–193.
11. A short summary of the theory of Lysenko and the dispute over it can be found in George Fischer, ed., *Science and Ideology in Soviet Society* (New York: Atherton Press, 1967), pp. 100 ff.

12. George Herbert Mead, *On Social Psychology,* Anselm Strauss, ed., (Chicago: University of Chicago Press, 1956); A. L. Strauss *et al.,* "The Hospital and Its Negotiated Order," in E. Freidson, ed., *The Hospital in Modern Society* (New York: Free Press, 1963); Herbert Blumer, "Society as Symbolic Interaction," in A. Rose, ed., *Human Behavior and Social Processes* (Boston: Houghton Mifflin, 1962); Howard S. Becker, *Outsiders* (New York: Free Press, 1963); and Fred Davis, *Passage through Crisis* (New York: Bobbs-Merrill, 1963).

13. Konrad Lorenz, *Das sogenannte Boese* (Wien: Vorotha-Schoele, 1963).

14. Max Weber, *The Protestant Ethic* (New York: Scribner, 1930), pp. 13–36, 76–78, 182–183, and *The Religion of China* (Glencoe: Free Press, 1951), p. 237, also Chapter 3, Part D.

15. The dichotomy between *Gemeinschaft* and *Gesellschaft* has been detailed by Ferdinand Toennies, *Community and Society* (Ann Arbor: University of Michigan Press, 1957).

16. Helmut Schelsky, "Ist die Dauerreflexion institutionalisierbar?" *Zeitschrift fuer evangelische Ethik,* 4 (1957), pp. 153 ff.

17. The concept of "empathy" has been applied very successfully to sociological inquiry by D. Lerner, *The Passing of Traditional Society* (Glencoe: Free Press, 1958).

18. Developed by David Riesman, *The Lonely Crowd* (New Haven: Yale University Press, 1950).

19. See the various essays in Maurice Stein, Arthur Vidich, and David M. White, eds., *Identity and Anxiety* (New York: Free Press, 1960).

20. This point has been well developed by Lerner, *op. cit.*

21. Robert K. Merton, *Social Theory and Social Structure* (Glencoe: Free Press, 1949), pp. 265 ff.

[8] Revolutionary Ideas

IT is a commonplace observation that today's world is full of revolutionary ideas. And the two most visible ideas (or, more accurately, ideational complexes) are nationalism and communism, as a glance at the morning newspaper will show. Both nationalism and communism are vitally involved in the revolutionary transformations now taking place in many parts of the world. Obviously, it is not possible here to undertake a detailed historical analysis of two such complex phenomena. What we will attempt to do, however, is to show how both nationalism and communism relate to the process of modernization, which has been one of our focal themes. We will discuss nationalism first, as it is the historically older movement.

Nationalism

In today's world nationalism obtrudes most sharply on our awareness in the proliferation of new nations. To the casual observer of the so-called third world it may sometimes seem that a new nation emerges practically every month: maps quickly become obsolete; the number of flags in front of the United Nations Secretariat in New York grows ever larger; stamp collectors have their heyday. The maps, the flags, and the postage stamps, of course, all mark the juridical fact of the multiplication of sovereignties. Yet beyond the domain of international law and politics there is something else in the contemporary world; something of immense power—

the idea of nationalism. It is this idea and its social implications, rather than its relationship to legal and political institutions, that is of interest to us here.

What is a nation? For the sociologist an answer that refers merely to the juridical sphere is not satisfactory, as sociological questions generally cannot be adequately answered in terms of the "official" definitions of social reality. A definition by Stanislav Andreski is adequate for our purposes: "A nation is a population located within a certain territory, characterized by some features of culture which distinguish it from similar populations, and whose members conceive of themselves as forming a community which aspires to political unity and independence (in the sense of not being governed by outsiders)." [1]

The first elements of this definition, the demographic and the territorial ones, are clear and objective: either there is or is not a certain population in a certain territory. The further elements of the definition, however, introduce a more difficult, a subjective dimension. How is one to decide objectively whether a particular culture is sufficiently different from another one to merit the designation "national," and thus to serve as the foundation for political sovereignty? There are significant differences between the cultures of New York and Boston—yet New Yorkers and Bostonians (despite the fact that both can objectively be described as populations inhabiting certain territories) regard themselves as belonging to the *same* American nation, and they would conceive of anyone calling them separate nations as a crackpot, at least. On the other hand, there are people with almost identical cultures living on opposite sides of the Rhine, and, with few exceptions, those on one side regard themselves as belonging to the German nation and those on the other to the Swiss nation. A similar phenomenon occurs along the long border that divides the United States from English-speaking Canada. Clearly, objective criteria do not suffice here; it is the subjective notions of the populations in question that are decisive. In other words, nationality is a matter of what Émile Durkheim called "collective consciousness," that is, of the ideas that a group of people hold in common. [2]

Nationality, it appears, is a matter of consent. It is by consent that German-speaking people in Basel and French-speaking ones in Geneva regard themselves as members of the same Swiss nation. It is by consent that French-speaking people in Geneva and French-speaking people in Grenoble do *not* regard themselves as belonging to the same nationality. Implicit in the nature of consent is the possibility of change. Sometime, back in history, the idea of the Swiss nation was realized—if you like, invented. In principle, it is possible that the idea may lose its power—may, if you like, be "dis-invented." Indeed, something like this may be happening today in Belgium and in Canada. The idea of a united Belgian nation has become strained by a conflict between the French- and Flemish-speaking populations within the political territory of Belgium, just as the rise of separatist nationalism in French-speaking Quebec is threatening the idea of Canada, a nation that unites its French- and English-speaking people within a geographic territory. Of course, this consensual, subjective dimension of nationality is particularly obvious in the case of very recent nations, such as those just now emerging in Africa. It seems that there is something patently "artificial" about the use of ideas of nationalism and nationality in territories such as, say, Tanzania, Nigeria, or other emerging African states. It is important to understand, however, that the principle of Tanzanian nationalism is no more artificial than that of Swiss nationalism—the crucial difference is, quite simply, that Switzerland has had a much longer history, and her people have had a longer time to become habituated to the idea of being Swiss.

Nationalism, then, is a matter of a large number of people believing that they hold certain things in common: things which, as Andreski's definition of a nation suggests, lead them jointly to aspire toward political unity and independence. This purposive, activistic impulse lasts as long as the idea of their nationalism continues to be capable of inspiring them, and even after their political sovereignty as a nation has been achieved. Compared with prenationalistic attitudes, therefore, nationalism favors social change and, in consequence, accelerates it. Also, nationalism serves to weld together previously heterogeneous populations, enabling them to share a sense of belonging. To accomplish this, there must be powerful symbols capable of uniting the people in purposive action. Very often these are symbols of antagonism, because people who act against a common enemy often thereby come to accept their national oneness. These various elements of nationalism—its activism, its unifying function, and its propensity for antagonistic symbols—are of great importance in relationship to modernization. Before we examine this, however, we must look briefly at the historical roots of nationalism.

HISTORY OF NATIONALISM

Nationalism is a modern phenomenon and, in its origins, a peculiarly Western one.[3] It developed in Europe not much before 1800; during the French Revolution was the first time that people conceived of a "nation" in the modern sense, as opposed to the older sense that meant little more than a geographical or linguistic grouping. In the wake of Napoleon's conquests, the idea of nationalism became a potent force throughout Europe. The imperial title assumed by Napoleon nicely expresses the change in conception: he called himself *not* "Emperor of France" (as his predecessors had been "Kings of France"), but "Emperor of the French." In other words, political sovereignty was no longer to be rooted as a static, inheritable property, a dynastic territory, but was to spring from a dynamic organization of the people that constituted the nation. Tolstoy, in *War and Peace,* lucidly conveys a sense of the rapid spread and immense attractiveness of this idea during the Napoleonic period.

The reasons why nationalism arose so late in the historical development of European culture are, of course, forbiddingly complex. Nevertheless, although some of them are beyond our ken here, we can take note at least of the specific sociological conditions that had to be fulfilled for nationalism to emerge. The primary requisite is the existence of social structures that enable loyalties to *transcend* the loyalties to local community, region, or clan. That is, highly abstract, generalized identifications of people are required. The contrast with European feudalism in this respect is very clear.

Feudal society, and its continuation in the *ancien régime,* was held together by loyalties that were concrete, particular, personal, and therefore usually within one's immediate community, one's feudal fief, or one's burgh; and the people identified themselves socially in these immediate terms only. The aristocracy alone had a direct loyalty to any central political authority—say, the king of France. This loyalty, also, was the product of a very personal and particular allegiance, though over a broader distance, and *not* of an abstract adherence to the French "nation." The aristocracy itself was simply free-floating, what today we would call very international: there was no feeling that an aristocrat from Italy or Germany should not enter into a relationship of allegiance to the King of France, or that his loyalty would therefore be different in principle from that of an aristocrat who spoke French and was born in Paris. And, apart from this aristocracy and from the clergy (who constituted a special case), most of the population accepted their geographic limitations. This was especially true of the land-bound peasantry, which contained the great mass of the population. And, in all cases, physical immobility had its analogue in an immobility of mind and imagination. The peasant's sense of the world was for the most part circumscribed by the immediate community in which he lived his entire life, and he was hardly capable of identifying himself in terms that transcended these limits. Thus, there could be no development of national consciousness within the feudal system as such, nor on its fringes, in the bourgeoisie, whose loyalties were to the immediate family, guild, and town. The burgher was, furthermore, hardly in a position to identify himself with larger collectivities, since he had so strong an economic and political dependence on the aristocracy.

The reason we are attending so precisely to the localized, concrete, limited relationships fostered under feudalism is, of course, because nationalism is possible only on the level of *abstract* identifications. But, it could be argued that, in a fundamental sense, all social identifications are abstract and artificial, even those of family and kinship. It is not given in the nature of things that a man belongs to his cousin or even to his brother in a way that demands special loyalty. All the same, there is a difference between loyalty to individuals or groups that are available, face-to-face, in the individual's actual life, and loyalty to entities that cannot be experienced in everyday social life. The concrete kind of loyalty feels less artificial, more natural. In this sense, it is natural to feel a sense of community with the people in one's village or one's valley, but not to "fellow-Frenchmen" one has never seen and probably never will see.

In premodern Europe, only *religious* loyalties were founded on this degree of abstraction. The clergy was, of course, the social group that embodied and localized this, as it were, supraempirical allegiance, and the Crusades constituted the most dramatic actualizing of these transcendent loyalties. After the Reformation Protestantism frequently served as a vehicle and symbol of unification for the rising middle class, and both Protestantism and anti-Protestantism were used by the aristocracy to mobilize broad political support for its class interests. Religion thus provided a connecting link between traditional, particularistic loyalties and the transcendent loyalty of national consciousness. It still plays this role today in modernizing societies.

By the late eighteenth century a marked change in this "economy of loyalties" was coming about. The bourgeoisie now emerged as a carrier for the idea of nationalism, a role it maintained throughout the nineteenth century, so that the phrase "bourgeois nationalism" is an apt one. The middle class was most suited for carrying the banner and the life-style of nationalism because of its background in *trade*. With the expansion of capitalism, the trading class necessarily entered into ever more complex financial relationships which, by their very character, broke the limitations of the traditional social structure—and, by the same token, transcended the boundaries of traditional, particularistic loyalties. Indeed, it may be that capitalist economic activities, in and of themselves, have an abstract quality that permeates the consciousness of those who engage in them.[4] In any case, the new middle class was increasingly mobile in every sense of the word: physically, because of the geographically expanding arena of its economic activities; socially, because of the dynamism it introduced into the stratification system; and, most importantly, it also came to be ideologically mobile. Gradually the idea and feeling of nationalism spread beyond the middle class. The middle class used the new sense of nationalism to mobilize the general population, first against the groups representing the old regime, later in "national" struggles against other middle-class nations. The bourgeois-oriented governments were the ones who maintained their policies under the symbolic banner of nationalism—a fact that became tremendously significant during Europe's imperialistic expansion into the non-Western world.

NATIONALISM IN MODERNIZING NATIONS

So, nationalism is a Western invention, and it has served as an ideological focus for imperialism and colonial expansion. Yet, ironically, its offspring has been a variety of nationalisms centered *outside* the West and ultimately directed *against* the West. In most of the non-Western world, loyalties once were local and particularistic, or, when abstract and general, they were at least based on religious symbols of one kind or another; national consciousness was no more present than in premodern Europe. But nationalism was adopted from the West and has become a decisive factor in the recent development toward self-determination and modernization.[5]

The history of Asia is, in many ways, a model for non-Western development.[6] There were, of course, in Asia some strong loyalties based on general cultural identification, as in China or Japan, but these employed religio-political symbols rather than symbols of nationality. The lack of national solidarity is partly responsible for the lack of opposition to Western colonialism in the nineteenth century. What little there was generally took place under the banner of *religious* symbols, used to unite the various strata of the subject populations against the colonial powers: for example, the Indian Mutiny (1857) that ingeniously combined Hindu and Muslim religious grievances against the British; the Muslim-inspired uprisings against the Dutch in Indonesia; and the Boxer Rebellion in China (1899). In almost all cases, these prenationalistic movements were still led by traditional elites, whom the colonial powers were rarely unsuccessful in detaching from the general population by the granting of special recognition and privileges. (This political method was raised to a fine art by the British.) However, it was of little use against the unifying bonds of the nationalistic spirit.

In most Asian countries a new middle class began to appear about 1900.[7] Although this stratum became the carrier of nationalism, it was significantly different from the middle class that had earlier performed this role in the West. It had fewer merchants, fewer entrepreneurs, fewer professionals. Instead, there was a preponderance of clerks—what we would call white-collar workers —mostly employed in the governmental apparatus of the colonial regimes. In this group, status depended on individual achievement rather than on traditional criteria; its claims to leadership were largely based on the education its members possessed. Unlike the Western middle class, the clerks tended to scorn trade and commercial activities, as these were the precinct of the foreigners, the colonizers.

The social situation of this class had frustration built into it. Its aspirations were directed, above all, toward governmental careers; precisely these careers, however, were denied or strictly limited for natives under the colonial regimes. And, so, the new middle class became a reservoir of pent-up resentment and inhibited ambition. As this group was, because of its employment, open to ra-

Traditional Religion and
Modern Ideologies

The following excerpt describes the interplay between traditional religion and modern revolutionary ideologies. A similar process is experienced in many modernizing societies.

The dominant political ideologies of South Asia, nationalism, democracy, and socialism, have been readily reconciled with the major religions, Hinduism, Buddhism, and Islam. On the whole, Marxism has been held to be incompatible with the religions of South Asia, although serious efforts have been made in Ceylon to demonstrate its compatibility with Buddhism.

Almost any highly elaborated system of thought, whether a political ideology or a set of religious doctrines, will have some assumptions or ideas in common with other systems of thought. A basic compatibility between two systems is established, consciously or unconsciously, by emphasizing these common assumptions or ideas and minimizing differences. In the absence of a recognized authority with power to set rigid limits to doctrinal compatibility, such as exists in the Roman Catholic Church, the process of mutual accommodation by reinterpretation can ordinarily go quite far.

In South Asia the imported Western notions of nationalism, democracy, and socialism have been accepted and assimilated by Hindus, Buddhists, and Muslims with relatively little sense of conflict with the essential tenets of their religious faiths. While the Western impact produced considerable secularization, the new interpretations of Asian religion have sought to demonstrate that there was no need to abandon one's ancestral faith because it was quite compatible with modern values and ideologies.

One might think that Hinduism, to which the institution of caste is so closely linked, would be impossible to reconcile with democracy or socialism. Yet Dr. S. Radhakrishnan and others could point to the Hindu emphasis on individualism and freedom in the search for truth as an important value undergirding democracy. He found support for the idea of equality in the metaphysical assertion of Vedanta of the ultimate unity of all beings in the Absolute. If all individual souls are part of the same ultimate Reality, all are equal. Hinduism, therefore, teaches equality, and caste has nothing to do with religion.

Gandhian thought gave rise to the remarkable Sarvodaya movement led by Vinoba Bhave, a kind of Hindu socialism aiming at a radical transformation of society by noncoercive means. Sarvodaya is the ideal social order, a casteless and classless society with equal opportunity for all; it is also a stateless society. Unlike the Marxists, however, the leaders of the Sarvodaya movement seek the withering away of the state by declining to use the machinery of state power to attain their immediate goals.

Source: Donald E. Smith, *South Asian Politics and Religion* (Princeton: Princeton University Press, 1966), pp. 33 ff.

tionalizing values, and especially to the values of bureaucracy, nationalism was ideally suited to meet its needs.

The general form and use of nationalism was, of course, learned from Western experience, absorbed in the course of the Western-oriented education on which the position of the clerks rested. But now it was filled with non-Western content (say, the values of Indian culture, as understood or reinterpreted by this group) and with an anti-Western political focus (the liberation, say, of India from British colonial rule).

Nationalism could, at the same time, mobilize other social groups under the leadership of the new middle class. All feeling oppressed in one way or another, these other groups could now channel their various grievances into a unified struggle for national liberation; there could grow an expanding universe of loyalties, absorbing a great variety of social grievances—held together behind a single banner, national liberation. Nationalism became a movement of *total* liberation, not only from colonial rule, but from social and economic oppression, and from all traditional limitations. For example, Indian nationalism aligned itself against the native and traditional Hindu caste system, and Chinese nationalism proclaimed the abolition of traditional social inequities as well as the inequities brought about by colonialism. Nationalism identified itself with the liberation of women from traditional bondage, with the emancipation of the young, with enlightenment as against superstition and cultural "backwardness." The emphasis on youth was strong. Everywhere the protagonists of the nationalist movements presented themselves as a *young* elite, educated and forward-looking. This image has entered our language in the phrase "Young Turks," the self-designation of the modernizing Turkish

Nationalistic Values and the
Process of Secularization

Max Weber has drawn attention to the influence of secularized religious values on economic development. Neil J. Smelser, a sociologist
who studies social change, in an essay, "Mechanisms of Change and
Adjustment to Change," speaks of a similar process of secularization
in the development of nationalistic values.

"Nationalism seems in many cases to be the very instrument designed to smash the traditional religious systems—those like the
classical Chinese or Indian—which Weber himself found to be less
permissive than Protestantism for economic modernization.

On the other hand, nationalism, like many traditionalistic religious systems, may hinder economic advancement by "reaffirmation
of traditionally honored ways of acting and thinking," by fostering
anticolonial attitudes after they are no longer relevant, and, more
indirectly, by encouraging passive expectations of "ready-made
prosperity." We can distinguish among these contrasting forces of
"stimulus" and "drag" that such value systems bring to economic
development by using the logic of differentiation in the following
way.

In the early phases of modernization, many traditional attachments must be modified to permit more differentiated institutional
structures to be set up. Because the existing commitments and
methods of integration are deeply rooted in the organization of traditional society, a very generalized and powerful commitment is required to pry individuals from these attachments. The values of ascetic and this-worldly religious beliefs, xenophobic national
aspirations, and political ideologies (like socialism), provide such a
lever. Sometimes, these diverse types of values combine into a single system of legitimacy. In any case, all three have an "ultimacy"
of commitment, in whose name a wide range of sacrifices can be demanded and procured.

The very success of these value systems, however, breeds the conditions for their own weakening. In a perceptive statement, Weber
notes that, at the beginning of the twentieth century, when the capitalistic system was already highly developed, it no longer needed the
impetus of ascetic Protestantism. By virtue of its conquest of much
of Western society, capitalism had solidly established an institutional base and a secular value system of its own—economic rationality. Its secular economic values had no further need for the "ulti-

mate" justification they had required during the newer, unsteadier days of economic revolution.

Such lines of differentiation constitute the secularization of religious values. In the same process, other institutional spheres—economic, political, scientific, et cetera—become more nearly established on their own. The values governing these spheres are no longer sanctioned directly by religious beliefs, but by an autonomous rationality. In so far as this replaces religious sanctions, secularization occurs in these spheres.

Similarly, nationalistic and related value systems undergo a process of secularization as differentiation proceeds. As a society moves increasingly toward more complex social organization, the encompassing demands of nationalistic commitment give way to more autonomous systems of rationality. For instance, the Soviet Union, as its social structure grows more differentiated, is apparently introducing more "independent" market mechanisms, "freer" social scientific investigation in some spheres, and so on. Moreover, these measures are not directly sanctioned by nationalistic or communistic values. It seems reasonable to make the historical generalization that, in the early stages of a nation's development, nationalism is heady, muscular, and aggressive; as the society evolves to an advanced state, however, nationalism tends to settle into a more remote and complacent condition, rising to fury only in times of national crisis.

Hence there is a paradoxical element in the role of religious or nationalistic belief systems. In so far as they encourage the breakup of old patterns, they may stimulate economic modernization. In so far as they resist their own subsequent secularization, however, these same value systems may become an impediment to economic advance and structural change.

Source: Neil J. Smelser, "Mechanisms of Change and Adjustment to Change," in B. Hoselitz and Wilber E. Moore, eds., *Industrialization and Society* (Mouton: UNESCO, 1963), pp. 32–34. By permission of UNESCO.

revolutionaries of 1908, but equivalent names have been created in Persia, Burma, China, and elsewhere.

Somewhat later in the development of nationalism in each Asian country, two other new strata emerged in the cities, and joined the clerks: an industrial proletariat, and a stratum of "semi-intellectuals," consisting of lower-echelon white-collar workers, such as postal employees, railroad workers, and the like. The inclusion of these strata in the nationalist alliance meant that allowance had to be made for *their* social grievances, which were more acute financially than those of the middle class.[8] Thus, the nationalist movement took on an ever more radical and increasingly socialist coloration. Also, a new *rural proletariat* emerged as the traditional peasant structures of rural life were shaken by the development of a capitalist money economy, coupled with the population explosion caused by the still only modest introduction of modern medicine and hygiene. This was a stratum of landless peasants, which either subsisted on the margins of traditional rural culture or was eventually driven into the cities to swell the ranks of the urban proletariat. These ex-peasants, no longer bound by the traditional conservatism of their background, became quite susceptible to revolutionary slogans that were often couched first in religious terms. All these changes in the stratification system made it possible to include virtually all strata of the population.

It will be clear now that, despite nationalist unity and the shared goal of national independence, the whole movement has quite different meanings for the various participating groups. For the new middle class, independence means acquiring the governmental positions previously held by the colonial rulers, and therefore precludes commitment to radical changes in the social structure. For the industrial proletariat, the proletarianized peasantry, and for the "semi-intelligentsia," national independence is only a first step toward liberation from their particular social oppressions. For the old elites, as well as for the traditional religious leadership and the "intact" groups within the peasantry, national liberation means a return to an idealized past, to the true, underlying values of the indigenous culture once but no longer suppressed by pernicious Western influences.

So long as the nationalist movement is still struggling against the colonial power, these contradictions in purpose can be kept under control and possibly even out of consciousness. But they constitute, whether or not admitted, a tension leading naturally to instability. This is almost certain to manifest itself soon after national independence has been achieved, once the euphoria of national liberation has spent itself, and uninspiring, quotidien economic problems must now be faced by the new state.[9] Thus the united nationalistic movement may prove, as in many cases, only a temporary stay against confusion and its own ultimate disintegration. This accounts for the failure of the Kuomintang in China, of the Muslim League in Pakistan, and for what may be happening now to the Congress Party in India. And the consequence of this frequent weakening of the nationalist *élan* and of the movement that embodied it in the struggle for independence is that a wide field is opened up for the growth of revolutionary ideas that go beyond "bourgeois nationalism," namely, the ideologies of the socialist and communist movements.

Communism

It is in this connection with the aforementioned developments that one should understand the strong appeal of communism in underdeveloped countries today.[10] This is not always easy to do from a Western vantage point. The Westerner is likely to be, above all, attentive to the brutalities and sacrifices that communist revolutionary movements inflict on the populations of these countries. We would not want to deny that this perspective is justified, in an ethical sense, but it should be pointed out that matters often look differently from within the countries themselves—except when seen through the eyes of the direct victims of the revolutionary violence. That is, to the general population the brutalities of the revolutionaries are hardly different in kind from the brutalities practiced by the former supporters of the status quo. And, as to sacrifices, one's response to them depends on whether one believes they will prove eventually to have been worthwhile. If people do believe this, then their revolutionary hopefulness can unleash hitherto untapped energies and courage, even in those groups that had previously reacted passively and apathetically to their own social fate. And, of course, the revolutionary intellectuals always have ready-made justifications for their methods. A common legitimation of their own violence is in the argument that, after all, it is just as bad, or worse, for people to die of starvation as to be killed in battle or even to be executed. There is the additional argument that misery, in the old state of affairs, afflicted mainly the innocent, while revolutionary violence is directed toward and, for the most part, hits only those who have caused suffering and whose punishment will eventually benefit the vast majority. Also, it may be added, few revolutionary intellectuals expect to share in these sacrifices themselves, which adds to their moral calculations a certain personal comfort.

One must further understand that communist goals in the underdeveloped world are different from the traditional communist goal—the liberation of the working class—in the industrialized countries.[11] The new goal is, more and more, the liberation of *all* strata of the population in these countries. This goal has, of course, been linked to what are known as "wars of national liberation." It is particularly important in the Chinese and Cuban brands of communism, though the Soviets have also come to redefine their goals accordingly and to claim for themselves the leadership of these broadly conceived revolutionary movements.

Communism has thus become, above all, a part of the movement to overcome backwardness and to bring about modernization —that is, it now fills the very role that once was played by early capitalism. The believers in this redefined communism are from the same stratum that, as we have previously described, provides the exponents of nationalism—the "intellectuals," who in underdeveloped countries form a mushrooming stratum of partially educated (at least to the point of literacy) clerks, schoolteachers, and minor bureaucrats, as well as a proportionately smaller group of professionals and academicians. Among these people, nationalism and communism have become closely intertwined. The attempt to reseparate these almost identical strains (a common pastime of American policy makers) is more often than not a quixotic undertaking.

This pattern prevails not only in a number of Asian countries, but in other parts of the world as well. The Cuban case is illuminating.[12] There is good reason to believe that the communist component in Castro's revolution was negligible at first, whatever may have been the personal political sympathies of some of the leading individuals. The revolutionary regime became openly and self-avowedly communist only when it was confronted with difficulties in doing what previously it had simply been struggling to gain the power to do: there were external difficulties, in its relationship to the United States, but also internal difficulties, in its efforts to modernize the social and economic structure of Cuba. It is rather an idle question whether the regime is today more communist or nationalist in Cuba, or in the Castroist movements in other Latin American countries. These movements are *both* nationalist and communist, directed against an enemy that seeks to maintain the status quo. The enemy has an external aspect, represented by the United States as international guarantor of the status quo, and an internal aspect, the domestic "oligarchy" that is the stratum within

Latin-American countries with a vested interest in the status quo. The revolutionary movement is nationalist in its stance against the United States, communist against the domestic conservatives and the moderate reformers. And both nationalist and the communist ideologues are revolutionary intellectuals.

The "second revolution" is what this pattern is called.[13] A two-stage development is involved in these revolutionary upheavals: first, a nationalist revolution; then, a communist regime. Precisely this is what happened in China, where the communist revolution directly resulted from the failure of the Kuomintang (Nationalist party, 1912–1949) regime to modernize the country and to satisfy the expectations that it had aroused in the broad masses of the population. Not surprisingly, then, Chinese communism, as expressed in Maoist theory, has become the normative pattern for revolutionary development throughout the world.[14] It has placed critical emphasis on "wars of national liberation," and so has produced a nationalist and perhaps even a racist version of revolutionary ideology.

Because of the differential stage of development of the Soviet and Chinese societies, the popular Maoist version of communism has not been easily compatible with the Soviet regime and history. But it is important to note that the Chinese were not the first to merge nationalism and communism, that the merger had already occurred (albeit in a quite different context) in the Soviet Union, under Stalin.[15] In his early struggle with Trotsky's old-fashioned brand of communist *internationalism,* Stalin had coined the idea of "socialism in *one* country." Increasingly, communism became identified with Soviet patriotism—which apparently brought the political dividend of consolidating Stalin's rule in Russia, but also created unwanted difficulties in the Soviet regime's relationship with foreign communist movements, as became dramatically clear, for the first time, in the split between Stalin and Tito (in Yugoslavia). Soviet patriotism thence forward was identified with the still potent, the old motifs of *Russian* nationalism—including a glorification of the national past of the Russian nation, a resuscitation of pan-Slavistic ideas, and (in Stalin's last year) a resurrection of time-honored Russian antisemitism. This merger of communism and nationalism came to a head, understandably, during World War II (which the Soviets called the "Great Fatherland War"), but even since then strong traces of it have remained in the official ideology of the regime.

It may, at first, be difficult to understand the seemingly inexorable process whereby nationalism and its conversion into communism have occurred in so many parts of the world. It all makes sense, however, once we understand that behind the often tortured ideological arguments there is one overriding necessity today: to modernize. To be sure, in many parts of the world the conditions still exist that traditionally were the basis for the growth of revolutionary ideas—gross inequality between classes, exploitation, corrupt and incompetent government, and the like. But it is hardly an exaggeration to insist that the one fundamental revolutionary goal is modernization. First, one must remove what, rightly or wrongly, are regarded as the major obstacles to modernization; then, once this immediate goal has been achieved and political control acquired, one must actually modernize. The problem then is how to motivate people to make the requisite sacrifices and participate in the hard work. Probably the strongest argument for communism in the underdeveloped world is that it has been most successful in motivating people, because of its access to force, including terror, and its use of mass indoctrination. That this argument is dubious from the viewpoint, say, of the economist, is quite another matter. But, where it is *believed,* it is capable of legitimating both the means and the ends of communist revolutionary movements as opposed to any other method.

To repeat, modernization requires vast human efforts and sacrifices, for the motivation of which revolutionary ideas are often required. They can do this because whatever their ideological shading, they are marked by fervor, enthusiasm, and total solidarity—that is, by the characteristics that Max Weber called "charismatic." [16] But once there has begun a successful movement toward modernization, a very different social dynamic takes over. What is required is no longer the wild enthusiasm and self-sacrifice of the earlier phase. Instead, the society demands refined technical skills, cool intelligence, and, above all, stability. Revolutionary structures give way to bureaucratic structures, in the process that Weber called the "routinization of charisma." The revolutionary man becomes obsolete: society needs technicians and administrators, not heroic plotters and bomb-throwers. In other words, the *rational* demands of the new industrial system shape the social imperative. *Rationality* becomes the critical virtue, and the human types most needed are those that embody this quality.

The Soviet pattern of development illustrates this change most

The Red Executive

David Granick's study of the organization man in Soviet industry, *The Red Executive*, emphasizes the high educational level of the Russian industrial manager. This suggests the growing rationality of the industrial sector.

Although we have no current general statistics, I received the impression from conversations in the Soviet Union that a college education is virtually an absolute requirement for a candidate for an industrial management post. For example, I was told that at least 80 per cent of the entire staff of the Leningrad Regional Economic Council had college degrees, and that all plant directors were college graduates.

Statistics of the 1930s for heavy industry tend to confirm my impression. Back in 1936, 65 per cent of the heads of industry branches had engineering degrees; 90 per cent of the chief engineers of factories had engineering diplomas; and 80 per cent of department superintendents were in this category. Only plant directors had a lower educational level, with less than one third having regular degrees; but by 1939, the proportion in this group had been raised to 85 per cent in the industries of defense and ferrous metallurgy. Moreover, it seems certain that since the mid-1930s—in the Soviet Union as in the United States—the proportion of management with college degrees has been growing.

Some recent data, available for entire industries in the Soviet Union, offer general support for this view, although they do show that there are still a significant number of holdouts in management who have not had a college education. Of all plant directors in the Ministry of Machinebuilding on December 1, 1956, 89 per cent had a specialized high school or college education; in the Ministry of Heavy Machinebuilding, the proportion was 94 per cent. But in the Ministry of the Oil Industry, the figure fell to 78 per cent; and in the low-priority and low-salaried Ministry of Light Industry, only 45 per cent had this education. While some of the college-trained directors did not have the appropriate "specialized" education, and some of those with a specialized education were not college graduates, these groups probably cancel each other out reasonably well. The percentage of directors with college diplomas in these industries was presumably roughly at the levels indicated by the percentages.

Source: David Granick, *The Red Executive* (New York: Doubleday, 1961), pp. 46 ff. Copyright © 1960 by David Granick. Reprinted by permission of Doubleday & Company, Inc.

dramatically.[17] As Soviet society succeeded, after immense sacrifice, in transforming itself into a modern industrial state, the old revolutionary types became obsolete and, under Stalin, were liquidated with considerable efficiency. Since the death of Stalin and the decline in terror, the leading figures in Soviet society have become increasingly of the cool, pragmatic, rational type, those with whom Westerners "can talk," and *ipso facto* they have infuriated revolutionaries in countries still on the road toward modernization. Most observers agree that Mao's "Cultural Revolution" was motivated by a desperate desire to prevent this "changing of the guard" from happening in China. But, if our analysis is correct, Mao is fated to disappointment.[18] As modernization succeeds, a new mentality *inevitably* comes to the fore and replaces the figures with old revolutionary charisma. If this is frustrating to revolutionary intellectuals, it is, on the other hand, comforting to those who hope for some measure of stability in the course of world affairs.

In this chapter we have devoted special attention to Asia, because it manifests the basic pattern most clearly, and also because of the great importance of the area. However, although modernization and revolution are similar everywhere, special problems in Africa and in Latin America arise from the particular historical and social conditions in these countries.[19] For example, in Africa they must deal with tribalism's great tenacity in the face of modernizing changes, while in Latin America there is the problem of the overpowering presence of the United States' economic and political power. In the light of this, we must stress that the processes we have described are not unilinear or monolithic, and do not unfold with mechanical inexorability. In every society a variety of historical and cultural factors must be taken into account, and in all human events there is always the unexpected and the surprising. Nevertheless, an overall pattern can be discerned and is useful even in understanding those states that are divergent because of particular circumstances.

NOTES

1. Stanislav Andreski, *The Uses of Comparative Sociology* (Berkeley: University of California Press, 1965), p. 99.

2. Émile Durkheim, *The Rules of Sociological Method* (Glencoe: Free Press, 1950).

3. Hans Kohn, *Nationalism, Its Meaning and History* (Princeton: Van Nostrand, 1955); Louis L. Snyder, *The Meaning of Nationalism* (New Brunswick: Rutgers University Press, 1954); Karl W. Deutsch, *Nationalism and Social Communication* (New York: John Wiley, 1953); John H. Kautsky, ed., *Political Change in Underdeveloped Countries: Nationalism and Communism* (New York: John Wiley, 1962).

4. The abstract quality of capitalist activities has spread with capitalism to human interaction as well. This has been observed by Georg Simmel as well as by Karl Marx. Marx considered this development generally detrimental, whereas Simmel was more ambivalent. Georg Simmel, *Philosophie des Geldes,* 6th ed. (Berlin: Duncker and Humblot, 1928), *The Sociology of Georg Simmel,* ed. and trans. Kurt Wolff (Glencoe: Free Press, 1950). See especially the essay on "The Metropolis and Mental Life." Also, Karl Marx, *Das Kapital* (New York: Modern Library, 1953).

5. See the excellent analysis by W. F. Wertheim, "Nationalism and Leadership in Asia," in *East-West Parallels* (Chicago: Quadrangle Books, 1965); and Deutsch, *op. cit.,* which includes a large bibliography on studies of nationalism in non-Western societies. See also Kautsky, *op. cit.,* and Louis Hartz, *The Founding of New Societies* (New York: Harcourt, Brace, and World, 1964).

6. These explications are largely based on Wertheim, *op. cit.,* and Rupert Emerson, *Government and Nationalism in Southeast Asia* (New York: International Secretariat, Institute of Pacific Relations, 1942).

7. Wertheim, *op. cit.*

8. B. S. Cohn, "The Initial British Impact on India: A Case Study of the Benares Region," in I. Wallerstein, ed., "Social Change: The Colonial Situation" (New York: John Wiley, 1966); W. F. Wertheim and T. S. Giap, "Social Change in Java, 1900–1930," in Wallerstein, *op. cit.*

9. See especially Kautsky, *op. cit.,* Chapters 2 and 3, and Wertheim, *op. cit.*

10. Morris Watnick, "The Appeal of Communism to the Underdeveloped Peoples," in Kautsky, *op. cit.*

11. On the convergence of Communism and nationalism, compare Kautsky, *op. cit.,* Part III, and David E. Apter, *Ideology and Discontent* (New York: Free Press, 1964).

12. R. H. Phillips, *Cuba, Island of Paradox* (New York: McDowell, 1959).

13. See Kautsky, *op. cit.,* and John Kautsky, *Communism and the Politics of Development* (New York: John Wiley, 1968).

14. Kautsky, *Political Change,* pp. 79 ff.

15. Klaus Mehnert, *Stalin Versus Marx* (London: Allen and Unwin, 1952).

16. Max Weber, *From Max Weber,* eds. W. Gerth and C. W. Mills (New York: Oxford University Press, 1959).

17. Barrington Moore, *Soviet Politics: The Dilemma of Power* (New York: Harper and Row, 1965).

18. Compare especially the various interpretations of recent events in China as reflected in newspaper and magazine articles.

19. McCord, *op. cit.* James Petras and Maurice Zeitlin, eds., Latin America, *Reform and Revolution* (New York: Fawcett World Library, 1968).

[9] Changing Personality

I⊤ is a tenet of popular wisdom that individuals, in some degree and way not fully understood, *are* what they *do*. We say that someone is sober as a judge or shrill as a fishwife, and, although we all know that there are also intemperate judges and gentle fishwives, we still are inclined to accept in a general way the sociological proposition that being and doing are related. And there is good reason for doing so. We can restate it: the personalities of individuals are related to their positions in the social structure. We can further state that, in any given society, social structures and psychological factors interact. This means that we cannot fully understand any particular social structure unless we have some grasp of the psychological makeup of the people who exist within it. Conversely, our understanding of the individual will be deficient unless we can locate his personality in the particular social context in which it took shape. In other words, personality and social structure are in a dialectical relationship with each other; they reciprocally create each other.

Such a view of the relationship of the sociology and the psychology of situations is especially relevant to an understanding of social change. It is too common, when looking at these situations, to fix one's attention on the large, often spectacular, institutional processes—transformations of the state, the economy, the stratification system, and so on—and to forget that these processes are dependent on the thoughts, motives, and actions of many single individuals. Whatever else it may be and do, social change is also a process taking place in the consciousness and unconscious of individuals. Social change and changing personality are in a dialectical

Changing Society and Changing
Personality Structure

One of the most fascinating problems of comparative sociology involves the impact of modern society on the course of individual life.
Rapid social change, increasing social mobility, transformations in the
family structure, and the high level of rational organization of various
social institutions are not without effect on individual personality. A
theoretical consideration of this reality and of the sociological study of
it is the subject of Thomas Luckmann's *The Invisible Religion.*

What if the relation of the individual to the social order underwent
a radical transformation with the emergence of modern society? In
that case sociology would be confronted with a problem which
could not be resolved by simple application of the "universal" struc-
tural-functional theories of socialization and social change. The
theory of socialization posits generally identical processes of internalization of cultural "contents" in a given "social system." It is
predicated upon an ahistorical conception of the relation between
"social" and "psychological" systems. The theory of social change
explains specific institutional changes by reference to a functional
model of equilibrium within the "social system." Starting out from
a dialectic conception of the relation between individual and society
in history, however, one must be ready to inspect the hypothesis
that a fundamental shift occurred in the "location" of the individual
in the social order in modern society. If the possibility of such a
shift is granted, the discussions about the effect of "mass society"
upon "individualism" appear in a new light. They may be inter-
preted as symptoms of the relocation of the individual in the social
order. If there are qualitatively different patterns of location of the
individual in society and if institutional change may lead to qualitatively different forms of society, an ahistorical conception of socialization and institutional change no longer appears adequate and a
new theoretical effort is required of sociology.

A unifying perspective on the problem of individual existence in
society is to be found in the sociological theory of religion. This insight must be attributed, within the sociological tradition, to Emile
Durkheim and Max Weber. Both were profoundly interested in the
fate of the individual in modern society. Both recognized that the
character of modern society carried serious consequences for the individual. Their studies of the division of labor, bureaucratization,
suicide, and so forth, are characterized by this interest. No matter
that their methodologies were value-free—their grave concern for

the social conditions of individual existence in the contemporary world clearly expresses the moral engagement of their sociological theorizing. Different as their theories are, it is remarkable that both Weber and Durkheim sought the key to an understanding of the social location of the individual in the study of religion. For Durkheim, the symbolic reality of religion is the core of the *conscience collective*. As a social fact it transcends the individual and is the condition for social integration and the continuity of the social order. At the same time, only the internalization of that objective reality by the subject makes man into a social and, thereby, a moral and genuinely human being. For Durkheim man is essentially *homo duplex,* and individuation has, necessarily, a social basis. The problem with which we are concerned here is seen by Durkheim in a universal anthropological perspective and is articulated by him, correspondingly, in a radical manner. For Weber, on the other hand, the problem of the social conditions of individuation appears in a more specific perspective—that is, in the historical context of particular religions and their relation to historical societies. When it came to the question of the individual in modern society, however, both Weber and Durkheim linked it directly to the secularization of the contemporary world. It can be said that both Weber and Durkheim recognized what is presupposed in the present essay: that the problem of individual existence in society is a "religious" problem. We maintain, then, that the relevance of sociology for contemporary man derives primarily from its search for an understanding of the fate of the person in the structure of modern society.

Source: Thomas Luckmann, *The Invisible Religion* (New York: Macmillan, 1967), p. 11 ff. Reprinted with the permission of The Macmillan Company. © 1967 by The Macmillan Company.

relationship: changing social structures act on the personalities of their participants; in turn, changing personalities of individuals act back on the social structures that have changed them as people.

An incisive analysis of this interaction between social change and personality may be found in Daniel Lerner's study of modernization in the Middle East, *The Passing of Traditional Society,* most graphically in the section which Lerner calls "a parable," comparing two individuals: a village chief, and a grocer in a Turkish hamlet.[1] The village chief embodies the perspectives and ideas of the traditional society. His world is physically limited by the village and its immediate surrounding; his ideas are those of traditional Turkish culture, with its time-honored emphasis on military heroism. He is not happy about the changes that will engulf his village when a new road, linking it with the nearby capital city of Ankara, is finished, but he is prepared to face them with stoic resignation. The grocer, on the other hand, embodies the nascent modernizing spirit: he is enamoured of change, eager to find out about the outside world, impatient with traditional restraints. He says to the interviewer: "It is nice to know what is happening in other parts of the world. We are stuck in this hole, we have to know what is going on outside our village." [2] Why? Because what is going on is the advent of modernity, to which the grocer looks forward expectantly. And that advent, interestingly, was announced to him in something he saw in a movie: a vision of an American-type supermarket, "with walls made of iron sheets, top to floor and side to side, and on them standing myriads of round boxes, clean and all the same, dressed like soldiers in a great parade." [3] Both the village chief and the grocer live in the same small community. But while the consciousness and personality of the one are rooted immovably in a world that is dissolving around him, those of the other are moving eagerly toward the new modern world that is in the process of arriving from America via Ankara.

A HISTORY

The insight that personality is related to social structure is not original to modern sociology, but has been known for a long time and in many forms by historians and social philosophers. For instance, the medieval Muslim philosopher, Ibn-Khaldun, tried to show how, and why, settled people differ from nomads in their character traits.[4] His interest in this question developed from his effort to explain the particular history of the Arabs and of the Muslim religion. But in dealing with this limited problem, he was led to the more general insight that different kinds of individuals are to be found in societies of divergent natures. In modern Western thought there has been a deepening concern with such socio-psychological matters. Thus in the eighteenth century numerous thinkers and writers discussed the psychology of the peasant, while in the nineteenth century this interest shifted to the psychology of the industrial working class.[5]

Marx occupies an important position in this development.[6] Although Marx did not develop a systematic social psychology, his analyses are based on an implicit one. His analysis of the "alienation" of the worker as a result of capitalist exploitation assumes that society shapes the individual psyche: it is not the worker's social position alone that is alienated because of his subjection to the forces that control his labor, but his entire being, his very personality as well. We are not concerned here with the correctness of Marx's viewpoint, now or then: our point is only that Marxian modes of thought helped to focus interest on the relationship of society and personality. In Marx's wake, throughout the nineteenth century, the conception developed that different classes and social groups had different "mentalities" (today we would say personality patterns), and that these had to be accounted for, ultimately, in sociological terms. On the other hand, the personality traits of, say, the bourgeoisie and the working class came to be seen as cross-culturally consistent, since they were the fruits of social conditions that were similar from country to country.

In classical sociology, important insights into these matters were formulated by Pareto and Simmel.[7] Pareto believed that certain personality types succeeded each other in history, and as each personality type came into dominance, so did the particular social class that it represented become dominant in society. This is the essence of Pareto's theory of the "circulation of elites." He believed the motor force in this process was psychological rather than social—namely, the alternation between two personality types, which he called "foxes" (aggressive, innovative, adventurous) and "lions" (peaceable, conservative, prudent).

Simmel, on the other hand, was interested less in such universal generalizations than in definitions of the social psychology of modern man. Two works of his most significantly focus on these matters. One is his intriguingly entitled *The Philosophy of Money*, in which he argues that the introduction of a money economy transforms not only social institutions but also the prevailing personality type. The other is an essay on the psychology of urban life, which has had a lasting influence on social-scientific studies of city life. *The Philosophy of Money* directly contradicts Marx by arguing that the money economy creates individuals who are different and freer than their predecessors, while "The Metropolis and Mental Life" portrays urban man as hyperconscious, impersonal, and calculating, yet also freer than preurban man.

Once more, it is Weber who is particularly relevant to this subject. Without any question, it is certain that Weber did not intend to construct a social psychology; indeed, his view of the nature of social science makes it doubtful that he would have approved of such a project. All the same, there is in Weber's work an implicit social psychology in the sense we have been using, of a link between personality and social structure. This is particularly evident in his *The Protestant Ethic and the Spirit of Capitalism.*[8] Its actual thesis is historical, namely, that there is a causal relationship between the development of Protestant morality and the growth of motivation and attitudes that foster capitalist enterprise. But underlying the historical thesis is a general proposition of social psychology: that each religious system of values puts a premium on different personality traits, which are in turn relatively conducive to certain socioeconomic practices. For instance, Weber found that Protestantism encouraged a number of psychological patterns—discipline, self-denial, rationality, hard work—the sum total of which he called "inner-worldly asceticism." Weber then argued that the resultant personality type, whose prototype would be the Puritan businessman in early New England, was very much in place in, "fitted" well with, capitalism. *Mutatis mutandis,* Weber applied this same perspective to other historical situations, especially in his elaborate work on the comparative sociology of religion. Thus the orthodox Jew, the Brahman priest, the Confucianist bureaucrat, are not only embodiments of certain religious values, but are specific personality types who have a unique "fit" in their particular sociohistorical situation as well.

But Weber is relevant to our present undertaking because of the particular formulations as well as the general orientation he suggests. The contemporary social-psychological situation, that is, what we call the personality of modern man, can best be understood as deriving from a *secularization* of the Protestant prototype as analyzed by Weber. The explicitly religious ideas and motives, to be sure, have waned, but the psychological patterns that fitted with this religious constellation are still very much present. Once again, the concept of rationalization is the keystone to a grasp of this.

The Rationalized Self

We have discovered throughout our analysis the rationalization of society and of the economy to be the basic element in modernization. Now we will consider rationalization. What does this mean?

Essentially, it means that personality too is marshalled as a re-source, and an important resource at that, for the realization of the rational purposes of a modern society. Increasingly, then, this marshalling of personality is itself rationalized, that is, is under-taken deliberately and consciously. The rationalization of person-ality thus means two things: (1) personality becomes a more ra-tional entity; (2) personality becomes the object of rational manipulation, of a sort of psychological engineering. Probably the second meaning follows, both logically and chronologically, from the first.

A rather consistent set of features distinguishes the rationalized and rationalizing personality. First of all, his overall psychological orientation is toward success and achievement, and he has a built-in intolerance of failure and passivity.[9] Tension develops when-ever the individual is not involved in projects of one kind or an-other in the social world, and severe frustration ensues if these projects do not yield at least a modicum of success. This type of personality is strongly activistic, alienated from the more contem-plative values. Since his fulfillment is in action, rather than in in-tellectual insight or in aesthetic or mystical experience, even his pleasures are approached as matters to be achieved: happiness it-self is a task, often demanding complex organization. The preva-lent attitude toward sex in contemporary American middle-class society illustrates this.[10] Sexual pleasure is considered a worth-while goal. And, as a goal, it is approached with earnest applica-tion, as if by a businessman set on making his first million before he is forty. The double meaning of the phrase "on the make" nicely catches the psychological similarity between success in business and in bed. Orgasms are counted, classified, and carefully engineered, as apparently they are seen as an important moral obligation, and sometimes, one suspects, an irksome one.

The activism of the rationalized personality requires a general attitude of optimism toward one's own projects and toward the world, for otherwise all of one's furious activity might be mean-ingless. Only if world and self are, in principle, improvable does it make sense to apply oneself to their improvement.

This type of personality demands and is prepared to accept strong discipline. Externally, in terms of his projects in the social world, this involves applying rational methods to achieve his goals. Internally, in terms of how the individual marshals his psy-chological resources, this involves what psychologists call "ego

The Theory of the Achievement Motive

David C. McClelland, a psychology professor at Harvard University, in his book, *The Achieving Society,* uses the methods of the behavioral sciences to establish a factual basis by means of which to evaluate and explain the rise and fall of civilization. The achievement motive he considers the decisive factor in economic growth. There is a brief summary of the implications of his findings for the interpretation of society in the last chapter, "Accelerating Economic Growth."

Our analysis has been pursued to its logical conclusion. We have uncovered certain psychological forces that apparently contribute fairly universally to economic development, and have shown how they alter the activities of individuals in a society, particularly in the entrepreneurial class, and traced their origins to certain beliefs and child-rearing practices in the family. In the course of our study we encountered some great landmarks of historical thinking and came to a better understanding of how most of them represent partial insights into more general phenomena.

Thus the connection seen by Max Weber between the Protestant Reformation and the rise of the entrepreneurial spirit, which provided the jumping off point for this study, can now be understood as a special case, by no means limited to Protestantism, of a general increase in *n* Achievement produced by an ideological change. The profit motive, so long a basic analytic element among Marxist and Western economists alike, turns out on closer examination to be the achievement motive, at least in the sense in which most men have used the term to explain the energetic activities of the bourgeoisie. The desire for gain, in and of itself, has done little to produce economic development. But the desire for achievement has done a great deal, and ironically it was probably this same desire that activated the lower middle-class leaders of the Russian Communist Party as well as the bourgeoisie they criticized so intensely.

The whole view of history shifts once the importance of the achievement motive is recognized. For a century we have been dominated by Social Darwinism, by the implicit or explicit notion that man is a creature of his environment, whether natural or social. Marx thought so in advocating economic determinism, in arguing that a man's psychology is shaped in the last analysis by the conditions under which he must work. Even Freud thought so in teaching that civilization was a reaction of man's primitive urges to the repressive force of social institutions beginning with the family.

Practically all social scientists have in the past several generations begun with society and tried to create man in its image. Even Toynbee's theory of history is essentially one of environmental challenges, though he recognizes that states of mind can create internal challenges.

If our study of the role of achievement motivation in society does nothing else, perhaps it will serve to redress the balance a little, to see man as a *creator* of his environment, as well as a creature of it. Much of what the Social Darwinists have taught must be thought through again in terms of a new dimension—i.e., the motives of the men affected by an environmental change or a social institution. A defeat in battle means one thing to a people low in *n* Achievement, another to a people who are high. Discrimination leads to counter-striving among Jews in the United States who are high in *n* Achievement, but not among lower-class Negroes who are low. A bureaucracy filled with men low in *n* (Turkey, Italy) is a different kind of bureaucracy from one staffed by men high in *n* Achievement (the U.S., perhaps Poland). The focus changes. History must be written again, as it was in the nineteenth century, at least partly in terms of national character, in terms of what a people is trying to do or is more concerned with.

Source: David C. McClelland, *The Achieving Society* (New York: Litton, 1961). © 1961 by Litton Educational Publishing, Inc.

control," keeping a tight grip on one's irrational impulses, so that rational goals will not be jeopardized by eruptions of one's "lower" nature. In other words, the rationalization of personality entails, necessarily, a high degree of what Freud terms "repression." Again, the parallelism with economic rationality is very evident. Weber showed how important *saving* is for the development of a capitalist economy; the spirit of capitalism motivates individuals to save rather than spend their surplus income. The psychological analogue of saving is a capacity for delayed gratification, a readiness of the personality to forego immediate satisfactions for the sake of some future goal, sometimes for goals in a far-away future. In sum, the rationalized personality is capable of both social and psychological discipline. Simply, he is capable of hard work, including hard work on himself.

Furthermore, the rationalized personality possesses a high degree of consciousness, both of the world and of himself. The achievement of rational goals requires reflection, deliberateness, calculation. The modern individual cannot now, as he could in traditional societies, count on his life being adequately governed by the grand designs of the institutional networks. Instead, he must choose, plan, manipulate his course in society. One way to put this is that the institutions no longer "program" the individual as effectively and as completely as they once did; as a result, he must "program" himself, and be ready to change the "programs" in mid-action. A contemporary German sociologist has called this peculiar feature of modern personality its "permanent reflectiveness." [11] This is a kind of overconsciousness.

Overconsciousness extends into the very self. Rationalized man keeps on observing himself, scrutinizing his own conduct, questioning his own motives—in sum, he is a do-it-yourself psychologist and a perpetual candidate for the services of psychological analyst, therapist, counselor, and the like. Once more, the parallelism between the socioeconomic and the psychological is clearcut. One of the important innovations of nascent capitalism was the refinement of economic calculating techniques. The capitalist entrepreneur needs methods like double-entry bookkeeping to rationally calculate his resources, as he used them in the past and how he intends to use them to advance toward his future goals. This same kind of calculation has a psychological counterpart. Modern man's consciousness of himself can be aptly described as psychological bookkeeping: his ówn personality, its assets and its problems, becomes, as it were, scrutinized on the credit and debit sides of a psychological ledger. It is obvious that such self-consciousness and self-manipulation are functional for the disciplined pursuit of social goals. It should also be evident that a high propensity to anxiety will likely be the price.

MOBILITY

Wherever in the world man achieves or is permitted social and geographical mobility, we will find there the modern personality type which we have been discussing. That is, the type emerges when the social structure permits or encourages the geographical movement of the people as well as movement within the stratification system. This has the usual psychological concomitant of structuring social reality into the individual. These individuals develop a certain expansion of their imaginations, which Lerner wisely called "mobility" [12.] the modern personality type's imagination is capable of ranging beyond his immediate circumstances, just as his body is.

Traditional forms of mentality, of ideas, and of personality can, quite fairly, be characterized as "immobile." They are fixed, and call for little modification throughout one's lifetime. Ideationally, the individual's world is firmly defined, usually by a stable religious worldview. Psychologically, the individual's sense of himself is firmly and stably defined—he "knows who he is." He does not necessarily *like* what he is, but at least he *knows* it, as he has what we call character.[13] He is, of course, a stranger to identity crises. But with the onset of modernization, this stable ideational and psychological sense begins to shift: old ideas begin to shake; old personality patterns become more fluid; the world has begun to change, and so have its inhabitants. And these changes in the individual prove, more often than not, to be geographical and social mobility. As people move from one social stratum to another, what they think and what they are changes, almost inevitably. Their old ideas no longer meet the new conditions of their lives. The same holds for the predispositions, attitudes, and habits, the sum of which we call "personality." People come to experience reality in new ways and, in the same process, come to experience *themselves* differently.

Lerner, in his study of modernization in the Middle East, discussed imaginative mobility on the basis of some interesting data.[14] For example, his questionnaire asked respondents to place themselves in the position of their country's head of government, and then to say how they would act in regard to certain policy matters. This, of course, is the kind of imaginative exercise that Westerners regularly engage in, and it is the basis of, among other things, the business of public opinion polls. In the Middle East, Lerner found only individuals who were open to modernization could accomplish this feat of imagination; most of the traditional people were unable to imagine themselves in this impossible situation and some even became angry that such a sacrilegious suggestion had been made to them. In a parallel example, Lerner's questionnaire asked the respondents under what circumstances they would consider changing their place of residence. Once more, only the more modern types were willing to answer. The traditional types strongly affirmed that they would never move from their home village, and some became quite upset by the thought. One villager, after a long silence, replied: "I would rather die." What

Modern Industrial Society and the Mobile Personality

J. R. Seeley, R. A. Sim, and E. W. Loosley have studied the suburban culture of North American industrial society. They vividly describe the personality of the upper-middle-class individual, oriented to mobility and success in his career.

> Various social interests have a stake in the development of career-oriented persons. We have said that the complex contemporary division of labor requires certain components at the professional and managerial level which become essential to the smooth operation of an industrial society. The maintenance of this group is, in turn, assured, it seems, by three conditions: mobility in space and in social class; occupational opportunity with commensurate rewards in material objects and class position; and finally, personal flexibility and adaptability within fairly well defined limits respecting attitude, behavior, and occupational techniques. These are the prerequisites of the successful career.
>
> Mobility is, as we see it here, the highly developed pattern of movement from one job to another, from one place of residence to another, from one city to another, from one class position to another. To the individual, therefore, moving must not only hold the promise of material reward and added prestige, but, in spite of cost and labor, it should itself be "exciting." The chance to meet new friends, the known but as yet untried amenities in the distant city, together with the exhilaration of leaving behind the frustrations and jealousies of office, clique, and neighborhood, help to make moving more than tolerable. The man and woman of the Heights have few bonds that cannot be broken at the promise of a "promotion." They have been prepared for this from the cradle.
>
> Mobility must be matched by opportunity: opportunity for training, employment, and advancement. Training must be available if the mobile person, bent upon a career, is to acquire the expected and necessary technical skills and social graces. He must have, of course, at least a minimum standard of intelligence, energy, and poise; but, more importantly, he must be drawn toward the enterprises around which skill, grace, intelligence, energy, and poise will play, and out of which his own career will develop. He must wish to manage or cure—and be prepared to learn to cure or manage.
>
> The third prerequisite calls for a readiness in the professional and executive to abandon cherished usages and techniques as new ones

arise. Of course the desire for change must not be so strong as to impair the individual's performance at the level presently occupied; the costs and risks of moving may help to bridle his ambition, but the job itself has its own satisfactions. Nevertheless, he must be willing to acquire new conceptions of life and organization, and to revise constantly in later life his procedures within his chosen field. The differences between the career of the person who has risen by his own effort and the person who has been placed in Crestwood Heights by the parent have a relation to the flexibility which is so essential to the professional and executive person in a rapidly changing society, since the individual who "gets a good start" is more likely to accept current techniques and practices than the individual who is struggling upward. The latter must challenge the very arrangements which give advantage to the former. Personal flexibility is a valued characteristic, whereas rigidity is generally condemned. "Flexibility" allows the person to accept innovation, to maneuver in difficult situations where precedent gives little guidance, and to seek by his own efforts new solutions to social and technological problems.

Source: J. R. Seeley, R. A. Sim, E. W. Loosley, *Crestwood Heights* (New York: Basic Books, 1956), p. 119.

does all this mean? Quite simply, it means that a traditional individual is tied to his place in the world and to the social identity that goes with this place. Objectively, in his actual biography, he is very unlikely to move. Subjectively, in his imagination, he cannot move either. He is *where* he is and *what* he *is* with a finality that is actually hard for a Westerner to conceive of.

Lerner's notions about the psychological aspects of modernization are supported by various other studies. Fraser, in a study of urbanization in Africa, showed that, in a modernizing nation geographical mobility is directly related to status.[15] A young man, to be anybody at all, has to have been in the city. It is the city, with its violent overturning of traditional patterns, that draws the most energetic and aspiring individuals. The senses of mobility and modernity both focus on the city as the reality and as the symbol of a new world. Also, Kenneth Little showed how psychological mobility is directly related to achievement ratings.[16] The individuals whose imaginations were capable of ranging beyond their immediate surroundings were generally the ones who achieved success in their projects both in and out of their careers. To some extent, of course, this correlation could possibly be a matter of intelligence, except that the data suggest other things are involved. After all, traditional types can be of high intelligence. It is not intelligence as such that goes with modernization, but a specific *kind* of intelligence, namely, the kind that Lerner called mobile. Again, the fundamental difference is that the modern personality, unlike the traditional one, is ready *for* change and *to* change.

A curious consequence is also shown by data about Allied prisoners of war during the Korean war.[17] While, as is well known, a sizable group of American and other Western prisoners were successfully converted by the "brainwashing" techniques of their Chinese captors, not a single Turkish prisoner was so converted. There may have been a number of different reasons for this, but one reason was very probably the predominantly traditional personality of the Turkish soldier, who was usually a simple villager. Once again, the modern, other-directed individual was able to change, and be changed, while the tradition-bound individual could not "move," and thus resisted the social forces designed to change him.

In this comparison of traditional and modern personality types, the student or the sociologist, whatever his own values, should beware of romantic distortions. It is fashionable today to bewail the alienation and the identity crisis of modern man, and to contrast this longingly with the sense of belonging and the stable sense of identity of the traditional personality type. Generally, it is true that traditional societies produce people who are more secure and less anxious in their psychological makeup than are most contemporary Westerners. But it is well to keep in mind the cost of this psychological stability—the narrowness of perspective, the overall passivity in the face of whatever fate or government or nature does, and, often, a pervasive sense of hopelessness that things could ever be better. Sociology, of course, cannot itself evaluate these things for anyone, but it can help to assess the social and psychological debit/asset balance of the two personality types.

It should be clear by now that the structural characteristics of society are directly related to the personality types most common in it. For example, the relationship between a personality geared to achieving success and the objective possibilities of success in his society, is a reciprocal or dialectical one. The more individuals there are whose personalities are oriented toward success, the

greater the likelihood that the society will as a whole be successful, especially in its efforts to modernize itself. Conversely, the
more a society's structures allow the individual to succeed in his
life, to better his position and to achieve his aspirations, the
greater will be the multiplication of achievement-oriented personalities. This social-psychological dialectic, unfortunately, does *not*
mean that there exists a one-to-one relationship between objective
success possibilities and subjective success aspirations. If it did, of
course, we would be living in the best of all possible worlds—
nobody's grasp would be bigger than his reach.

In fact, however, matters are less harmoniously arranged. Typically, aspirations become modernized more rapidly than do the
means for their attainment. An important factor in this is mass
communications, for to give people an image of a better life (by
means of movies, radio, television) is much easier than to give
them the means of achieving it. As a result, people's mentalities
begin to change quite out of proportion to the actual, external
changes in their situations. And so, the dynamic of social-psychological modernization, which increases the sense of frustration
in large numbers of people, can be very explosive. This is the
phenomenon that has been called the "revolution of rising
expectations"—and it is an important factor behind the revolutionary explosions of our age, in the underdeveloped countries and
in the underdeveloped sectors of the industrialized countries.

The great differences between the modern and the traditional
personality types, which we have been describing in regard to industrialized Western versus underdeveloped countries, exists also
within the modernized nations themselves. There the lower stratum often develops personality traits that are antagonistic to the
modernizing processes that the middle class is oriented toward.[18]
This is particularly clear in their child-rearing practices.[19] In the
middle class, children are reared in a way that facilitates achievement, at the same time that it creates anxieties and identity crises.
The workings of this process are vividly pictured in Seeley's study
of child-rearing in an upper-middle-class suburb of Toronto.[20]
Here an entire community is frantically pushing its young toward
achievement and success; home is a kind of pervasive kindergarten
in which the mobility anxieties of the parents are fully matched by
those of their children. The antipodal story is told in various social-psychological studies of Black American children.[21] In sum,
these studies show that Black children in the slums are reared

under conditions that make it almost impossible for them to be successful in the modern occupational world. School is the institution in which this failure of the child first is revealed, but its roots go further back, even to the earliest stages of socialization. This is not the place to discourse on the complex social, political, and educational problems with which this situation confronts American society; we will only point out that here, within an enclave of one of the most industrialized and modernized societies in the world, we have the paradigm for the social-psychological problems faced by every underdeveloped society.

THE RATIONALIZED SELF IN ITS WORLD

Now that we have established the fact of parallelism between the modernization of society and the modernization of personality, we will describe it more specifically in regard to several of the major processes of modern society. The three processes that we consider as crucial are urbanization, industrialization, and bureaucratization.

Urbanization and life in the city have played the most marked role in modernizing the human personality.[22] The city produces psychological behavior quite unlike that produced by preurban and nonurban communities, and indeed it is considered the symbolic home of modern man. The fundamental quality of life in the city is that it subjects the individual to a remarkably large variety of social experiences and groups. Of course, this has always been true of cities, even in ancient times, but the multiplicity of urban experiences and groups has vastly increased in the modern city, not only because of the latter's absolute size, but also because of its social complexity. What this means for the individual who lives an urban life is role segmentation. That is, the modern urban individual has to perform many different and mutually segregated roles in the ordinary course of his life. The most highly visible separation occurs between roles connected with work and roles pertaining to private life, which are commonly not only rather unrelated in nature, but also in geographical location: few people live where they work. The dissimilar nature of vocational and domestic life leads to the development of different personalities at work and at home. It goes without saying that this can become a strain, but the strain is reduced by keeping the discrepant roles physically far apart.

It should be stressed that the modern individual experiences role segmentation at a fairly early stage of his socialization—rarely later than when he enters school, and frequently earlier. The learning of role segmentation is an important facet of the process of personality formation, as the individual's identity is crucially linked to the roles he plays in his social life. Role segmentation, therefore, necessarily entails identity segmentation.[23] Simply, what this means is that the modern urban individual, even when still a child, must be different things with different people: he must act differently, must play different roles. Inevitably, then, an element of multiplicity (if one wishes, of duplicity) enters his conception of himself. He becomes unsure of just what or who he is.

The insecurity caused by segmentation is compounded by the fact that most urban relationships are highly anonymous and impersonal, and necessarily so, as it would be emotionally and even physiologically impossible to have a profoundly personal relationship with the numerous people available and unavoidable in city life. As we have seen, Simmel viewed the city as a society of strangers, people, who, in passing, brush against each other lightly. The sociologist expresses it this way: most urban social relations take place in secondary groups, that is, in groups or situations with which the individual has no deep or abiding ties. Understandably, then, urban life is always threatened by what Durkheim called *anomie*—a state of feeling lost, without secure human ties, and without stable norms.[24] The city is experienced as, above all, a faceless crowd, potentially hostile, generally indifferent. To forestall anomie, the urban individual must be able to entrench himself in a few primary groups, that is, groups with which he feels an abiding sense of belonging and within which he can have intensive face-to-face experiences. These serve as the fortresses of his identity. And the most important of them is, of course, the modern family. But even under the optimal condition of having established and maintained a primary, anomie-forestalling set of relationships, the urban situation still can produce both insecurity about identity and general anxiety. The modern city is a neurosis-generating place *par excellence*—what Karen Horney called the "neurotic personality of our time" is, above all, an urban phenomenon.[25]

The movement toward urbanization usually involves an economic transformation, as a cash economy comes to replace a system based on land tenure. This too has far-reaching psychological

Personality of the Urban Japanese

The Tokugawa peasant was not fully an individual. He had few private emotions, and few private ambitions. The pattern of his life was more or less determined at birth. He had only to follow the course that was expected of him. In a closely regulated system of social relations, situations which presented themselves to him as offering or requiring a conscious choice between alternative courses of action were rare. When such situations did arise, it was as a representative of the family that he acted, and the responsibility for the choice was as much his family's as his own. The possibility of incurring the displeasure of, and becoming emotionally isolated from, his family and his neighbours was sufficient to prevent him from departing from the established modes of conduct. For on these people he was both emotionally and economically dependent.

But his great-grandson Mr. Risookei, in modern Tokyo, is a very different person, and his life is lived under different conditions. His neighbours are simply people who live next door and in whose economic or emotional life he shares as little as they in his. His employer is simply the man to whom for the moment he sells his labour. His livelihood depends on no one's goodwill, but only on the fact that it continues to be in the interest of his employer to employ him, of his shopkeepers to serve him, and of his bank to maintain its reputation by safeguarding his savings. What employer he shall serve, which shop he shall patronize, how he shall spend his leisure time, whom he shall make his friends—these become questions which offer a conscious choice of alternatives. And, provided that his choices are not proscribed by the laws of the country, few people outside his immediate household will be concerned to show either approval or disapproval of his actions; perhaps only a small circle of workmates or neighbours, a circle which, small and constantly shifting with changes of job and of residence, is less important to his emotional well-being and has less power to influence his conduct by its expressions of approval and disapproval than was the case with the Tokugawa peasant and his fellow-villagers. "The Risookei family" means little to such circles of acquaintances, and the fear that by exciting their disapproval he will bring dishonour on the good name of his family weighs little with Risookei himself.

Tradition, then, does not provide Mr. Risookei with clear directions for leading his life or regulating his relations with his fellow men; nor does his social environment provide pressures which serve to keep him moving in traditional grooves. His sources of direction are internal. It is a duty to himself to live up to the aims which he has set himself, and it is he who blames himself if he fails to achieve his ambitions to acquire wealth, or prestige, or saintliness, or power, or academic qualifications. It is his own conscience whose disapproval is excited if, in dealing with the manifold situations of choice which face him, he fails to live up to certain generalized standards of conduct which he has internalized.

Source: R. P. Dore, *City Life in Japan* (Berkeley: University of California Press, 1958), pp. 376–377. Reprinted by permission of the Regents of the University of California.

consequences. The individual's status and identity, what and who he is, become less visible, less concrete, less secure, and more easily convertible; purchasable commodities become status symbols and, as such, part of what Erving Goffman has called the individual's "identity kit." [26] All of this is, of course, related once again to the high geographical and social mobility of urban society. Like jobs and homes, status and identity also become objects to be achieved. As the individual must strive to attain a certain social position, so must he strive to become a certain kind of person. In a way that would be unimaginable in traditional societies, identity has become a *project*. The individual works on his self, or finds an expert in the proliferating American psychotherapeutic profession to do the work for him.

As society is a mobile place, so is the individual self. Both biography *and* personality are seen as escalators, which move toward social and personal fulfillment. The individual is inclined not only to change the milieu, but also to consider possible change of his own self.[27] The familial and institutionalized educational processes by means of which individuals are socialized not just into their stratum of origin, but also into (or rather, *toward*) a stratum they aspire to, have grave psychological consequences, which we call the "deepening" of individual subjectivity. (We will examine this more closely in the final chapter.) One point should, however, be reiterated here: the family is not capable of providing this sort of socialization by itself and for this reason educational institutions of one kind or another become tremendously important in this situation. We have previously referred to this fact but should remember it once more in connection with the social-psychological dynamics of modernization.

Industrialization also has a potent effect on personality. Industrial work and the social organization it requires both place a premium on specific psychological traits.[28] The preeminent ones are rationality and discipline. Industrial work demands consistent and logical relationships between means and ends; it also demands discipline, from the external level of punctuality and precision to the internal level of high frustration tolerance and a capacity for delayed gratification. Thorstein Veblen, in a classical work of American sociology, called this the "discipline of the machine." [29] Of course, it is not the machine, in the end of itself, that has these effects, but the social organization that is required for machine production. In any case, industrialization can proceed only where enough individuals are psychologically prepared to work under its conditions.

Bureaucracy, a form of social organization, is the primary condition of work in an advanced industrial society; indeed, it is required even in the noneconomic institutions of modern life. It demands specific personality traits, which society helps create for it.[30] The traits are basically impulse controls of an exceptionally far-reaching kind. To use current American idiom, bureaucracy requires and produces "uptight" people. They are orderly, systematic, and cautious. And they exercise manipulative controls not only over the world (*what*ever it is they administer) and the world's people (*who*ever it is they administer), but even administer their own selves as well. The bureaucratic personality's administrations are founded on a certain sense of time, symbolized by the ubiquity of the watch and clock; not surprisingly, a wristwatch is an important symbol of modernity, as is the pen, in underdeveloped countries. And, bureaucracy requires highly specified role definitions (I'm only competent to deal with area "x"), thus further aggravating what we have called the segmentation of identity.

Sociological and psychological literature generally deal with the phenomenon of the bureaucratic personality in quite negative terms. For example, see the writings of Erich Fromm and William H. Whyte.[31] Their concern has been that—with the bureaucratization of personality—drive, enterprise, and spontaneity may disappear. This generally is an accurate characterization. Also, since in American society the school system, and especially higher education, is structured so as to foster the bureaucratized personality type, trouble may potentially come from those who do not fit into this mold.[32] On the other hand, it must be recognized that modernization could hardly exist without this type of man. In underdeveloped countries, the critical role of the military may derive partly from the fact that military officers are the only bureaucratic executives. A major problem of modern society may be to develop a *modus vivendi* between the social-psychological requirements of bureaucratic organizations and the demands of those people who cannot or will not live in accordance with those requirements.

NOTES

1. Daniel Lerner, *The Passing of Traditional Society* (Glencoe: Free Press, 1958).

2. *Ibid.*, pp. 27 ff.

3. *Ibid.*

4. Ibn-Khaldun in the *Muggadimah* insisted that differences in customs and institutions depend on the various ways in which man procures for himself the means of subsistence.

5. In the late seventeenth century we find in the writings of the Frenchman Marquis de La Fare, living at the court of Louis XIV, the argument that the personality and mentality of people differ in accordance with their social background, and especially their work: *"L'esprit particulier de leur profession."* M. de La Fare, *Mémoires et réflexions sur les principaux Evénements du regne de Louis XIV et sur le Caractère de ceux qui y ont eu la principale part,* Nouv. ed. (Amsterdam: 1782), pp. 6 ff. Early reflections on the personality of peasants can also be found in eighteenth-century Germany, in such writings as Christian Garve, *Ueber den Charakter der Bauern und ihr Verhaeltnis gegen die Gutsherrn und gegen die Regierung* (Breslau: Korn, 1786), p. 5. Here Garve claims that the social factor is more important than the national factor.

In the industrializing societies the attention shifted to the question of the new kind of personality emerging with the newly created industrial worker. See, for instance, Adam Ferguson, *An Essay on the History of Civil Society* (Basel: Tourneisen, 1789), p. 279; Adam Smith, *An Inquiry on the Nature and Causes of the Wealth of Nations* (London: Dove, 1826), pp. 609–610; Jules Michelet, *Le Peuple* (Geneva: Fallot, 1846), p. 33.

6. Marx and Engels formulated this notion first in a rigid form in their famous *Communist Manifesto.* Together and independently in their subsequent years they elaborated this notion.

7. Vilfredo Pareto, *The Mind and Society,* 4 vols. (New York: Harcourt, Brace, 1935), especially 1:426, 2:276–277 and section 870, and IV, on the "Circulation of Elites." See also Georg Simmel, *Die Philosophie des Geldes* (Berlin: Duncker and Humblot, 1958) and "The Metropolis and Mental Life," in Kurt H. Wolff, ed., *The Sociology of Georg Simmel* (Glencoe: Free Press, 1950).

8. Max Weber, *The Protestant Ethic and the Spirit of Capitalism* (New York: Scribners, 1930).

9. David C. McClelland, *The Achieving Society* (New York: Free Press, 1967).

10. Articles in *Commentary,* Spring 1965.

11. Welmut Schelsky, "Ist die Dauerreflexion institutionalisierbar," in *Zeitschrift fuer Evangelische Ethik* (1957): 4, pp. 153 ff.

12. Lerner, *op. cit.,* pp. 43 ff.

13. Cf. the concept of "inner-directed" personality in David Riesman *et al., The Lonely Crowd* (New Haven: Yale University Press, 1950).

14. Lerner, *op. cit.,* p. 415, Appendix A: "The Questionnaire."

15. T. M. Fraser, "Achievement Motivation as a Factor in Rural Development: A Report on Research in Western Orissa" (unpublished paper, Haverford College, 1961). A short summary of essential findings in this paper can be found in McClelland, *op. cit.,* pp. 271–273, 380–381.

16. Kenneth Little, *West African Urbanization* (New York: Cambridge University Press, 1965), Chap. 1, "The Lure of the Town."

17. Edward Hunter, *Brain-washing in Red China* (New York: Vanguard Press, 1951).

18. Cf. McClelland, *op. cit.,* on U. S. A. and Italy. See also the findings of S. M. Lipset and Reinhard Bendix, *Social Mobility in Industrial Society* (Berkeley: University of California Press, 1963); also W. Lloyd Warner *et al., Social Class in America* (Chicago: University of Chicago Press, 1949); and the many recent community studies in America which attempt to show that the personality is, to a decisive degree, formed by the class subculture of the individual.

19. See Donald Gilbert McKinley, *Social Class and Family Life* (New York: Free Press, 1954); A. B. Hollingshead, *Elmtown's Youth* (New York: John Wiley, 1949); Herbert Gans, *The Urban Villagers* (New York: Free Press, 1962); J. R. Seeley et al., *Crestwood Heights* (New York: Basic Books, 1956); and Jessie Bernard, *Marriage and Family among Negroes* (Englewood Cliffs: Prentice-Hall, 1966).

20. Seeley, *op. cit.*

21. Bernard, *op. cit.*

22. Simmel, "The Metropolis and Mental Life."

23. George Herbert Mead, *Mind, Self, and Society* (Chicago: University of Chicago Press, 1934).

24. Émile Durkheim, *Suicide* (Glencoe: Free Press, 1951). Also see Robert Merton, "Social Structure and Anomie," in *op. cit.*

25. Karen Horney, *The Neurotic Personality of Our Time* (New York: Norton, 1937).

26. Erving Goffman, *The Presentation of Self in Everyday Life* (New York: Doubleday Anchor, 1959).

27. Cf. the concept of "anticipatory socialization" in Robert Merton, *Social Theory and Social Structure,* 4th ed. (New York: Free Press, 1961), pp. 265–268.

28. Karl Mannheim, *Essays in the Sociology of Knowledge* (New York: Oxford University Press, 1952).

29. Thorstein Veblen, "The Industrial System of the New Order," in *Absentee Ownership* (Boston: Beacon Press, 1967).

30. See Mannheim, *op. cit.;* Merton, *op. cit.*

31. Erich Fromm, *Escape from Freedom* (New York: Holt, 1941), and William H. Whyte, *The Organization Man* (New York: Doubleday Anchor, 1957).

32. The argument is convincingly made by F. Musgrove, *Youth and the Social Order* (Bloomington: Indiana University Press, 1965), especially the introductory chapter.

[10] The Pluralistic Situation

EVERYTHING we have studied in the preceding chapters contributes to a single peculiarly modern phenomenon: pluralism.[1] In common usage, when we speak of America as a pluralistic society, we mean that it has a plurality of ethnic and other social groups, of religions, of beliefs and value systems, or centers of political power. In this very broad sense, the same term is even enshrined in the American motto *E pluribus unum,* where the oneness of the society is affirmed through the plurality of its constituent groups. But, although this is not incorrect, a narrower understanding of the term is generally more useful for the sociologist. For him, pluralism exists preeminently in terms of belief and value systems. The pluralistic situation is one in which different beliefs and values coexist, side by side—or, from another perspective, in which no worldview successfully maintains an ideological monopoly.

The basic features of pluralistic society become quite clear as soon as one thinks, by contrast, of a nonpluralistic, homogeneous society—an intact tribal society. In the latter a common worldview, religious in character, unites the entire society, and all beliefs and values are essentially coextensive and universal throughout the society. There may be individual deviants here and there, or even marginal groups that deviate from the common universe of discourse, but none of these constitute a threat to or are in serious competition with this universe. The various institutions have a high degree of integration—the same "logic," as it were, permeates all of them. The crucial point for our study is that in such a society, socialization takes place in a context that is both institutionally and ideologically unified. And, therefore, it proceeds in a

stable and consistent manner, to produce stable and consistent personalities. Man in a tribal society feels that he knows his world
and knows who he is.

If we conceive of tribal society as being at one end of a continuum and our own society as at the other, most traditional societies
would belong at points much closer to the first pole than to our
own. But, the process of modernization would then constitute a
speedy movement away from tribalism and toward America. In
terms of the social structure, the reason for these relative distances
lies in the rapid multiplication of institutions that occurred when
the division of labor was accelerated by the onset of industrialism
and urbanism. We have already discussed this, explicitly and implicitly, in Part I—on social change and institutional structures.
The level of ideas and personality is what interests us now.

Religious Pluralism

On the ideational level it is in regard to religion that pluralism
first manifested itself, and religious pluralism may still be considered paradigmatic for pluralism in general.[2] In Western history,
religious pluralism has its origin in the disintegration of Christendom and of the medieval ideal of a society integrated by its common religious symbols. As is always true, the actual European society in the Middle Ages did not correspond fully to the lofty
ideal; profound divisions, heresies, and schisms occurred throughout the period. Nevertheless it is certain that medieval Western society had an institutional and ideological unity that it has never
had since then. The Renaissance and the Reformation, each with
its particular challenge to the monopolistic authority of Catholic
Christianity, were crucial in the disintegration of this unity. In the
more recent period the critical factor in the deepening and diffusion of pluralism has been secularization. Indeed, secularization
and pluralism are today almost inseparable phenomena.[3]

Secularization is a process in which religious institutions and
religious symbols withdraw, usually against their will, from sectors
of the society which they previously held sway in. Thus education,
which the Church once controlled, has been progressively emanci-
pated from ecclesiastical control. Not only has the institution of
the Church withdrawn from education, but Christian symbols, val-

Religious Pluralism in America

The peculiar characteristics of religious pluralism in America have
been analyzed by Will Herberg in *Protestant, Catholic, Jew.*

> It must be remembered that in America the variety and multiplicity
> of churches did not, as in Europe, come with the breakdown of a
> single established national church; in America, taking the nation as
> a whole, the variety and multiplicity of churches was almost the
> original condition and coeval with the emergence of the new so-
> ciety. In America, religious pluralism is thus not merely a historical
> and political fact; it is, in the mind of the American, the primordial
> condition of things, an essential aspect of the American Way of
> Life, and therefore in itself an aspect of religious belief. Americans,
> in other words, believe that the plurality of religious groups is a
> proper and legitimate condition. However much he may be attached
> to his own church, however dimly he may regard the beliefs and
> practices of other churches, the American tends to feel rather
> strongly that total religious uniformity, even with his own church
> benefiting thereby, would be something undesirable and wrong, in-
> deed scarcely conceivable. Pluralism of religions and churches is
> something quite axiomatic to the American. This feeling, more than
> anything else, is the foundation of the American doctrine of the
> "separation of church and state," for it is the heart of this doctrine
> that the government may not do anything that implies the pre-emi-
> nence or superior legitimacy of one church over another.

Source: Will Herberg, *Protestant, Catholic, Jew* (New York: Doubleday, 1955), pp. 98 ff.

ues, and beliefs have also been "retreating." Contemporary education in America is now largely secularized. Secularization also occurs in individual consciousness. There, too, religious symbols,
values, and beliefs have tended to disappear totally, or to become
irrelevant and meaningless. Our age is characterized by secularized institutions, by entire societies that can properly be called
secularized, and also by a new secularized man—a type of man
who seems to get along very well without religion. Originally a
Western phenomenon, secularization is today a seemingly inevitable accomplishment of modernization, and therefore appears everywhere in the world. Secularization and pluralism may be said

The Secularization of Modern Life

By secularization we mean the process by which sectors of society and culture are removed from the domination of religious institutions and symbols. When we speak of society and institutions in modern Western history, of course, secularization manifests itself in the evacuation by the Christian churches of areas previously under their control or influence—as in the separation of church and state, or in the expropriation of church lands, or in the emancipation of education from ecclesiastical authority. When we speak of culture and symbols, however, we imply that secularization is more than a social-structural process. It affects the totality of cultural life and of ideation, and may be observed in the decline of religious content in the arts, in philosophy, in literature, and, most important of all, in the rise of science as an autonomous, thoroughly secular perspective on the world. Moreover, it is implied here that the process of secularization has a subjective side as well. As there is a secularization of society and culture, so is there a secularization of consciousness. Put simply, this means that the modern West has produced an increasing number of individuals who look upon the world and their own lives without the benefit of religious interpretations.

While secularization may be viewed as a global phenomenon of modern societies, it is not uniformly distributed within them. Different groups of the population have been affected by it differently. Thus it has been found that the impact of secularization has tended to be stronger on men than on women, on people in the middle-age range than on the very young and the old, in the cities than in the country, on classes directly connected with modern industrial production (particularly the working class) than on those of more traditional occupations (such as artisans or small shopkeepers), on Protestants and Jews than on Catholics, and the like. At least as far as Europe is concerned, it is possible to say with some confidence, on the basis of these data, that church-related religiosity is strongest (and thus, at any rate, social-structural secularization least) on the margins of modern industrial society, both in terms of marginal classes (such as the remnants of old petty bourgeoisies) and marginal individuals (such as those eliminated from the work process). The situation is different in America, where the churches still occupy a more central symbolic position, but it may be argued that they have succeeded in keeping this position only by becoming highly secularized themselves, so that the European and American cases represent two variations on the same underlying theme of global secularization. What is more, it appears that the same secularizing forces may now become worldwide in the course of westernization and modernization. Most of the available data, to be sure, pertain to the social-structural manifestations of secularization rather than to the secularization of consciousness, but we have enough data to indicate the massive presence of the latter in the contemporary West.

Source: Peter L. Berger, *The Sacred Canopy* (New York: Doubleday, 1967), pp. 107 ff. © 1967 by Peter Berger. Reprinted by permission of Peter Berger, Doubleday & Co., and Faber and Faber Ltd.

to be in a dialectical relationship, in that they reciprocally reinforce one another. Whichever may have appeared first historically, today they mutually produce and augment each other. Secularization produces pluralism by weakening the religious monopoly that once dominated most societies. Only in rare instances is the specifically American form of pluralism produced, in which a large variety of religious and quasi-religious groups coexist. However, it is also pluralism where a society contains both adherents to the old religious tradition and those who no longer adhere. More precisely, pluralism exists when the nonadherents become large enough to form a specific subculture or subsociety of their own. For example, in France, which never had America's large variety of churches and sects, pluralism is largely the consequence of secularization, which led whole segments of the population to turn away from the formerly monopolistic Catholic culture and to form their own secular (*laique*) subculture. And, of course, pluralism also produces secularism in turn, because the very fact of the coexistence of beliefs and values weakens the plausibility of any one of them, implicitly calls an *absolute* truth into question. The plausibility of even a nonreligious perspective on the world must be entertained.

Ideational Pluralism

Pluralism produces, in effect, a sort of market of world views. The term "market" is not intended to suggest that worldviews simply become a matter of economic motives or manipulations. The term refers to the fact that all worldviews must compete with each other, since the individual is now in a position to choose freely among them. In a sense, man has become a consumer of worldviews. This pluralism has institutional support, at least to the extent that the state has given up the idea of enforcing one particular religion on its population. The refusal to enforce such a monopoly may take legal and political forms. All of them tend toward some sort of separation of state and church in that the state lets all religious groups fend for themselves, and no longer puts its police powers at their disposal. Often this has a chastening effect on ideological militancy, for every group must accept the existence of its competitors and perhaps even enter into some form of tolerant cooperative relationship. Sociologically, therefore, regardless of their theologically absolute self-interpretations, religious groups become voluntary associations. Of course, an individual's religious choice will still not be altogether free of family and ethnic loyalties, upbringing, and personal experiences. But in the last resort no one is *compelled* to adhere to any religious group; adherence is voluntary in a legal and in a personal sense. After all, it is at least *possible* to shrug aside loyalties, upbringing or habit, and individuals are increasingly taking advantage of this possibility.

Religious pluralism is paradigmatic because it was historically the first form of pluralism and because it may well be the necessary foundation for all other forms of pluralism. In contemporary society, however, there coexists a variety, not only of systems of religious belief, but also of thoroughly secularized *Weltanschauungen* of moralities and values, of personal life styles, and of political and social ideologies. Thus the contemporary American may choose among various religious affiliations, or may choose to forego all religious affiliation; or he may choose, for instance, to adhere to a particular psychotherapeutic group (which may touch every area of his life, even career or morality or child-rearing), to commit himself to unconventional forms of sexuality or aesthetics, to organize his private life in a highly idiosyncratic way, or even to accept an ideology that radically rejects the status quo.

As in the matter of religion, one's choices are not merely personal, individual heresies. Often they lead to membership in a subculture, frequently quite highly organized. So, we have in America today subcultures of Reichians, homosexuals, urbanite swingers, hippies, or the New Left. Needless to say, these all have particularly individualized contents and differing degrees of deviance from the majority norms. What makes the whole situation pluralistic, though, is the voluntary way in which individuals join all their groups, and the competitive coexistence which all are compelled to accept.

An interesting sociological question is whether there may not be an upper limit to pluralism, beyond which a society will be threatened with general collapse. After all, don't we all assume that every society is a society because it has some shared beliefs and values. A society can, for instance, allow variations in sexual morality; it is hardly possible to imagine a viable society that allows different moral choices concerning homicide. On the other hand, the history of modern totalitarianism seems to indicate that efforts to reverse the trend toward pluralism and to use state power to impose new monopolistic belief systems have not been notably successful. Soviet Russia certainly learned to allow some choice. It would seem that whatever the upper limits of pluralism may be, certain strong forces in modern industrial society make a good measure of pluralism nearly inevitable.

The effect of such pluralism on ideas and values is, as we have seen, to militate against certitude and security. Sociology and social psychology can tell us why this is so.[4] As soon as we move away from immediate sense experience, certainty is strongly dependent on social support. We do not require other people to support us in our sure belief that, say, we have a toothache, or that we shall fall to the ground if we step off the roof. But we do require social verification in order to be certain of, say, the divinity of Christ or the superiority of the capitalist system. Our *degree* of certainty is directly related to the strength of our social support: it is easier to "know" that capitalism is best in a milieu in which almost everyone believes it than in one in which there are many strident anticapitalists. In a supportive situation, it is, in fact, possible to be as sure of this as of the facts of physical nature. The belief may then feel natural, in the sense that it will be taken for granted, accepted unquestioningly.

It is precisely this quality of naturalness in regard to ideas, values, and beliefs that is endangered in the pluralistic situation. By definition, pluralism breaches the unanimity of social support. It brings in discordant voices of nonsupport and disconfirmation, and, as a result, doubts and ambiguities insinuate themselves. Even if the system of belief is not threatened with change or collapse, at the very least it will be held in a novel, more tentative, uncertain manner. This progression from pluralism to skepticism we see as one of the principal causes for the crisis of religion in modern society. Religious beliefs are at the farthest remove from direct sense experience, and, therefore, are especially dependent on social unanimity. Where religious beliefs are nearly unanimous, stable, and consistent, they may even feel like natural facts, as indeed they were in traditional societies. But where pluralism has begun to breathe, there is inevitably a sharp decline in the credibility of religion. One may still be a natural Catholic in some remote Spanish village, but hardly in New York City, or, for that matter, in Barcelona. Not surprisingly, comparative data indicate that secularization (at least in the more easily measurable sense of institutional differentiation) is strongest in those social sectors most affected by urbanization and industrialization.[5]

Pluralism's most interesting consequence is not, however, that religious beliefs are abandoned or modified in *content;* rather, it is that the manner in which they are felt in the mind changes. One might say that they have floated up from those levels of unconsciousness on which rest our certainties to those conscious levels where we entertain ideas, hypotheses, opinions that we are not fully committed to. A German investigator called this type of belief "opinion-religion." [6] Actually, American usage has an apt phrase for it, "religious preference." The phrase nicely catches the fundamental uncertainty we have about religious beliefs today. One may have a preference for religious position "X," but that implies that positions "Y" and "Z" are not, at any rate, beyond the range of possibility. One may change one's preference at a later stage. The suggestion of the consumer's attitude is, as we mentioned before, appropriate to the pluralistic market situation. It goes without saying that, if one is certain of something, one can not have a preference for it—for one can conceive of no alternative to it.

Again, this paradigm of the psychology of religion applies equally to other ideas and belief systems in a pluralistic universe. "Natural" assumptions and convictions about morality, about aesthetics, about politics have also profoundly declined. Generally speaking, certainties are hard to come by in our age of rapid change, skepticism, and uncertainty in the realm of ideas. At the same time, if only because of the scope of communications, the mental horizon of people has vastly expanded. We know about more and more—and are certain about less and less. In a very im-

portant sense, then, this is an age of *opinion*. To many, especially
young people, this is not a very satisfactory state of affairs. There
is a considerable hunger for new simplicities and certainties,
which may potentially cause the age of opinion to become the age
of fanaticism. For most people, however, the craving for certainty
remains latent or unfulfilled, or, at best, precariously satisfied by
the individual's personal efforts, and supported, typically, by a
small group of private associates, such as family members, friends,
and fellow-adherents to voluntary associations. In other words,
Weltanschauungen have generally lost their traditional status of
self-evident objectivity; instead, they have become "subjectivized"
and private and, by the same token, tenuous.[7]

Pluralism and Personality

Pluralism's effect on personality is similar to that of mobility, discussed in Chapter 9, for the two are clearly related, at least in
their structural and institutional bases. As is mobility, pluralism
is injected into the very socialization process through which
the individual becomes a member of society and, indeed, becomes
a person.[8] In traditional societies, where there is a high degree of
unity and integration in the institutional structure, this is not so.
There, all the people who constitute what may be called the socializing personnel embody and represent the *same* models, role
expectations, and values. In other words, in such societies there is
no disagreement as to what is expected of the individual, in terms
of both his conduct and his identity. He is clearly, continuously,
and unambiguously *identified*.

The clarity and the continuity of socialization are undermined
in the pluralistic universe, and identity, as a result, is much more
ambiguous. The entire social context, even in the experience of
very young children, is quite fragmented. Discrepant role definitions and role expectations are presented to the child: he is supposed to be "X" in one context, "Y" in another. What is more,
there is a great amount of uncertainty among his socializers about
their roles in the child-rearing process, and especially among contemporary parents. As the child grows older and moves outside
his family, his experience of the plurality of the social world becomes almost bewildering. He finds a variety of conflicting models

and expectations—in the school, in the peer-group, in the mass media, to mention only the three most obvious sources.

The consequence of all this is fairly straightforward: the individual is forced to *choose* a self, himself, just as we saw that he was forced to choose his ideological perspective on the world. That is, there is a sort of identity preference, as there is religious preference, among those available in the identity market. For example, the American adolescent may exercise consumer-like preference with respect to a number of socially obtainable identities —junior-hippie, junior-swinger, careerist, serious student, athletic-extrovert. And, each choice is by definition a tentative, not a final one. Identity and personality are open-ended, inconclusive, always prone to radical change.

The personality type that has the best "fit" with the pluralistic situation is, quite naturally, the same one we previously described as the high-mobility type. Perhaps now its general portrait will be even more distinct. This type has an unstable identity. The individual is prone to recurrent identity crises, which are related to his perpetually changing social milieu: he is chronically unsure of just who and what he is. The dynamics of social life make his uncertainty contagious. It communicates itself to those who associate intimately with him and is especially crucial in the socialization of his children. It is then self-perpetuating and self-multiplying. This is further intensified by this personality type's extreme capacity for self-observation, the product of his identity's not feeling natural and *fait accompli*. Thus today an increasing number of individuals reflect almost unceasingly on themselves and manipulate themselves with a variety of psychological techniques, since to them identity is a *problem* and a *task*.

The diffusion of this personality type is the basis of what we call subjectivization—the individual has developed an all-consuming interest in himself. This intense self-regard has also been called "psychologism." Theoretically, it is expressed in the radical subjectivization of art and literature.[9] Practically, it shows itself in the great vogue of psychotherapeutic activities and movements.[10] In its extreme expressions (as, for instance, in some abstract forms of contemporary art and literature), objective reality has actually been denied—the whole of reality has been reduced to individual consciousness and its subjective perceptions, emotions, and states of being. Politically, the turn to subjectivity is linked to all ideologies of individual freedom and autonomy, and to call for an alleged right to untrammelled, spontaneous self-expression. These conceptions have, to some extent, become institutionalized in the educational system, from baby-care *à la* Dr. Spock to the permissive university, and on this formal level—self-perpetuating and self-multiplying. We need only to glance at current youth unrest for an indication of how explosive a force this social-psychological constellation potentially is.

The pluralization and fragmentation of personality expresses itself for most people in modern societies in one basic dichotomy: the separation of their lives into private and public spheres.[11] Since for most people their public life is coextensive with their work, this dichotomy means that an individual is one thing at work and quite another at home. Not only does he perform different roles, but he actually experiences a different identity. The sharp contradictions between these two lives sometimes lead to intolerable psychological tensions and crises of one kind or another. Being given to reflection about himself, the simple expedient of physically segregating the two lives often does not suffice to quiet modern man's urge somehow to integrate the discrepancies: he must try to "rationalize" them, both in the Freudian sense of finding reasons for what he does unreasoningly and in the Weberian sense of seeking a rational *modus operandi* in the complexities of his existence.

The private sphere, it may be said, did not exist before the modern age, at least not in the way we now experience it. In terms of our overall social structure, the private domain is a kind of interstitial area, related only indirectly to the economic and political institutions. Historically, it was the rationalization of these major institutions that led to the creation of the private sphere, by eliminating from them everything that was personal, private, and familistic. The emergence of the modern factory is a prime example of this development: production was taken out of the home, away from the context of family life. As a result, home and family became private in a new way: on the one hand, they were deprived of their traditional public functions; but, on the other hand, they were freed for new functions pertaining to the private aspirations and pleasures of the individual.

Viewed by itself, the private sphere is characterized by a high degree of autonomy, at least as compared with the sphere of public institutions. This does not necessarily mean that it is a realm of perfect freedom. But it does mean that the individual has, in this

The Rise of the Private Sphere in Modern Society

Most analysts of the role of religion in modern society see it as facing an inevitable decline in importance. Thomas Luckmann, in his *The Invisible Religion,* takes a divergent view. Following Durkheim, he argues that religion is a constant element in all of men's attempts to find "ultimate" significance. He believes that what is happening today is not the disappearance of all religion, but its emergence in a new, secular form. This form of social religion is anchored in the private sphere. In the following we have selected a few passages describing some of the aspects of the "private sphere," (p. 109 ff.).

The dominant themes of the modern sacred cosmos bestow something like a sacred status upon the individual. . . . This, of course, is consistent with our finding that "ultimate" significance is found by the typical individual in modern industrial societies primarily in the "private sphere"—and thus in his "private" biography. The traditional symbolic universes become irrelevant to the everyday experience of the typical individual and lose their character as a (superordinated) reality. The primary social institutions, on the other hand, turn into realities whose sense is alien to the individual. The transcendent social order ceases to be *subjectively* significant both as a representation of an encompassing cosmic meaning and in its concrete institutional manifestations. With respect to matters that "count," the individual is retrenched in the "private sphere." It is of considerable interest that even those subordinate themes in the modern sacred cosmos that are derived from economic and political ideologies tend to be articulated in an increasingly "individualistic" manner—for example, the responsible citizen, the successful business "operator."

The theme of individual "autonomy" found many different expressions. . . . In the modern sacred cosmos self-expression and self-realization represent the most important expressions of the ruling topic of individual "autonomy." Because the individual's performances are controlled by the primary public institutions, he soon recognizes the limits of his "autonomy" and learns to confine the quest for self-realization to the "private sphere."

Luckmann identifies a number of these themes of self-realization— the prevalent mobility ethos, status achievement, realization of self in sexuality, the new meaning of self-realization in the family, et cetera.

Source: Thomas Luckmann, *The Invisible Religion* (New York: Macmillan, 1967), pp. 109 ff.

sphere, much greater scope for arranging his life according to his own taste—indeed, his own *preferences*. At work—as in all highly rationalized sectors of society—the individual must perform functions that are firmly structured and that leave relatively little leeway for personal modifications. This is because rationalization demands, among other things, the assurance of smooth continuity; the individual must, in principle, be replaceable, which means that stringent limits must be set on the degree to which a man may "personalize" his role performance. Thus the individual's identity during work becomes extremely impersonal, anonymous. At home, in the private sphere these fundamental imperatives prevail, if at all, to a much lesser degree. The freedom is not absolute even here, but to a considerable degree the individual may fashion his life as he sees fit. Original or eccentric ways are not barred, so long as they do not interfere. Indeed, the argument can be made that eccentricity in private life supports conformity in public, because it provides a safety valve for one's frustrated individualism. Many people today regularly "commute" between conformity and eccentricity, the former being a necessity of their economic existence, the latter a necessity of their psychological economy.

To the degree that work has become rationalized, has become regulated by impersonalizing mechanical procedures, to that degree it has become meaningless and frustrating of personal fulfillment. This is especially widespread on the middle and lower levels of the occupational structure.[12] By way of compensation, it is in the private arena that most people seek personal meaning and fulfillment. The quest for private satisfactions takes many forms. On the most obvious level, it is manifested in consumption for happiness—satisfaction is derived from the possession and use of the material goods that are increasingly available to everybody in affluent modern societies. Personal identity here becomes attached to material possessions. Despite the lamentations of moralists and intellectuals, this can be quite satisfying to an individual, so long as he can successfully maintain a certain level of affluence. After all, there is no intrinsic reason why a steady stream of commodities should be any less fulfilling than, say, the possession by a traditional peasant of a plot of soil.

It is safe to assume, however, that such material possession *alone* is not enough for most modern people, just as it was not sufficient for most peasants either. Therefore, the private sphere also offers a range of nonmaterial satisfactions and sources of personal identity; they differ widely in nature, but the sophistication and meaningfulness one sees in them are dependent on one's personal hierarchy of values. There are the joys of family life, of sexual gratification, of intellectual and aesthetic pursuits, and of activities ranging from organized religion to do-it-yourself hobbies. Some of these satisfactions are legitimated by complex and highly sophisticated ideologies; contemporary familism and sexualism, for example, in which the individual's identity is felt to derive from his successes as, respectively, a family man (a good father and husband) and a sexual being (a perfect embodiment of the *Playboy* ideal). In a pluralistic society there are, of course, many options, many consumer choices as to which of these private activities, sources of identity, and ideologies one "prefers."

We will conclude this discussion by pointing once again to the phenomenon of convergence. To be sure, pluralism takes a different form in different societies. Its basic effects, however, are everywhere similar, on the levels of both ideas and personality. To some this may be reassuring, to others frightening. The consequence is, in either case, very significant sociologically: the world is becoming all of one piece, not only structurally but ideologically and psychologically as well. All of the world's problems resemble each other more and more. And this allows for the hope that such solutions to these problems as may be found in one place will also have relevance everywhere. This insight is of especial importance for Americans. America represents the most advanced type of modern industrial society—not, to be sure, in the sense of moral superiority, but in the sense that the forces of modernization have gone furthest here. America has become a laboratory for the future of our planet. This may not make for tranquil living, but it has an undeniable element of challenge in it. The challenge lies in the recognition that the problems we face and the solutions we may be able to find are likely to matter, vitally, for mankind as a whole.

NOTES

1. On the general conception of pluralism, see Peter Berger and Thomas Luckmann, "Secularization and Pluralism," *International Yearbook of Religion* 2 (1966): 73–86.

2. On religious pluralism in America, see Will Herberg, *Protestant, Catholic, Jew* (New York: Doubleday, 1955); Gerhard Lenski, *The Religious Factor* (New York: Doubleday, 1961).

3. On the interconnection between secularization and pluralism, see Peter Berger, *The Sacred Canopy—Elements of a Sociological Theory of Religion* (New York: Doubleday, 1967), pp. 105 ff.; Thomas Luckmann, *The Invisible Religion—The Problem of Religion in Modern Society* (New York: Macmillan, 1967); Berger and Luckmann, *op. cit.*

4. In American social psychology, the work of Solomon Asch and Muzafer Sherif is of basic importance in dealing with the problem of the social support of belief systems. See Asch's *Social Psychology* (Englewood Cliffs, N. J.: Prentice-Hall, 1952), and Sherif's *Social Interaction* (Chicago: Aldine, 1967).

5. A large variety of comparative materials on secularization, mainly in Western societies, may be found in the following journals in the sociology of religion: *Archives de sociologie des religions* and *Social Compass* and *Sociological Analysis*. Some of the best work on this has been done in France, in the school of Gabriel Lebras: for some English selections, see Louis Schneider, ed., *Religion, Culture, and Society* (New York: John Wiley, 1964). For an interesting study of the relationship between urbanization and secularization in Africa, see Kenneth Little, *West African Urbanization* (New York: Cambridge University Press, 1965).

6. The term was coined by Hans-Otto Woelber, *Religion ohne Entscheidung* (Goettingen: Vandenboeck & Ruprecht, 1959).

7. The term was coined by Arnold Gehlen and developed in various works of his, none of which is presently available in English. For reference to modern society, see especially *Die Seele im technischen Zeitalter* (Hamburg: Rowohlt, 1957).

8. On the theoretical presuppositions underlying our discussion of pluralistic socialization, see Peter Berger and Thomas Luckmann, *The Social Construction of Reality* (New York: Doubleday, 1966), pp. 119 ff.

9. A considerable part of Gehlen's work is devoted to subjectivization in art and literature, e. g., his *Zeit-Bilder* (Frankfurt: Athenaeum, 1965).

10. Peter Berger, "Towards a Sociological Understanding of Psychoanalysis," *Social Research* 32 (1965): 1.

11. The concept of the private sphere was developed in recent German sociology, under the influence of Gehlen. On privatization in non-Western societies, see R. P. Dore, *City Life in Japan* (Berkeley: University of California Press, 1958), pp. 374 ff.; Herbert Barringer, "Increasing Scale and Changing Social Character in Korea," in Scott Greer et al., eds., *The New Urbanization* (New York: St. Martin's Press, 1968).

12. On the meaning of work in modern society, see Everett Hughes, *Men and Their Work* (Glencoe: Free Press, 1958); Sigmund Nosow and William Form, eds., *Man, Work and Society* (New York: Basic Books, 1962).

Index